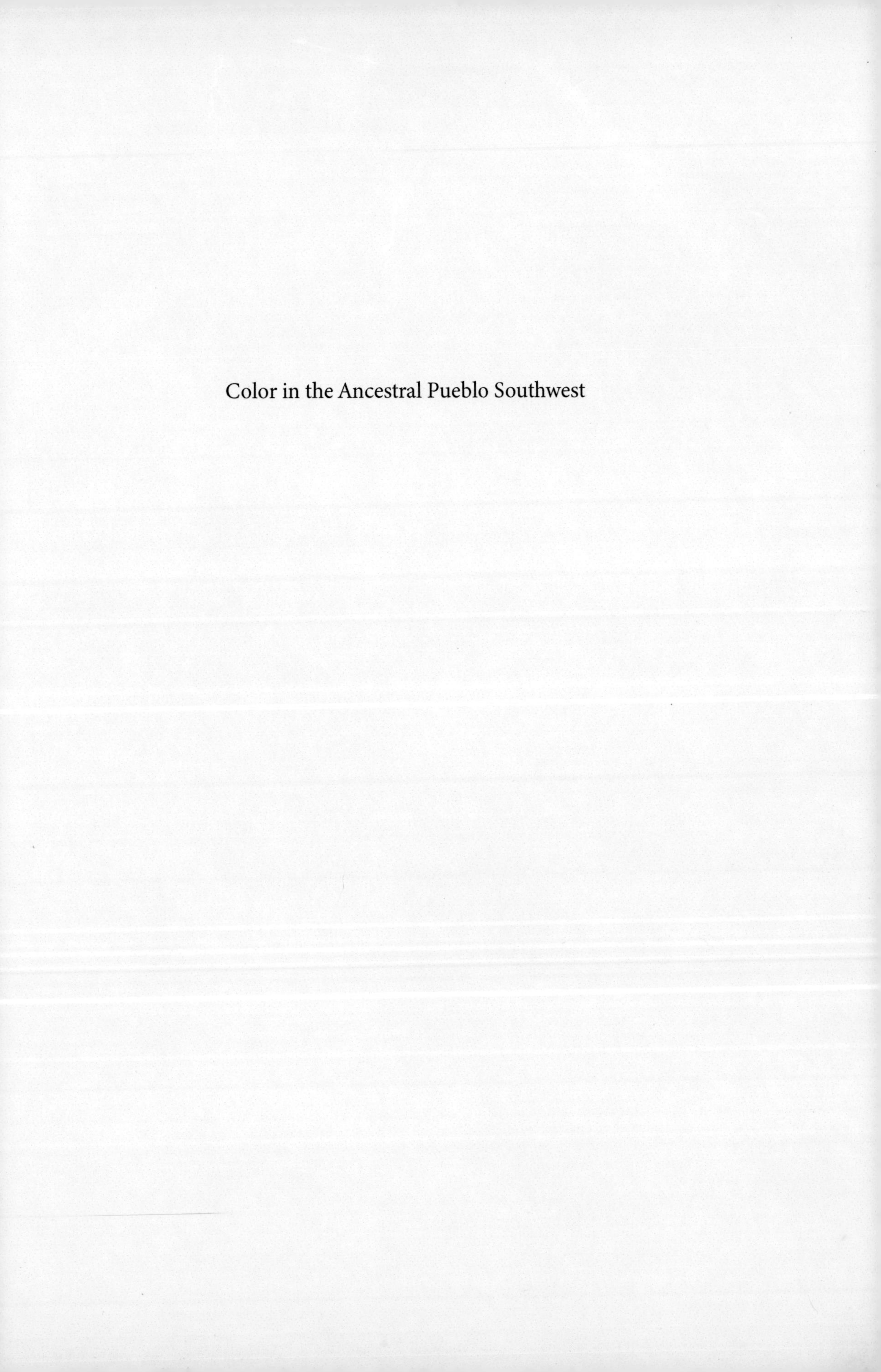

# Color in the Ancestral Pueblo Southwest

# Color in the Ancestral Pueblo Southwest

Edited By

Marit K. Munson and Kelley Hays-Gilpin

The University of Utah Press
*Salt Lake City*

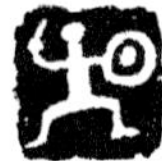

The Defiance House Man colophon is a registered trademark of The University of Utah Press. It is based on a four-foot-tall Ancient Puebloan pictograph (late PIII) near Glen Canyon, Utah.

LIBRARY OF CONGRESS CATALOGING-IN-PUBLICATION DATA

Names: Munson, Marit K., editor. | Hays-Gilpin, Kelley, 1960– editor.
Title: Color in the Ancestral Pueblo Southwest / edited by Marit K. Munson and Kelley Hays-Gilpin.
Description: Salt Lake City : The University of Utah Press, [2019] | Includes bibliographical references and index. |
Identifiers: LCCN 2019008119 (print) | LCCN 2019009892 (ebook) | ISBN 9781607817215 ( ) | ISBN 9781607817208 (cloth : alk. paper)
Subjects: LCSH: Ancestral Pueblo culture. | Symbolism of colors—Southwest, New—History. | Color—Social aspects—Southwest, New—History. | Pueblo Indians—Material culture—Southwest, New. | Pueblo art—Southwest, New. | Color in visual communication. | Pueblo Indians—Antiquities. | Southwest, New—Antiquities.
Classification: LCC E99.P9 (ebook) | LCC E99.P9 C686 2019 (print) | DDC 978.9004/974—dc23
LC record available at https://lccn.loc.gov/2019008119

Errata and further information on this and other titles available online at UofUpress.com

Printed and bound in the United States of America.

# Contents

# Figures

# Tables

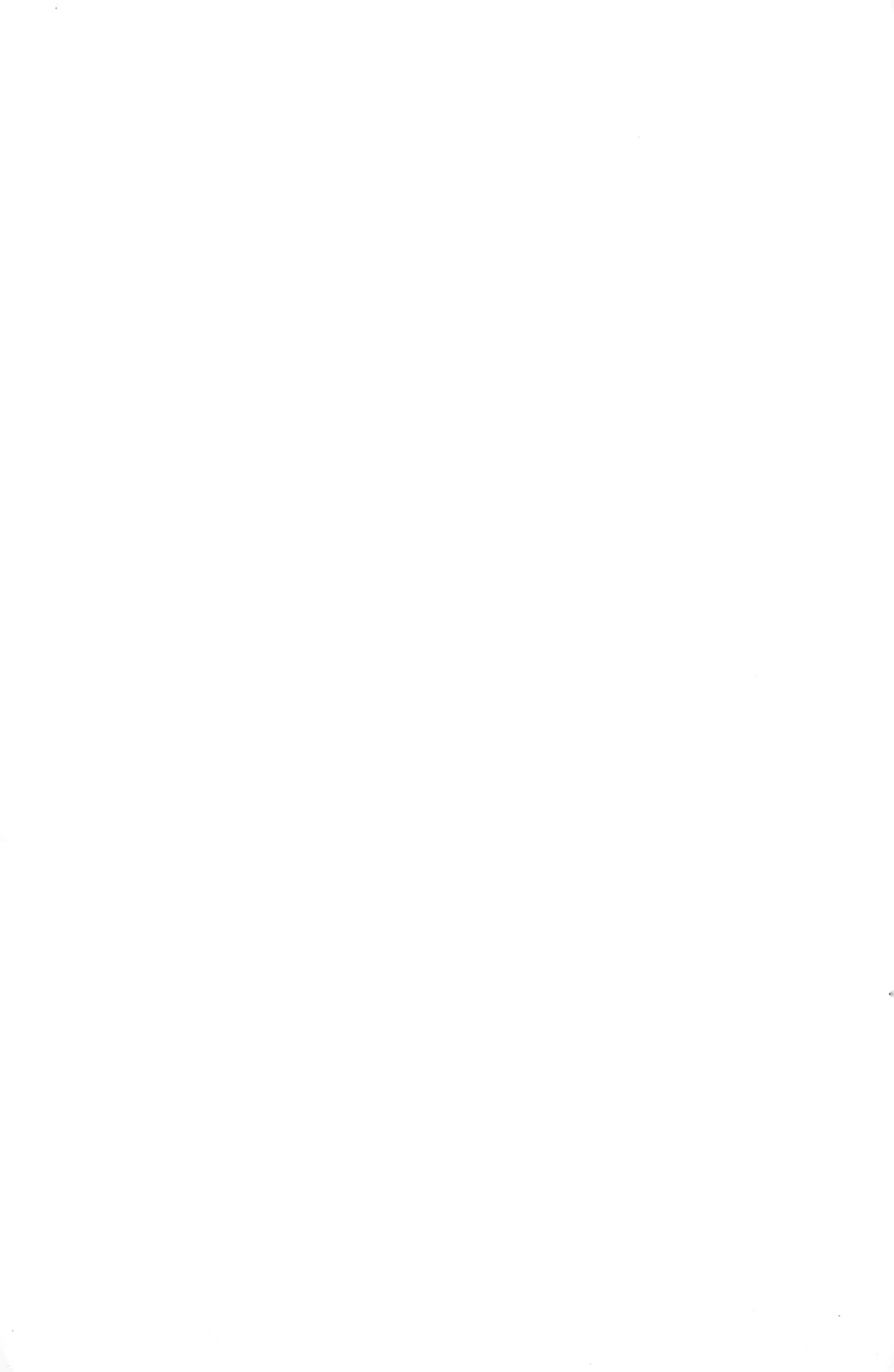

# Acknowledgments

We extend heartfelt appreciation to the participating authors and Reba Rauch at the University of Utah Press for their expertise, patience, and persistence. Will Russell's thoughtful comments on several drafts strengthened the manuscript and are gratefully acknowledged, along with those of an anonymous reviewer. Jill E. Neitzel is more than a contributing author—many thanks for her editorial suggestions and encouragement throughout the volume. Paul Reed and Lori Stephens generously answered queries about Aztec and Salmon Ruins, as did Samuel Duwe, Severin Fowles, Judith Habicht-Mauche, Curt Schaafsma, Polly Schaafsma, and Lucy Schuyler about sites in the Rio Grande Valley.

Thanks to the many individuals and institutions who provided assistance with photos and illustrations: Phil Geib, David Grant Noble, Robert Mark, John Pitts, Curtis Schaafsma, Polly Schaafsma, and Patricia Vivian; the staffs of the Dallas Museum of Art and Museum of Northern Arizona; Nina Gregorev, Anna Semon, David Hurst Thomas, Lori Pendleton Thomas, and Barry Landau at the American Museum of Natural History; Jannelle Weakly and Arthur Vokes at the Arizona State Museum; Don Cole at the Fowler Museum at the University of California, Los Angeles; Diane Bird at the Museum of New Mexico; Nathan Sowry at the National Museum of the American Indian; David Rosenthal at the National Museum of Natural History; Christian Downum at Northern Arizona University; and Laura Holt at the School of Advanced Research. We are also grateful to artist Robert Schultz for his skill and patience in transforming ideas into drawings.

Polly Schaafsma is particularly indebted to Patricia Vivian for the generous loan of her thesis on the Pottery Mound murals from which she has granted permission to use extensive quotes. As well, Vivian has provided mural imagery from her personal collection of slides and drawings.

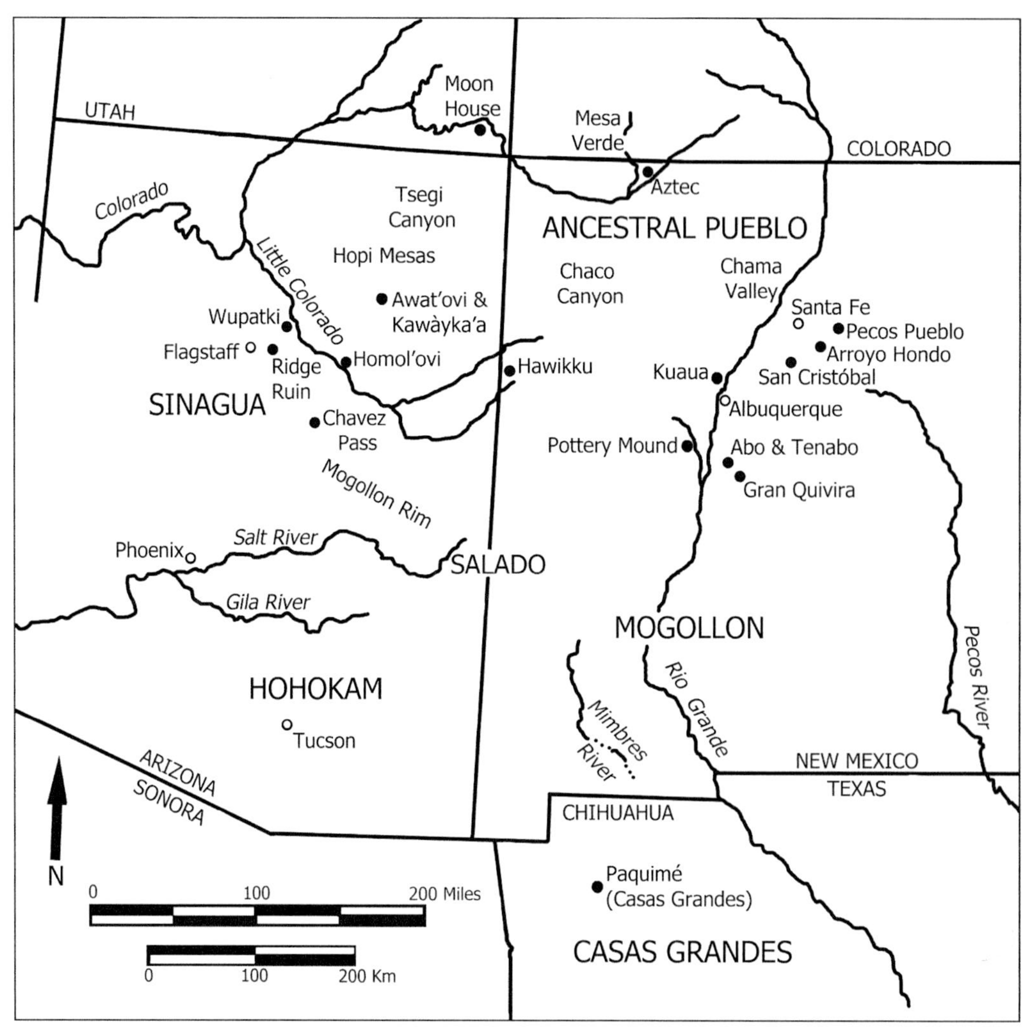


FIGURE 0.1. Key sites and geographic features of the U.S. Southwest. Map by Marit K. Munson.

INTRODUCTION

# What Is Color?

Marit K. Munson

We are in a time of heightened interest in color in North America—witness the availability of paints mixed to match an infinite array of hues at the hardware store, the apps that allow one to extract a decorative palette from a photograph, and the publicity that surrounds (at least in certain circles) the announcement of the Pantone color of the year (Blaszczyk 2012). Ironically, despite this interest, we are still not accustomed to imagining the past in color (DeBoer 2005:66; Jones and Bradley 1999:112; Pastoureau 2001:8). Some of this comes about, quite literally, because of black and white illustrations, which have prevailed in books and articles because they are less expensive to print. But part of this bias is rooted in the notion that color is superficial and frivolous (Taussig 2009:3), and therefore irrelevant to important questions about the past.

A search through the scholarly and popular literature soon puts this idea to rest, as publications in a range of fields document the multitude of ways in which color is implicated in all aspects of society: color attracts attention, evokes emotions, conveys information, carries symbolic meanings, displays technical knowledge, and makes things beautiful (Ball 2001; Clarke 2001; Davidoff 1997; Finlay 2003; Gage 1993, 1999; Lowengard 2007). Color is both style and material; it is rooted in technology and swayed by economic forces, even as it reflects deeply held meanings and reinforces religious and social values. Above all, color is "first and foremost a social phenomenon" (Pastoureau 2001:7).

Exactly *how* color accomplishes its many social, practical, and symbolic purposes touches on a broad range of subjects, including physiology, aesthetics, chemistry, cosmology, neurobiology, art, and human evolution. This Introduction, together with the first chapter, draws on a broad array of fields to examine how color is perceived and conceived, how it is produced technically and socially, and how it carries a multitude of meanings, in general and for Pueblo people in particular. In doing so, it lays the foundation for the remainder of the volume, which examines the archaeological evidence of color in the Ancestral Pueblo world, from kiva murals and rock paintings to pottery and ornaments, demonstrating how systematic explorations of color can contribute to and enrich our understanding of the past.

## Vision, Light, and Biology

In 1666 Sir Isaac Newton famously placed a prism in a beam of sunlight shining through a shutter into a darkened room, producing a rainbow of color. He then passed that rainbow through a second prism, reuniting the colorful spectrum into a beam of white light (Newton 1704). In doing so, he resolved a question that had long plagued his contemporaries, demonstrating that color consisted of different wavelengths of visible light (Fraser 2019:5–8; Livingstone 2008: 12–14). This led to the idea of the spectrum, with color ordered by wavelength. When light of a relatively short wavelength is reflected from an object to the eye, the item appears violet; at the other end of the spectrum, where the reflected wavelengths are much longer, the object appears red. More recently, scientists have learned that colors may also be produced when waves of light interact with the fine structure of an object. These structural, or interference, colors create striking visual effects such as the iridescence of hummingbird feathers and of opals (Fraser 2019:48; Livingstone 2008:20–23).

The perception of colors, whether created by reflection or interference, is based in fundamental biology: light enters the eye, where photoreceptors called rods and cones translate it into signals that travel to the brain. The exact details of how this happens are the subject of considerable debate (see Thompson 1995), but most vision scientists concur that there are two complementary theories that explain how we see color (Fraser 2019:24; but see Jameson and D'Andrade 1997): trichromacy and opponent-process theory. Trichromacy refers to the fact that color vision in primates is based on three different kinds of cones, each responding to different wavelengths of light that correspond roughly to blue, green, and red (Livingstone 2008:26–27). When information from all of the photoreceptors is combined, it allows people with normal color vision to distinguish as many as a million different colors across the visible spectrum (Kuehni and Schwarz 2008:6).

However impressive *distinguishing* a million colors may sound, we simply do not acknowledge that many colors in daily life (Sivik 1997: 163). Indeed, experiments under tightly controlled conditions suggest that most people can only *identify* about six to eight hues. Those hues, or what we would colloquially think of as colors, are modified by variations in value (lightness or darkness) and in saturation, or the intensity of the color. Taken together, these add up to about 30 colors that can be identified under tightly controlled experimental conditions (Kuehni and Schwarz 2008:6). This surprisingly limited scope of identifiable colors may perhaps be explained in part by opponent-process theory (Hering 1964), the second theory about how color vision works. Opponent-process theory focuses on how specific cells in the brain process light (Fraser 2019:23–24). One type of cell responds to wavelengths corresponding roughly to red, green, or blue, while another responds to lightness and darkness. An additional kind, called Type 2 cells, acts in a more binary fashion; a given Type 2 cell that is excited by one color will also be inhibited by another color (Livingstone 2008:61). The result is that red and green cannot be perceived simultaneously, nor can blue and yellow—an opposition of colors that explains why we cannot conceive of a color as being a reddish-green or a yellowish-blue. Opponent-process theory therefore suggests that there are four elementary hues: yellow, red, blue, and green (Hering 1964).

Linguists and other researchers continue to argue over what opponent-process theory might mean in terms of universals of color language (see Hardin and Maffi 1997; Kay 2005). Regardless of the details of this debate, Kuehni and Schwarz (2008:7) believe that these elementary hues may help to explain how humans are capable of distinguishing so many colors, yet typically identify and name a considerably smaller set. They suggest that the six to eight hues that people are able to identify experimentally consist of four elementary colors (red, yellow, green, and blue), plus additional colors that are named in the parts of the spectrum that lie between those colors. For example, there is sufficient perceptual distance between red and yellow that English speakers recognize and name a distinct intermediate hue, orange. Similarly, the space between red and blue is perceived as being occupied by the category purple.

In the region of yellow, green, and blue, however, "no intermediate categories have established themselves early and strongly enough to result in simple, generally understood hue terms" (Kuehni and Schwarz 2008:93); instead, we are left with descriptors like yellow-green and blue-green, or color terms that are "arbitrary and largely culturally determined" (Kuehni and Schwarz 2008:7), such as lime or turquoise. In many languages, green and blue are considered variations of a single color. This color, which linguists refer to in English as "grue" (Jameson 2005:160–163), provides an excellent reminder that the conceptualization of color is far more involved than biology alone would suggest (Pastoureau 2008:16). As we will see, color systems—modes of conceiving of and organizing colors—are far from universal (Kuehni and Schwarz 2008; Lucy 1997b:322).

### The Importance of Value

Prior to Newton's experiments in the seventeenth century, the Western world lacked a coherent color system; that is, there was no general agreement about what colors existed and how they related to each other (Kuehni and Schwarz 2008:28–30). For example, writers in ancient Rome could not settle on the colors in a rainbow. Various authors proposed anywhere from three to six colors, and, even more surprisingly, no one could agree about the order in which the colors occurred (Pastoureau 2001:31), despite the fact that it would seem to be a simple matter of observation.

In fact, Western color space from the ancient Greeks and Romans into the twelfth century centered more on value (lightness or darkness) and saturation (intensity), than on hue ("color," as used colloquially). People were concerned primarily with the distinction between dark and light (Gage 1993:11–16) and with red as a saturated color that stood in contrast to white (Pastoureau 2001:16). Effectively a three-color system, this concept led to odd use of terms in classical texts, causing some scholars to propose that the ancient Greeks and Romans were all color-blind (see Pastoureau 2001:23). This misunderstanding occurred because the researchers ignored "the often considerable gap that exists, in all eras and cultures, between 'real' color (as it is objectively seen), color as it is perceived, and color as it is named" (Pastoureau 2001:26–27). Colors such as yellow, blue, and green existed, of course, but were less important socially, economically, and symbolically and therefore were not named and acknowledged as distinctive hues.

In early medieval Europe, color concepts focused primarily on the contrast of light and dark. Old English (ca. AD 600–1150), for example, effectively recognized six colors. Of the six basic terms, green was the only one that referred entirely to hue. Red had meanings related to both brightness and hue, while black, white, yellow, and blue were described in terms that focused on brightness, such as *leoht* (light), *deorc* (dark), and *scir* (light, shining). That is, most Old English "color terms" actually referred exclusively to brightness and darkness, *regardless of hue* (Casson 1992).

### The Emergence of Hue

Over time, Europeans began to reconceptualize color, reorganizing their color system as they started to pay more attention to hue. As blue, yellow, and green became more important, some Old English terms related to brightness gained hue-dominated meanings in Middle English (AD 1150–1500). Other terms dropped out of use or lost their color association entirely (Casson 1997). These changes arose in part due to technical innovations and the availability of new materials, which made it possible to produce certain colors more reliably and economically than before (Pastoureau 2001:63–72). As new colors became available and socially relevant, new vocabulary words sprang up to describe them (Casson 1994).

As color possibilities expanded, medieval Christian authorities became embroiled in violent arguments over the nature of color and its appropriate use in the church. On one side were those who believed that color was light and therefore an immaterial, and quite beautiful, expression of the divine. The most famous of these chromophiles was the Abbot Suger (ca. AD 1081–1151), who believed "that nothing was too beautiful for the house of God" because "the illumination, beauty, and visual splendor needed to worship God were expressed most effectively through colorful objects" (Pastoureau 2001:44). Indeed, Suger's enthusiasm for colorful ornamentation encompassed a wide range of precious materials, including silks, purple and gold cloths, and gemstones such as sapphires, all valued for both color and rarity (Gage 1993:70–73). "Medieval people were," Gage (1993:75) tells us, "no strangers to the glamour of expense."

The chromophile philosophy was made tangible in religious architecture such as the famous Sainte-Chapelle in Paris, completed in AD 1248, which continues to dazzle visitors with its soaring stained glass windows and ceilings richly painted in blue and gold. Blue and gold were also used widely in illuminated manuscripts and paintings of saints, a choice that reflected religious beliefs as much as aesthetics (Ball 2001). Applying gold leaf to an image required considerable expense and resulted in a bright, luminous surface that was prized as a tangible manifestation of the light of God. Blue, in contrast, had been used for centuries but did not gain widespread favor until the twelfth and thirteenth centuries, when it was increasingly considered an appropriate color for the Virgin Mary's cloak (Pastoureau 2001:50–55). Like gold, the best blue pigment, lapis lazuli, was costly; it was known as ultramarine ("beyond the sea") because the mineral was imported to Europe from the Middle East (Gage 1999:13–14).

The most precious colorants, including blue and gold, were seen as appropriate expressions of piety and reverence that would increase the potency of paintings that were "invested with the power to intervene in everyday life" (Ball 2001:85). In fact, contracts for paintings in the Renaissance period often specified how much gold and ultramarine was to be used for specific parts of the image, as well as the grade of materials (Gage 1999:13).

The chromophiles' delight in color and precious materials was not universally shared in medieval Europe. In fact, they were roundly condemned by Bernard of Clairvaux and other church authorities, who felt that color was "both immoral and dangerous" (Pastoureau 2001:42). These chromophobes, mostly members of the Cistercian order, believed that color was matter, amounting to no more than "a futile artifice applied by man to the surface of God's creation" (Pastoureau 2001:42). Far from divine, color was base and deceitful, drawing people farther from communion with God. As a result, the Cistercian tradition eschewed color in religious architecture.

Theological debates about color and creation played out in the experiences of dyers as well. Dyers, of necessity, mixed different materials together, combining dyestuffs with mordants and other ingredients to change the color of cloth. As a result, they "were viewed with fear and suspicion because they seemed to be manipulating matter" (Pastoureau 2001:72), therefore violating God's established order of creation. Dyers had considerable practical knowledge of the materials that they manipulated, as well as more ideological stances that governed what could or could not be mixed (Brusatin 1991:57–60). The result was a general division of the dyers' trade—and of colors themselves—into two mutually exclusive spheres. The process of producing red cloth, known as dyeing in the red, required madder as the dye, combined with a mordant during a lengthy period of boiling. Using woad or indigo to produce blue cloth, in contrast, required little or no mordanting and could be done without boiling. Dyeing in the red or in the blue were such different techniques that they were rigidly specialized, sometimes with regulations prohibiting the same individual from working with both colors (Pastoureau 2001:69).

Other colors were aligned to red or to blue based on process. For example, dyeing yellow, using weld as the dyestuff, required the same mordant–boiling water process as dyeing in the red, thereby demonstrating to medieval thinkers that red and yellow were linked. Green was usually produced by using naturally green dyestuffs, such as buckthorn, or by treating blues or blacks (Pastoureau 2001:72); green was therefore aligned with blue. As a result, the European color system from the 1100s to the 1500s effectively consisted of two different spheres: yellow, red, and white in one and green, blue, and black in the other. Each set was considered distinct from the other, and the mere idea of mixing colors to produce a new hue was counter to prevailing religious beliefs, which saw mixing as diabolical and dangerous (Pastoureau 2001:72).

### *Science Harnesses the Rainbow*

The 1600s marked the "secularization of color" (Finlay 2007:425) in Europe, as concepts of color shifted to incorporate new ideas generated by Renaissance thinkers. Over the span of about a century, scientists began to explore the notion of primary colors, proposing that mixtures of certain colors would produce others; their ideas were supported by the practical experience of painters, color printers, and dyers, which seemed to indicate that red, blue, and yellow were in fact primary (Gage 1993:153–176). Newton's experiments with light solidified the foundation for a new, unified theory of light and color. First published in 1672, his work circulated most widely with the publication of his *Opticks* (Newton 1704).

Although Newton's work helped to move color out of the realm of religious thought and into the world of science (Brusatin 1991:90–100), eighteenth-century scientists were far from unanimous regarding the meaning of Newton's discoveries. Some authors believed that color could only be understood through physics; others insisted that it be addressed through the lens of human perception (see Gage 1993; Livingstone 2008).

Curiously, it took more than a century after Newton's discovery for scientists to resolve the question of which colors were primary (Lowengard 2007:Ch. A3). In fact, the practical challenges faced by "colormen" trying to produce good colors for new markets (Lowengard 2001) proved critical in shaping the developing scientific consensus on color throughout the eighteenth and nineteenth centuries, just as new trade routes, mistakes in chemical laboratories, and novel manufacturing processes brought about a veritable explosion in the variety of available colors (Christie 2015:6–15; Finlay 2003; Lowengard 2007; Pastoureau 2001). These new discoveries had a democratizing effect, as synthetic materials replaced "that which was rare, dear, or unique" (Brusatin 1991:116) with a great array of new pigments and dyes that were more accessible to the middle classes (Christie 2015: 6–13; Orna 2013:69–90). Artists also reveled in the novel materials, experimenting with new artistic practices and ultimately launching Impressionism, pointillism, and other art historical movements focused on exploring color and its effects (Fraser 2019; Gage 1993).

The emergence of synthetic colors was not an entirely positive development. The popularity of the new colors established dyeing as a major commercial enterprise. Centered in Germany, this new chemical industry had ripple effects on the economics, politics, education system, and social structure of Europe in the tumultuous decades of the late nineteenth and early twentieth centuries (Brusatin 1991:119–121; Orna 2013:91).

## Contemporary Color Systems

As chemists gained control of the rainbow and artists deployed color in new ways, contemporary thinkers began to create corresponding ways of organizing and recording color. This resulted in an enormous array of different color systems, each an attempt to account for particular physiological facts or experimental data (Baty 2017; Jameson and D'Andrade 1997:296–298; Kuehni and Schwarz 2008; Sivik 1997). The most familiar of these, for archaeologists at least, is the Munsell system, developed in the early twentieth century as a means of ordering colors within a three-dimensional solid.

### *The Munsell System*

The Munsell system was initially created by American artist and educator Albert Munsell (1907, 1915) as a teaching tool; the system was later modified several times and published in its modern form in 1943 (Newhall et al. 1943; also see Kuehni and Schwarz 2008:114–115, 160–161). The Munsell system conceives of color as consisting of five hues (yellow, green, blue, red, and purple), each modified by value, or relative lightness or brightness, and by chroma. Chroma is usually thought of as saturation, although the two are technically different properties (Kuehni and Schwarz 2008:94–95). For the purposes of this book we use "saturation" or "intensity" as a general term and "chroma" only when referring to the Munsell system.

The Munsell system is considered a perceptual color space in that it was designed to reflect individuals' understanding or interpretation of the similarities (and differences) between colors, regardless of how the colors are generated or how they stimulate the visual system. The distance between any adjacent color chips should, in theory, "correspond directly to the perception of how similar the colors are" (Jameson and D'Andrade 1997:297). For various technical reasons, this is not entirely possible in practice (Sivik 1997), and in fact there is considerable variation in individuals' judgment when recording Munsell colors for the same objects (Frankel 1980; Giardino et al. 1998).

Nevertheless, the Munsell system is a clear improvement over the days in which people described color in colloquial terms. Some of the color names in use in the early twentieth century, such as grass green or cadet blue, are still relatively clear, but others like bice, solferino, or mummy are bewilderingly opaque (see Baty 2017). As long as Munsell color charts remain in circulation, they provide an accessible and highly practical means of recording differences in color among raw materials, artifacts, and archaeological deposits (Jones and MacGregor 2002:6).

The very ubiquity and practicality of the Munsell system means that it has been far more than a simple research tool; as the dominant color system in many of the sciences (Kuehni and Schwarz 2008:161), the Munsell system has in fact shaped anthropological understandings of color cross-culturally (Saunders 2000). Conceptually, it both creates and reinforces the notion of color as defined by the three dimensions of hue, value, and chroma. It has also had the very practical impact of providing a useful—and purportedly objective—tool for cross-cultural studies of color terms. As a result, it enabled some of the most influential research ever conducted into cross-cultural perspectives on color: the famous linguistic studies of Berlin and Kay.

### *Universalists: Berlin and Kay*

In the 1960s, linguists Brent Berlin and Paul Kay (1969) set out to discover cross-cultural universals in color thought. Armed with color chips from the Munsell charts, they elicited color terms from native speakers of 20 different languages, all of whom were living in California at the time. Berlin and Kay were interested in compiling basic color terms, defined as terms that are common in a given language, that apply to many different kinds of objects and that have been in use for a long time (Berlin and Kay 1969:5–7). In English, for example, "brown" and "red" are basic color terms; words that are more specialized in use, such as "brunette" or "roan," are not. To identify basic color terms, Berlin and Kay presented individuals with an array of 320 colored chips, along with 10 "neutral" chips that reflected shifting value from black to white. They asked each person to provide color terms, to map out all of the chips that were encompassed by each term, and to indicate the best example, or focal point, for each color.

Based on this research, Berlin and Kay (1969) proposed that there is a limited and universal set of basic colors in cultures around the world, with the simplest color concept distinguishing between white and black (or possibly light and dark). They believed that the number of color terms within a given language increased over time, following an evolutionary sequence that related to increasing degrees of sociopolitical complexity. Beyond the first "stage" of white and black (or light and dark), red was the next named color, followed by additional color terms added in a standard order.

The maximum number of basic colors, according to Berlin and Kay's model, is 11: black, white, red, green, yellow, blue, brown, purple, pink, orange, and gray. As Kuehni and Schwarz (2008:7) point out, these colors fall into three broad categories: those that are achromatic, or without hue (white, black, and gray); those centered on hue (red, orange, yellow, green, blue, and purple); and those that encompass lightness and saturation (brown and pink).

Over the years, entire generations of researchers repeated Berlin and Kay's experiments, with slightly modified methods, presenting individuals around the world with hundreds of color samples and recording color terms in dozens of languages. These data led to various revisions of Berlin and Kay's model (see Kay et al. 1997; MacLaury 1992), including attempts to downplay the proposed link between color terms and cultural evolution. Despite these revisions, researchers in a wide range of fields have embraced the original 1969 publication; although it was originally intended as a contribution to linguistic semantics, *Basic Color Terms* has become a staple of color research, cited by researchers in sociobiology, evolutionary psychology, and color science in general as seemingly incontrovertible evidence of universals of human nature (see discussion in Saunders 2000:81).

### *The Critique of Berlin and Kay*

Despite the dominance of the Berlin and Kay model in discussions of color cross-culturally, their work has been subject to criticism. Some researchers, such as art historian John Gage (1999:107), simply reject the search for basic colors as "remarkably inconsequential," adding that such study is "freighted with a heavy burden of ideology which seems far from the concerns of the ordinary user of colour-language." Among those more heavily invested in research on color language, researchers have three main criticisms: "how linguistic categories are *characterized*, how they are *compared*, and how they are linked to *cognition*" (Lucy 1997b:322, emphasis in original). In short, they argue that Berlin and Kay's work includes critical methodological and conceptual flaws (Chapman 2002; Jameson and D'Andrade 1997; Lucy 1997a; Saunders 1992, 2000; Wierzbicka 2005).

For archaeologists, the most important issue centers on the way Berlin and Kay rely on the fundamental assumption, derived from the Munsell system, that color is a universal concept that can be fully described with just three dimensions: hue, value, and chroma (Lucy 1997b:323). In doing so, Berlin and Kay's model flattens the "richness and variety" (Gage 1999:107) that is typical of color-thinking around the world. In fact, linguists and cultural anthropologists have documented numerous examples that highlight the nuances that are lost when researchers fail to consider the grammar of color language and whether color terms are central or merely a part of broader concepts (Anter 2008:333; Lucy 1997b:331)—including whether or not color is even a salient category (Wierzbicka 2005).

#### The Complexity of "Color" Systems: Maya

The Maya languages offer a good example of the complexity of color concepts that get masked by focusing on exclusively on hue, value, and saturation. Yucatan Maya initially seems to correspond neatly to the Berlin and Kay system, with five basic hue-focused color terms (black, red/orange, yellow/orange, white, and green), which can be modified to indicate brightness and saturation. However, Yucatan Maya speakers also modify basic terms to indicate the color of an object relative to its texture (soft, hard, smooth, lumpy, or prickly), its humidity (wet or dry), its reflectance (dull or shiny), and its relationship to light (opaque or translucent). In addition, their terms for color vary depending on the relative discreteness of the objects or materials in question, with different modifiers for small discrete objects, small clustered objects, large undifferentiated objects, or a broad expanse of color (Bricker 1999:286).

As Bricker points out, concepts important in Yucatan Maya have been "systematically excluded from studies of basic color terms," in large part because of methodological limitations of color chips as small, flat, opaque, smooth surfaces (Bricker 1999:297). Researchers typically present about 330 of these opaque color chips, devoid of any natural context, and ask for extraordinary discrimination of colors, far beyond what an individual would typically do in daily life. Ironically, the researchers do so to try to identify the focal point of each color, reducing the rich array of visible light into simple categories such as red, yellow, or blue. As a result, Lucy (1997b:331) argues, researchers end up imposing modern English hue-based terms onto conceptual systems that are in fact built upon other visual properties. For example, light and dark categories in various languages often get glossed as white/black color terms, even though a conceptual system based on distinguishing darkness and lightness is not the equivalent of a color system based on black and white.

### Color as One of Many Visual Properties: Hanunóo

Berlin and Kay's initial evaluation of the Hanunóo language, spoken in the Philippines, provides an interesting example of the flattening effect of simplification. Ironically, they opened their book by acknowledging "that Hanunóo 'color' words in fact encode a great deal of non-colorimetric information" (Berlin and Kay 1969:1). Having dismissed the relevance of these details, they then designated four basic Hanunóo color terms: white, black, red, and green (Berlin and Kay 1969:64). What is lost in their dismissal becomes clear when one examines Conklin's (1955, 1964) publications based on fieldwork with native speakers. He noted that the basic Hanunóo "color" terms correspond to concepts of lightness, darkness, "relative redness," and "relative greenness," with each term encompassing important meanings beyond color. The term for relative greenness, for example, incorporates materials that are wet, fresh, or succulent, while relative redness conveys the meaning of something dry or desiccated. A piece of freshly cut bamboo, which is a wet, shiny brown, would be described in terms of relative greenness; a dried-out piece of bamboo that has become yellowed would be referred to as having relative redness.

Hanunóo speakers recombine these dimensions of light and dark and wet and dry along another dimension that focuses on the permanence of a material's appearance. Objects with deep, indelible, or permanent color are associated with the terms for darkness and relative redness, while those that become pale, faded, or colorless are thought of in terms of lightness and relative greenness. In addition, Conklin noted that the Hanunóo pay considerable attention to qualities like visual texture, iridescence, sparkle, and dullness, adding that these aspects of appearance were "considered of primary importance," with color "serving only as secondary attributes" (Conklin 1964:191). With its focus on universals, Berlin and Kay's concept of evolutionary color space disregards such variability, glossing complex concepts with English terms for hues.

### Color as Process: Zuni

The Zuni language, like Hanunóo, raises concerns about the assumption that color is an intrinsic, unchanging property. When Berlin and Kay (1969:103) discussed Zuni, they listed 11 basic color terms: white, black, red, green, yellow, blue, brown, purple, pink, orange, and gray. This list has been criticized, however, on methodological and conceptual grounds. Barbara Saunders (2000:87) feels that Berlin and Kay "revamped" the linguistic data, incorporating words that are not basic color terms, while John Lucy (1997b) argues that Berlin and Kay's concept of color as static and unchanging ignores the rich reality of Zuni color language. In fact, most of the Zuni vocabulary that Berlin and Kay cited is based on color terms that combine a sense of hue with an interest in "processes of change or 'becoming'" (Hickerson 1975:328). For example, a verb-based color term is best translated as "to be or become blue, green" (Hickerson 1975:325). Such verbs can be modified with particles that convey considerable nuance about an object's current color state and even whether or not it seems likely to change.

In addition to verb-based color terms, Zuni also has nouns that "refer to intrinsic color, specific to a substance or object, and unchanging" (Hickerson 1975:328), such as malachite, red cedar wood, or bluebirds. For example, the word for malachite—usually categorized in English as green—can be modified by suffixes to convey the meaning of "pale blue (like blue paint stones)." This construction, referred to as "entity-for-entity's-color" (Casson 1994), often leads to new vocabulary for color, as a term that was initially used for naming a physical entity has its meaning expanded to encompass the hue of that entity. Over time, the entity meaning may be retained, as in the English color term "orange," based on the fruit, or it may drop out, leaving just the color name (Casson 1994).

The important aspect of dual verb- and noun-based Zuni color vocabulary—and the point that critics argue Berlin and Kay missed—is that it "reflect[s] two basically different types of experience" (Hickerson 1975:328): one about intrinsic properties and the other about change over time. Zuni speakers can therefore use one term to refer to an object that is inherently yellow and a different term for something that has ripened, aged, or faded into a yellow, rusty, or pale hue (Newman 1954:87–88), even if the two objects in question appear to be the same color. In other words, Zuni concepts of color are not static but reflect "a cultural concern with the origin of the color and various specific cultural associations" (Lucy 1997b:336).

In the Maya, Hanunóo, and Zuni cases, the language of color (and therefore color concepts themselves) are far more complex and intriguing than Berlin and Kay address, encompassing many qualities beyond hue, value, and saturation. The Yucatan Maya example affirms, on one level, the idea of basic color terms; at the same time, it demonstrates that additional dimensions are necessary if one is to capture the complexity of color-thinking. In similar fashion, the Hanunóo case shows how universalist models based on Western scientific thinking tend to reduce complicated concepts about seeing and the appearance of things to a narrow focus, primarily on hue. Finally, the Zuni example demonstrates a concern with color as incorporating both intrinsic properties and change through time. Taken together, these examples highlight how researchers' biases can cause them to overlook or dismiss interesting variability in how speakers of different languages notice, value, and discuss a wide range of visual properties in conjunction with color (Lucy 1997b).

## Color in Archaeology

Archaeologists' track record with color is not particularly distinguished. Since the 1950s, we have embraced the Munsell system as *the* single means of treating color objectively (Shepard 1956:107), dutifully recording Munsell codes as a standard research practice. The perceived importance of color data is predicated on the notion of color-as-indicator: that is, that color reflects some aspect of the material type or the production process, such as the kind of stone, the composition of paint, or the firing atmosphere of ceramics (e.g., Jernigan 1978; Shepard 1956; Smith 1952:21–24; Tanner 1976).

When possible, some researchers sought to identify the materials used to produce paints; Watson Smith's (1952:22–32) thorough documentation of pigments in the murals of Awat'ovi and Kawàyka'a was the most notable in its scope. Such studies were relatively uncommon, however, perhaps reflecting an unwillingness to address "squishy" or "unscientific" topics such as color. This attitude began to shift in the 1980s and 1990s, when post-processual archaeologists began to focus more on understanding the lived experiences of individuals in the past (Jones and MacGregor 2002). Rejecting the evolutionary- and biology-based interpretations of their predecessors, these researchers began to explore color as a meaningful part of the human past.

Intrigued by a range of published material that clearly demonstrated the emotional and symbolic power of color, post-processual archaeologists leaped directly to the issue of addressing the meaning of color in the past—a task that proved to be extremely difficult. In 1999, for example, the *Cambridge Archaeological Journal* published a series of pieces in a special section on the meaning of color in the past (Gage et al. 1999). The articles in this issue all wrestled with the issue of meaning, noting a range of approaches from the use of written records to "cautious appeal to common human experience" (Gage et al. 1999:109).

Unfortunately, most archaeologists seemed to forget the caution, transposing ethnographic and historic details directly into the past or, when such information is not available, relying heavily on purported universals. Ironically, this meant that many archaeologists who eschewed evolutionary trajectories ended up embracing Berlin and Kay's universalist model, operating under the assumption that black, white, and red are universally important colors for cultures around the world and far back in time.

This idea was further reinforced by the work of Victor Turner (1967:59–72), whose ethnographic research documented the symbolism of red, black, and white among the Ndembu of central Africa. Published shortly after Berlin and Kay's *Basic Color Terms*, Turner's *The Forest of Symbols* has had considerable influence on the topic of color and meaning. Archaeologists citing Turner often gloss his work as highlighting universal meanings in which red, black, and white symbolize, respectively, blood, darkness or evil, and milk or semen (e.g., Barber 1999:119; Tilley 1996:322). The confluence of these ideas, combined with the prominence and incredible time-depth of red ochre in the archaeological record, has meant that researchers have focused considerable attention on an assumed link between ochre as a natural symbol for blood and, by extension, perhaps for life (e.g., Bradley 1998:Ch. 2; Scarre 2002:228–229; also see Jones and MacGregor 2002:7–8).

One of the difficulties with such work, though, is that interpretations based on universals oversimplify meaning, sometimes to the point of caricature. Much as Berlin and Kay ignored the complexities of color speech in Zuni and other languages (Lucy 1997b:326), archaeologists' superficial citations of Turner's research strips his work of the nuance that makes it so valuable. Far from identifying universal meanings of red, black, and white, Turner's work is best understood as an exploration of those colors as "sacred, theatrical, and mysterious" (Taussig 2009:8). Indeed, anthropologist Michael Taussig (2009:8) argues that Turner's work demonstrates that the whole "idea of a color code is inappropriate" because "far from being symbolic, distinct from their referents, the colors *are* those referents in a deeply organic sense" (emphasis in original). Indeed, anthropological research on color demonstrates, above all, that color is meaningful for all (or most) cultures worldwide—even though the specific meanings of particular colors are contingent, complex, and sometimes surprisingly fluid.

In this volume, we consider the relationship of Pueblo peoples to color in the past, documenting the ways in which the archaeological record reflects color choices across time and space and working to understand color as a meaningful property. When possible, we address meaning by drawing on the ethnographic and historic record of the Pueblo Southwest, where the breadth and depth of material provides a rich source of insight into the past (see Chapter 1). In addition to considerable information on color symbolism, ethnographic accounts from Hopi, Zuni, and other pueblos provide clear examples of the power of paints and of the use of colorful materials as chromatic prayers. These accounts provide a direct parallel with archaeological evidence for both plastering of kiva walls and the painting of murals (see Chapter 1 and Solometo 2010). As a result, archaeologists and Pueblo people interested in kiva murals often address color explicitly, from scientific analysis of pigment composition (Smith 1952: 21–24) to detailed studies of iconography, worldview, and visual metaphor (Crotty 1995; Hays-Gilpin et al. 2010; Newsome and Hays-Gilpin 2011; Sekaquaptewa and Washburn 2010). Discussions of color in other media usually cite related ethnographic material, suggesting that the significance of paints as powerful materials extends to rock paintings (Schaafsma 2010:27) and painted clay-lined baskets (Odegaard and Hays-Gilpin 2002).

Curiously enough, Southwestern archaeologists studying pottery have not fully engaged with the idea of paints as meaningful materials. Pottery color is most often part of discussions about glaze wares and other late prehispanic polychrome vessels (see Chapter 3), tending to focus on technical aspects such as identification of paint recipes and the potential relationship of color, communities of practice, and identity (Cordell and Habicht-Mauche 2012; Habicht-Mauche et al. 2006; Huntley 2008; Huntley et al. 2012). Ironically, some of the most overt explorations of color in Southwestern pottery actually center on black-on-white or black-smudged vessels, which are commonly thought of as lacking color. Based on a suggestion by art historian J. J. Brody, Stephen Plog (2003) explored whether hachure in black-on-white Chacoan pottery may have been used as a stand-in for blue/green, which could not be produced on Southwestern pottery due to technological limitations. More recently, Will Russell and his colleagues (2018) and Stephanie Whittlesey (2014) have tackled similar questions about the color of

TABLE 0.1. Time periods referred to in this volume. The specific dates of these broad periods varies across the Pueblo Southwest, and transitions between periods usually played out over a few generations.

| Time Period | Approximate Dates |
|---|---|
| Contemporary | 1890s–present |
| Pueblo V/Historic | AD 1540/1600–1890s |
| Pueblo IV | AD 1300–1540/1600 |
| Pueblo III | AD 1130–1300 |
| Pueblo II | AD 900–1130 |
| Pueblo I | AD 700–900 |
| Basketmaker III | AD 500–700 |
| Basketmaker II | 1000/500 BC–AD 500 |

Mimbres Black-on-white vessels, while Tammy Stone (2018) has considered the importance of iridescence in black-smudged Mogollon bowls.

The most comprehensive discussion of color in Southwestern archaeology comes from Brody's (1991) broad overview of painting in multiple media, from the Archaic period through to the early 1900s. He noted that painted murals and pottery prior to AD 1300 tend to be monochromatic, or bichromatic if one considers the color of a slip or a plaster surface. After 1300, he argued, painting underwent a great "florescence," with radical changes in all media; color became increasingly important in pottery and murals, while rock paintings declined in favor of monochrome petroglyphs.

## The Structure of This Volume

In this book, we examine patterns in the use of colors through time and space, systematically comparing multiple media to expand our understanding of color in the Ancestral Pueblo world. Drawing on ethnographic and historic information, Chapter 1 discusses the uses and meanings of color as documented in Pueblo ethnography, discussing mimetic symbolism, the use of paint as chromatic prayer, and the relationship between color, material, and landscape. It also establishes the groundwork for understanding the process of acquiring and working with colorful materials, exploring pigments, paints, and dyes as technologies that required specialized knowledge and a great deal of skill to use successfully.

The remaining chapters examine color in a specific medium, focusing primarily on the Pueblo I to Pueblo IV time periods (roughly AD 700–1600; see Table 0.1). We also draw on additional archaeological and ethnographic material, especially from neighboring groups, such as the Hohokam, Mogollon, and Sinagua, who share histories of interaction, trade, and migration (Cordell and McBrinn 2012).

In Chapter 2, I examine the presence of pigments and paints in the archaeological record, as well as the tools used for processing and preparing them. I summarize the current state of knowledge regarding the distribution of different colors through time and space, highlighting the extensive, if somewhat inconsistent, record of colorants in the published literature.

In Chapter 3, Kelley Hays-Gilpin and Jill E. Neitzel discuss the use of color in pottery, from single-color vessels beginning about AD 600 to more formal bichrome white ware and red ware traditions a century or two later. They argue that a meaningful opposition arose between black-on-white and black-on-red in pottery as pottery traditions became regionally distinct in the late Pueblo II and Pueblo III periods, possibly reflecting symbolism of clouds and earth. Polly Schaafsma documents similar uses of color for wall paintings (Chapter 4) and rock paintings (Chapter 5) dating to the Pueblo II and Pueblo III periods; as Brody noted, most were bichrome, involving various combinations of white with red, tan, or occasionally black. Schaafsma argues that the act of smearing or spreading paints may have expressed meanings related to moisture and clouds.

This limited palette of Pueblo II and III stands in distinct contrast to the elaborate polychrome murals of the Pueblo IV period, which surely represent the most dramatic color shift ever to have occurred in the Pueblo world. In Chapter 4, Schaafsma outlines how the expansion of colors in mid-fourteenth-century murals allowed painters to add detail, to highlight important features, and to evoke symbolic meanings. This theme is echoed in her discussion in Chapter 5 of Pueblo IV to protohistoric painted rockshelters from the Rio Grande Valley, which make similar use of color to represent detailed human figures, including clear katsina iconography, and elaborate animal images.

Despite these prominent examples, however, there was not a single, unified trend toward polychromy in all media. As Neitzel and Hays-Gilpin describe in Chapter 3, the shift to polychrome in pottery was more complicated, as potters first combined existing red ware colors in new ways in the 1200s and then, by the late 1300s, threw out the color rules entirely to produce a range of bright polychrome pottery, which increased in intricacy into the 1400s. And, as Neitzel and David E. Witt discuss in Chapter 6, the colors of ornaments seem to have been relatively immune to the shift to polychromy; the distribution of the various stones, shells, and other materials used to make jewelry varied primarily due to large-scale patterns of trade and exchange, with some striking polychrome examples associated with elite contexts.

Indeed, all of the chapters highlight important exceptions to the bichrome "rule" of Pueblo II and Pueblo III, as well as the persistence of black and white as an important pairing alongside the bright polychromes displayed in Pueblo IV kivas, plazas, and rockshelters. Our goal in this volume is to document the varied uses of colors across the Ancestral Pueblo world, to better understand how meaningful materials shaped the past.

# 1

# Color in the Pueblo World

Marit K. Munson

Color is central to Pueblo religion and worldview and, therefore, life itself. Color symbolizes directions, identifies group affiliations, cures ailments, affects the weather, and manifests katsinas and other spiritual beings, among other things. Outsiders have tended to think of color in the abstract, but Pueblo ethnography makes it clear that color is much more than disembodied hue. When a Keres man painted a prayer stick with blue-green paint, he created chromatic prayers for fertility and the growth of plants, evoking the direction west, vegetation, and maleness; when a Hopi woman finished a painted pot, the transformation of its colors through firing was a visible sign that it had become animate.

This chapter discusses how color was and still is a tangible expression of Pueblo cosmology, produced from powerful materials obtained from meaningful locations, as accessible as a wash next to the village or as esoteric as the underworld or place of Emergence. Under the supervision of knowledgeable specialists, Pueblo people laboriously transformed these materials into paints and dyes that, when used in appropriate ways, made manifest the powers that move through the world.

## Color Symbolism in Pueblo Ceremonialism

The cultural associations of color among the Pueblos are deep and complex, as considerable ethnographic fieldwork has made clear. Perhaps the most profound association is between color and direction. Like most other North American indigenous groups, Pueblo peoples associate colors with the cardinal directions or, in the case of Hopi, intercardinal directions associated with the sun's position during the summer and winter solstices (Ford 1980:19–20; Hieb 1979:577; Ortiz 1969:19; Reyman 1971; Stephen 1898:261; Tedlock 1979:499). Parsons explained that "other colors are recognized and named, but the direction-colors are paramount in thought. They would be named first, and you might even be told by somebody that there were no other color terms" (Parsons 1939:99).

Most of the Pueblos associate north with yellow, west with blue, south with red, and east with white (Table 1.1). Below, or the underworld, is generally associated with black or dark, while the zenith, or the world above, is variably represented by black, brown, yellow, or multiple colors. There are differences in directional symbolism from Pueblo to Pueblo, however, particularly among Tewa and Tiwa speakers. Even within a single group, colors might be deployed in different ways or "swapped in and out of the system" (Hays-Gilpin et al. 2010:127).

In addition to colors, the directions were associated with a range of phenomena, creatures, spirits, and places. Writing about Hopi, Stephen described it thus:

> At the North sits a chief wearing a yellow cloud as a mask; it covers his head and rests upon his shoulders; a multitude of yellow butterflies flutter constantly before his face

TABLE 1.1. Directional color associations among the Pueblos (based on Parsons' comments in Dumarest 1919:182; Harrington 1916; Lange 1990:230; Parsons 1939:99; 1964 [1933]:67; Stephen 1898:261; Stevenson 1904:350; White 1942:83). Note that some Pueblos use intercardinal directions related to the solstices, rather than the cardinal directions listed here.

| | North | West | South | East | Above | Below |
|---|---|---|---|---|---|---|
| Hopi | yellow | blue | red | white | black | variegated |
| Zuni | yellow | blue | red | white | variegated | black |
| Laguna | yellow | blue | red | white | brown | green |
| Tewa | blue-green | yellow | red | white | all colors | black |
| Cochiti | yellow | blue | red | white | all colors | black |
| Acoma | yellow | blue | red | white | black | gray |
| Zia | yellow | blue | red | white | light yellow | dark |
| Santa Ana | yellow | blue | red | white | brown | black |

> and everywhere in that region yellow corn grows perpetually. At the West sits a chief wearing a blue-green cloud. At the South, another with a red cloud; and at the East, another with a white cloud. At all these places butterflies of appropriate colour flutter before the chiefs, and corn of like appropriate colour grows at each of these points. At the Above sits a black chief wearing a black cloud and before him flutter countless black butterflies. Below sits Mu'inyiñwu [Muy'ingwa] on Sihchomo [Sitsomo], Flower mound. He wears a mask of clouds of all these five colours, and before it flutter all the sacred birds and all the butterflies. Speckled corn and sweet corn grow there and melons, cotton, beans, squash, etc. [Stephen 1936:333]

Appropriately colored clouds, butterflies, and crops represented each direction, as well events happening in that direction (Hays-Gilpin et al. 2010:129). Directions and colors became linked to sacred mountains where spirits resided, to flowers, trees, and animals of the appropriate color, and to weather phenomena and seasons (see Parsons 1939:172).

For Hopi people, unlike most other groups, the critical directions are not cardinal but are tied to the points on the horizon that are marked by sunrise and sunset during the summer and winter solstices, or roughly equivalent to northwest, southwest, southeast, and northeast (Hieb 1979). Thus, at Hopi the northwest is linked, by virtue of yellow, to orioles, with their bright yellow-orange feathers, and to the mariposa lily and many other kinds of flowers. In addition to this flowery symbolism, the northwest is linked to mountain lion, an emblem of war and the hunt. The blue of the southwest, the direction of sunset on the winter solstice, evokes bluebirds, with their bright feathers, the flowers of blue larkspur, and bears. The southeast, where the sun rises on the winter solstice, is associated with the red of the Indian paintbrush, known in Hopi as "maiden flower." This is also the direction associated with summer weather and the sun, as well as the scarlet macaws who were traded from the warm land of Mexico. The white of the evening primrose represents the northeast, the direction of the sunrise on the summer solstice, along with the distinctive white breast and shoulders of the magpie. Above, represented by the color black, is tied to sunflowers and the yellow-headed blackbird or, in some accounts, the eagle, while Below, the realm of Muy'ingwa, the germinator spirit, encompasses flowers, birds, butterflies, and clouds of all colors (Hays-Gilpin et al. 2010:129, 131).

### Color as Chromatic Prayer

The four directions, the multilayered worlds of Above and Below, and the colors and entities associated with them are central principles in Pueblo religion (Ortiz 1969; Parsons 1939).

The fact that colors are so closely tied to different plants, animals, locations, directions, and contexts makes it possible to create nuanced, context-specific meanings by drawing on some or all of those associations. Stevenson (1904:189) outlined some of the complex associations of color and design when she described a painted kilt belonging to a bow priest at Zuni that "has a broad band of blue-green (symbolic of the vegetation of the world) painted across it," along with a design, painted in yellow and black, representing a ritual game. "The yellow," Stevenson continues, "indicates the north country, whence the A'shiwi [Zuni] came, over which the... Shi'wanni of the North has care, whose breath must be pure so that this region may always be fruitful and beautiful to look upon. The black is symbolic of the earth over which the Shi'wanni of the Nadir has care, whose prayers must be pure that the earth may be made good for man to walk upon."

In this way, the use of color in ritual paraphernalia—and in everyday life—could be seen as a form of chromatic prayer, a term that Stephen (1898:265) coined when he described the yellow, green, red, and white paint used on a katsina as "a direct appeal to the clouds at the four directions to hasten with rain to the Hopi land." Indeed, the symbolic power of color in the Pueblo world is derived in part from the knowledge that colors are meaningful materials that hold the power to affect events, even to compel action, through the key ceremonial principle of like causing like (Parsons 1939:168). When the faces of katsinas at Laguna were painted yellow, for example, the paint simultaneously represented corn pollen and brought rain to the village: "corn pollen through rain, and so in turn causing rain" (Parson's note in Dumarest 1919: 181; also see Parsons 1939:xxxiii).

This highlights a key point regarding color in the Pueblo world: color matters because of its symbolism and association with directions, animals, plants, and natural phenomena—but color is not enough. In a world where all colors were derived directly from the natural world, not a chemist's lab, material was an integral and crucial aspect of color.

## Color as Material

For the vast majority of human history, color has had to be found or created, often through difficult and time-consuming processes. When people wished to use a particular color—say, red—they might seek out a material that is inherently that color, such as the feathers of a scarlet macaw, or naturally red minerals. Inherent colors are satisfying when the colored material is in a desirable or usable form, such as when the symbolism of feathers and of bright red corresponds or when argillite can be shaped into a pendant or nose plug. In other cases, people might choose to apply color to an object or person. Some colorants can be transferred to an object by rubbing, such as soot or certain grades of red ochre (e.g., Stephen 1936:651; Stevenson 1904:450, note b). In most cases, however, it is more effective to transform colorants into a dye or paint.

Safely and successfully creating a paint or dye requires advanced planning, along with a great deal of skill and specialized knowledge (Colton 1965; Odegaard and Hays-Gilpin 2002: 323). Paints are typically made from a pigment combined with a variety of binders, liquid vehicles, and sometimes other additives to help with coverage or adhesion. Pigments may be organic or inorganic materials, but they are by definition insoluble (Rapp 2009:201). When added to other materials, mixing happens on a mechanical, not chemical, level; the particles are suspended in the mixture, maintaining their original physical properties. Pigments therefore tend to make relatively permanent paints (Mayer 1981:30) that resist fading when exposed to light. However, they may still be susceptible to moisture, acidity, and alkalinity (Rapp 2009: 201). The most famous example is lead white, a common paint for millennia, which turns from bright white to brown or black when exposed to the air (Mayer 1981:48).

While most paints are based on pigments, there is a special kind of paint, known as a lake, that is produced by using dye to add color to a white base material, such as clay, aluminum hydroxide, chalk, or gypsum (Mayer 1981:33, 98). Dyes are complex organic compounds that impart color to other materials by bonding chemically (Rapp 2009:201); because they are soluble, dyes tend to be fugitive, fading through washing and exposure to UV radiation. They can, however, produce intense colors that are otherwise difficult to obtain—the most famous example being Maya Blue, a lake that consists of a white clay base dyed with indigo (Houston et al. 2009:65–66).

### *Making Paint*

Museum collections of Pueblo material from the nineteenth century are awash in color, created from a wide range of colorants applied in vivid, appealing manner. When Alexander Stephen began documenting the production and use of colorants in the Hopi villages in the 1880s, making color was still a laborious process, involving a range of natural materials prepared and mixed by hand. Even as commercially produced aniline dyes, synthesized in laboratories, became more readily available in the Southwest (Amsden 1934:88), painters continued to use traditional processes to create paints that were full of meaning and even power.

To produce a paint, Pueblo people began by assembling the pigments, dyestuffs, and other necessary materials. Some colorants were widely available, particularly ones based on local clays or materials such as charcoal or soot. Others were collected from more limited sources, such as pieces of copper carbonate that were used to make blue-green paints (White 1962:249–250) or special clays used as body paints by religious societies (Harrington 1916:251). The locations of valued pigment sources were widely known and were often named after the pigment itself, such as Whitewash Mountain, Red Earth, and Yellow Earth Gap (Harrington 1916:323; Stevenson 1904:233, 234, 426).

Some particularly prized colorants came from farther afield, such as a high-quality red ochre from the Grand Canyon and blue-green copper carbonate from central Arizona. Regardless of their location, pigment sources were often accessed by multiple different indigenous groups, as in a source of red pigment near Taos that was used by people from Taos, Picuris, Tewa, and Keres pueblos, as well as Jicarillas, Utes, "and other tribes" (Harrington 1916:175). Parsons (1939:32–33) noted that the Hopi made special trips to trade with the Havasupai to get buckskins, baskets, and the ochre, which they called *Kohonini shu'ta (Kòonina suta)*, or Havasupai red (Stephen 1936:1195). It seems likely that this is the same "special red ochre" that Lange (1990:132) noted people at Cochiti buying from the Hopi; the price in the 1950s was "a dollar per teaspoonful," which is the equivalent in today's dollars of about $10 a teaspoon, or more than $900 per pound.

Once the ingredients were assembled, the painter needed to process them and prepare the paint or dye according to the recipe. Depending on the materials being used, this might involve grinding pigments, preparing binders or other additives, mixing ingredients, and heating or cooking the materials. Mineral pigments could be ground on an informal grinding surface, such as the stone cover of a niche or the floor or bench of a kiva, or by using a dedicated mortar and pestle or mano and metate (e.g., Stephen 1936: 92, 541, 820, 878). Grinding pigments required a certain amount of skill and judgment, for the quality of paint could depend on how finely or coarsely the materials were ground (Rapp 2009: 202). The mano and metate used for preparing ceremonial paint at San Felipe were so valued that the stones "constitute[d] a kind of altar," exhibited in the room where preparations for the dances took place (White 1932:29).

Paints were prepared from ground pigments, a liquid vehicle, and a variety of additives, from saliva to bear grease, that served a range of practical and religious purposes. For example, men might chew the seeds of melons or cotton, then spit the mixture onto the pigment. According to Stephen (1898:265), the Hopi say, "speaking secularly, that the saliva arising from seed-chewing causes the pigments to adhere to the painted object, but they also say, this practice has the purport of a votive offering."

Some paint recipes also involved elaborate cooking processes, necessary to extract and fix color. Lakes, or paints made by using dyes to stain a base material, were particularly complicated. At Hopi, for example, Stephen watched as an "old expert priest" made a yellow lake using rabbitbrush flowers (Stephen 1898:262). The process began by combining alum, a mordant often used in dyeing, with a fine white material similar to gypsum, talc, or clay. These ingredients were added to a jar of hot water, then stirred constantly with a gourd ladle while the mixture boiled and foamed. When the foam settled, the priest crammed in as many rabbitbrush flowers as possible, boiling the mixture for another half hour before straining out the flowers with a yucca sieve. The resulting liquid, a dull yellow color, was returned to the pot and all of the steps repeated again. From time to time, the paint-maker tested the color by dabbing it on his skin, adjusting the ingredients to lighten or darken the mixture as needed. After about four hours of work, the liquid was reduced to about a pint of creamy, bright yellow paste (Stephen 1936:271). The paint could be used as soon as it was cool, or might be shaped into a small cake and left to dry for later use (Stephen 1936:1294).

The most labor-intensive and specialized paint was copper resinate, a special green paint made with pine resins and copper carbonate (Kühn 1970). As Stephen (1898:263; 1936:1192–1194) described, the process began with roasting a mass of piñon gum in a jar over the fire, with a little bit of water added to keep it from burning. After the gum melted completely, it was left to boil for about 10 minutes, then poured through a sieve lined with horse hair or shredded yucca fiber into a pot of water. The piñon gum quickly congealed into a sticky white mass, which the man preparing the paint then kneaded and stretched for about 15 minutes, until it was soft and glistening. In the meantime, one or two men ground copper carbonate into a fine powder, eventually adding water to make a thin liquid. The paint-maker dipped the gum briefly into the blue-green liquid, then heated it again over the fire. As soon as the gum began to melt, he poured in the rest of the copper carbonate liquid, stirring constantly while the whole mixture came to a boil. As the gum began to take on the color of the copper carbonate, the paint-maker occasionally fished it out of the pot to check the color, which got darker the longer the mixture boiled. When he judged that the color was correct, after about 20 minutes, he poured out the hot water and replaced it with cold, causing the now blue-green gum to coagulate once again and allowing him to shape it into a rough cake which hardened into a slightly brittle mass with a glossy, almost plastic, appearance.

The recipes for yellow lake and copper resinate clearly required a great deal of knowledge about ingredients and process, as well as judgments about when the paint had reached the appropriate color. Indeed, Hopi paint-makers were not indifferent to minor variations in hue, modifying ingredients or tweaking recipes to ensure that their paint was not "drab" or "off color" (Stephen 1936:1193). In fact, while the Hopi maintained traditional recipes for both yellow lake and copper resinate in the 1890s, Stephen (1936:542) recorded "the lamentable fact" that they were also willing to add aniline dyes to intensify the paint's color. "They call the aniline medicine and say" that its use in copper resinate "makes the fine...rich deep green... they especially desire" (Stephen 1936:923).

### Using Paint

Once paints were finished, they could be used immediately or stored for later use. The method of storage depended on the type of paint. Some paints were formed into a mass, then wrapped in corn husks or shaped into cones or cakes and left to dry (Stevenson 1904:160, 375). The names of the yellow lake and the copper resinate paint from Hopi effectively translate to yellow cake and blue-green cake because the paints were shaped into "little round cakes, five or six inches in diameter and one-half to three-fourths inches thick" (Stephen 1936:470). Such paints had to be reconstituted before use, usually by breaking up the cake and grinding it to a powder, then mixing in water or saliva and chewed seeds. When Stevenson (1904:221) observed copper resinate paint being reconstituted and mixed at Zuni, the process took two young men a full hour, with "one grinding while the other scrapes the paint toward the center of the paint stone."

Other paints, probably those that could be easily reconstituted by adding water, were stored in pottery vessels. James and Matilda Coxe Stevenson collected a great number of paint jars from Zuni, describing them as small jars or cups, about four to eight centimeters high. Some of the vessels were actually multiple jars or cups, joined together in pairs, triples, or even quadruples, with each part containing a different paint (Stevenson 1883:362–363). Observations of the double paint jars in the collections of the National Museum of Natural History suggest that they often contained yellow and black paints, implying that they may have been used for painting pottery (with the yellow paint firing to red in oxidizing conditions). However, Anna Shepard (1929:6) later reported that a Zuni man described two small jars joined together as being for body paint, while four small jars joined into a quadruple vessel were said to be used for "yellow, blue, red and white paint" and were reserved for the use of "the medicine man, cacique, or katsina."

Once prepared, paint was applied directly with the fingers or by using a brush of yucca, a twig, or a bone. The specific method of applying paints affects final color; painting on wet plaster, for example, results in more intense colors than applying the same paint to dry plaster (Rapp 2009:204). Certain paints or clays were applied by blowing, spraying, or spitting them onto a surface, a process that took advantage of the liquid consistency of the paint and in doing so evoked moisture-related symbolism by mimicking droplets of rain (Stephen 1936: 470). This method was especially preferred for applying copper resinate paint to dance moccasins, katsina regalia, and other ritual paraphernalia. At Zia, for example, the copper resinate was ground to a powder, mixed with water, and sprayed from the mouth. The paint was then set by spraying it with a second liquid, made of chewed pumpkin seeds and water; the milky liquid was said to make the copper resinate paint "look darker and greener" (White 1962: 250). Ingesting copper can cause stomach upset and other troubling symptoms; indeed, Stevenson (1904:221) reported that one man at Zuni became sick from spraying copper resinate paint onto dance paraphernalia.

The dangers of paint—on both physical and metaphysical levels—meant that the production and use of paints was done under the supervision and guidance of ritual specialists (Lange 1990:238; Parsons 1939:113; White 1932:15, 29) who had the knowledge to make and use them properly. This role was so significant that the kiva head at Santo Domingo had just a single item of ritual paraphernalia: "a grinding stone on which he grinds his blue-green paint" (White 1935:48, also see 95). The men responsible for gathering pigments to use on ritual paraphernalia at Cochiti were referred to with the word for "blue" (Lange 1990:290; also see 310, 349; and Goldfrank 1927:94, 113), indicating a close tie between color, material, and ceremonial role. At Zuni the Shi'wannakwe, or rainmakers, prepared themselves before touching a jar of stored paint by rubbing prayer meal on their hands (Parsons 1964[1933]:18, note 62).

The correct disposal of paint was also important. When men at Hopi scraped paint off of items before repainting them, the used material was collected in a basin and later placed into a shrine (Stephen 1936:395, 397, 519). The sand and pigments used in dry paintings on altars at Zuni were treated in similar fashion, being gathered up along with other ritual items and deposited in a hole outside the village (Stevenson 1904:576). The correct disposal was important, as certain paints used to paint ritual paraphernalia at Hopi might be "made taboo" and could only be touched by elders. "If a young man touched it," Stephen (1936:309) explained, "he would swell up and perhaps die." A similar prohibition may have been in place at Zuni, where altars and dry paintings "are referred to as *tesh'kwi* (not to be touched)" (Stevenson 1904:425)

## Color and Material in the Pueblo World

Organized by basic color terms, this section examines the pigments, paints, and dyes used to produce color in the Pueblo Southwest, drawing on ethnographic information from Alexander Stephen's time at Hopi, supplemented by other sources. It also considers the symbolism of various paints and the materials used to make them.

### *Red*

Pueblo people had several different reds available, some based on mineral pigments and others on plant dyes. The most important was probably red ochre, a general term for a range of materials, such as hematite, some goethite, and some clays, that are colored red by iron oxide. One of the most widely used pigments on earth, iron oxides can range in color from dull yellow to reds, purples, and browns, depending on factors such as the level of hydration, particle size and shape, and the presence of other mineral compounds (Rapp 2009:207–211). Iron oxides of all kinds are quite stable. They are resistant to alkaline conditions and to weak to moderate acids, as well as being lightfast (Rapp 2009:207).

The Hopi recognized multiple grades or versions of ochre red. Stephen (1936:1292) recorded the term *shu'ta* (*suta* in today's orthography) as referring to red ochre in general, while *ko'honini shu'ta* (*Kòonina suta*) referred to a special hematite from the Grand Canyon. Red ochre was "in constant use" at Hopi (Stephen 1898:264; also see Voth 1903:279, 286, 308, 322, 330, 334), as well as at Zuni (Stevenson 1904:212, 338, 451, 504, 517). Ochre might be rubbed directly onto a person or object, ground for use as an offering or a dry pigment, or mixed with binders such as animal fat to be used as paint (Stevenson 1904:504, 517; White 1962:18, 257, 303). The Hopi also used a red earthy paint that they called *pala'chka* (*palatsöqa*), a naturally occurring mixture of clay and iron oxide that they obtained from locations near their villages and prepared by rubbing it down with water (Stephen 1936:1195). The same term, *palatsöqa*, could also refer to a manufactured version of the paint, made by adding *Kòonina suta* to a clay base to create "a deep red or a paler tint according to purpose or fancy" (Stephen 1936:1194). Both versions were used as body paint for katsinas, often in a pale pink version (Stephen 1936:1195)

Stephen also recorded a third Hopi term for a mineral red: *kas'til shu'ta* (Castilian or Spanish red, now spelled *Kastil suta*), which he translated into English as vermilion. Vermilion, or cinnabar, is mercury sulfide, a soft greasy mineral that was usually extracted from silver mines (Rapp 2009:216). It is not clear whether vermilion was used in the Pueblo Southwest, as the term was often mistakenly applied to high-quality iron oxides (Smith 1952:27). The confusion over vermilion in the Southwest highlights the potential differences between scientific definitions of minerals and folk classifications of pigments; the two ways of knowing colorful materials do not always coincide, making clear discussion of materials difficult.

In addition to mineral reds, Pueblo people also used organic colorants to create red dyes and paints for a variety of purposes. Painters at Hopi made a red lake body paint by dyeing a white base with a mixture made from dark purple corn and dried sumac berries (Stephen 1936:233). The final color varied from red to pink, as "the result of the process as practiced by different men is not always quite the same" (Stephen 1936:1194). People at Hopi also used melted piñon gum mixed with a red substance from an oak tree to make a red paint used in decorating arrows (Stephen 1936:1238), as well as birch bark and roots to dye leather red (Stephen 1936:1274). A similar reddish-brown dye at Cochiti was produced from the bark and sometimes roots of mountain mahogany, boiled and mixed with a small amount of lime (Dumarest 1919:199; Lange 1990:147; White 1945:562). Even wafer bread might be colored red by adding a particular species of amaranth to the batter (Stevenson 1904:353, 363).

Red in general, and red ochre in particular, was associated with warfare, blood, epidemics, starvation, and hail (Lange 1990:279–280). It was widely reported in association with warriors and hunters in many pueblos, where it served as an offering to scalps, as face paint, or as coloring for prayer sticks (Dumarest 1919:184, note 6; Lange 1990:132; Stephen 1898:265; 1904:583, 585, 597, 606; White 1942:33, 308; White 1962:16). In some of the Keres pueblos, red could be used on prayer sticks for the sun, but it was inappropriate in prayer sticks for lightning or on paintings that were designed to bring rain (White 1935:163).

During initiation into the Bow Priesthood at Zuni, men offered red prayer sticks "to the Gods of War for the destruction of the enemy" (Stevenson 1904:585), while women offered black prayer sticks "to the deceased warriors [to ask] for rain" (Stevenson 1904:598). In the same ceremony, people offered sticks colored for each of the directions to ask "for the destruction of the enemies of the six regions" (Stevenson 1904:598). The pairing of red and black was strongly associated with warfare as well, including Morningstar, Venus, scalps, and Knife Wing (Schaafsma 2000).

At Cochiti, Dumarest (1919:159) noted that "witches" were referred to as "the dark reds" because they painted their hands and legs with red and black paint mixed together "when [they] are to engage in working evil." When Parsons edited Dumarest's notes for publication after his death, she commented that his overall description of witches seemed more like that of *koshare*, or sacred clowns (see Dumarest 1919:164, note 1). Either way, it seems that red and black mixed together were associated with the breaking of social norms. The combination of red and black together is particularly interesting in light of special forms of hematite, known as specular and botryoidal hematite, which combine both colors with sparkling and metallic effects.

### *Black*

The ethnographic literature mentions numerous black paints, used at many different pueblos (Goldfrank 1927:93; White 1962:311) in ways that pose what seem to outside observers to be interesting contradictions. At Zuni, the Tewa-speaking pueblos, and many of the Keres pueblos, it is the color of the nadir, or underworld; at Hopi and Acoma, however, it is the color associated with the sky, or Above. Black is the quintessential cloudy color, for it represents the color of storm clouds heavy with rain and, in some cases, "clouds of all colours" (Stephen 1936:824). Black also represents seeds and is therefore used to paint the seed-like eyes of katsinas; in other contexts, its use is associated with war. In fact, as discussed later in this chapter, black seems to be a complicated color for some of the Pueblos—or, more accurately, Pueblo people used a wide variety of different black pigments, paints, and dyes, often making fine distinctions among visually similar materials.

Archaeologists have long recognized that pottery painters had two basic means of creating black on their vessels: carbon paints or mineral paints (Hawley 1929; Shepard 1956). The specific composition of inorganic pottery paints varied, but most involve manganese- or iron-bearing minerals that fired to dark brown or warm black hues when used on Pueblo pottery. Carbon paints used on pottery were often made from Rocky Mountain beeweed or other plants boiled into a sticky black paint (Hawley 1929:738; Lange 1990:147; Parsons 1964[1933]:18, note 66; Stevenson 1904:375, 491; White 1945: 559). It could be used as-is, or the color could be reinforced by mixing in a mineral black in the form of manganese-bearing clay.

Plant materials were also used in textile dyes and paints used on ritual paraphernalia and as body paint. One Hopi recipe for black dye involved boiling sumac twigs and sunflower seeds, then combining them with a mixture of roasted piñon gum and "a kind of ochre found in shale" (Stephen 1936:1187).

Carbon compounds provided an array of blacks used for purposes other than pottery, including charcoal, soot, and corn smut (Dumarest 1919:199; Stephen 1936:751, 1195). Charcoal from burned corn cobs or wood could be rubbed into a powder on a grinding stone and used as a pigment for dry painting (Stevenson 1904:507, 560); like the other carbon blacks, however, it was powdery and prone to smearing. Painters mitigated the problem by mixing the pigments with a variety of ingredients, including saliva, chewed melon seeds, melted piñon pitch, and egg white (Stephen 1936:211–212, 426, 751).

Charcoal could also be mixed with white clay or similar materials to produce a gray-blue color (Mayer 1981:69), as Smith (1952:23) noted in some Pueblo IV murals in the Hopi Mesas. Other grays came from special clays and ashes used at Hopi and at Zuni (Parsons 1964[1917]b: 230–231, 233, 270, note 2; Parsons 1964[1933]:45–46, note 174). One particular clay, used as body paint for the Zuni Galaxy Society, comes from a spring that is named Ashes Spring (Parsons 1964[1917]b:230–231, 233; Stevenson 1904:430).

Pueblo people also used a range of naturally occurring black or dark gray stones and clays. Ritual practitioners at Hopi and Zuni made use of a naturally black mud or clay, obtained from the bottom of a spring at the place of Emergence (Stephen 1936:510, note 1, 753), representing "the undermost world" (Stevenson 1904:172). The identification of black stony pigments at Hopi was not always clear; Stephen (1936:470) variously recorded the use of shale, lignite coal, and "a coal shale or shaly coal." The recipes for the different varieties of dark stone seem similar: the material would be pulverized by pounding or grinding, then mixed with saliva generated by chewing the seeds of melons or cotton. This process made the black coal or shale paint appropriate for use on ritual paraphernalia, as the combination of ingredients served as kind of offering (Stephen 1898:265). Melon seeds in particular were an important ingredient in black paint for the eyes of katsinas, which symbolize the seeds of plants (Stephen 1936:215–216). When an elder mixed ordinary black shale paint with white cornmeal to use in painting an effigy of Paalölöqangw, however, the paint became dangerous; elders could touch the paint, but young men were prohibited from doing so (Stephen 1936:309).

Perhaps the most striking aspect about black paints among the Pueblos was the diversity of pigments and other ingredients. Although black made from coal, charcoal, soot, and corn smut would appear to be essentially the same color and even texture, the Hopi considered them to be distinct and took great pains to ensure that they were "never mixed together; but are used separately for different occasions" (Stephen 1936:1195). Corn smut, for example, was used as a body decoration because it was "a form of chromatic prayer for rain, because when rain is very plenty corn smut abounds in the corn; when there is but little rain, there is no corn smut" (Stephen 1936:708).

A similar phenomenon is documented at Zuni, where the rain priests, or A'shiwanni, maintained separate pots of special earth paints that came from the underworld, including two kinds of black and one red. These paints were used according to strict terms: prayer sticks "offered for cold rains and snows are colored with paint from one of the black pots and those for the summer rains are colored with paint from the other, an exception being when neither paint is used, but instead paint used by laymen. Should the paint of the A'shiwanni be used in the month of May, cold winds would come and destroy the fruit" (Stevenson 1904:172). Black paint and eagle down, used by Buffalo Dance participants at Cochiti, were similarly effective at bringing cold; they were not used during dances in the spring, for fear of bringing an unwanted late snowstorm (Lange 1990:328).

### *Sparkling or Metallic*

The associations of black and red come together in unusual pigments that combine those two hues with sparkling or metallic effects. This includes black minerals such as galena, some kinds of mica, and magnetite, as well as certain special forms of hematite.

Pueblo painters used mica or naturally sparkling minerals as an ingredient in face paint for warriors and katsina dancers, as well as medicine men and society initiates in certain circumstances (Goldfrank 1927:56; White 1942:175). Sparkling pigment might be used alone or in combination with red ochre, black paint, or a dark yellow ochre (White 1932:45, 46, 53). At Cochiti, for example, katsina faces were painted black, then sprayed by mouth with "the juice obtained by straining the contents of pumpkin seeds.... This darkens the paint and 'fixes' it. While this is still moist and sticky, the worker chews mica and sprays it evenly...to give it a glistening appearance" (Lange 1990:291, also 258, 510). Ritual specialists at San Felipe, Santo Domingo, and Zia achieved a similar effect by using a black sparkling pigment that White (1962:16) identified as a natural combination of magnetite and hematite, which could be ground and applied over black paint (White 1932:53, note 66; 1935:124). At Zuni Parsons (1939:70) noted that an "iridescent black paint" was used for painting katsinas, though she did not identify the material.

War symbolism was perhaps most strongly expressed in special forms of hematite. The hematite discussed previously as red ochre is an earthy mineral; however, hematite comes in other forms, which differ completely in appearance. Some hematite is a deep, reddish-purple color, often with sparkling inclusions. Specular hematite is a dark, glittering version that appears to consist of small black crystals adhered together (Houston et al. 2009:64). Another form of the mineral, botryoidal hematite, is even stranger in appearance. It consists of a series of spheres that have overlapped and grown together, like a cluster of grapes. The globular surface has a dark gray or deep purple-red metallic luster that is quite unworldly. The various combinations of dark red and metallic black must have been deeply significant, especially when one considers the association of those colors with stars and warfare (Schaafsma 2000).

Sparkling hematite and other metallic red-black minerals were special pigments. Called "star medicine" at Zuni, they served as a symbol of leadership for members of religious societies and were deemed "specially acceptable to the Beast Gods" (Stevenson 1904:415, also see 333, 542–543, 590). In the 1920s Frederick Hodge noted that Zuni workers excavating at Hawikku regarded glistening or glittering black paint as sacred (Smith et al. 1966:284). At Hopi metallic forms of hematite, called "sky stone," were associated with warriors (Stephen 1936:55–58, 76, 92). Deep red paint made using glittering black was seen as a "hard" paint and was used on special prayer sticks that were "stuck into the rafters, 'to make the house strong'" (Parsons's footnote in Crow-wing 1925:16).

### *White*

For Pueblo people, black and white are closely tied together (Parsons 1939:102), not as opposites as they are considered in Western thought today, but as two states of clouds. White symbolized "the clouds of the world," along with materials that are white or fluffy, such as cotton, down, and kaolin clay (Stevenson 1904:499; also Stephen 1936:853). White was also used to represent falling rain when streaked over black, the zigzags of lightning, or, when spotted, "the heavens" (Stevenson 1904:208, 509, 537).

Pueblo people used a variety of clays, gypsum, talc, and other chalky deposits as white paint, as a slip for pottery vessels, and as whitewash for walls. Researchers tend to label many of these materials as kaolin, a white clay that is free of iron oxides (Rapp 2009:187). As with many other colorants, however, the scientific classification is not necessarily always relevant, as most pueblos had a source of white clay or other pale earthy materials nearby (Dumarest 1919:199; Goldfrank 1927:94; Harrington 1916: 290, 329; Lange 1990:53; Stephen 1898:264; Stephen 1936:25; Stevenson 1904:233; White 1962:250). Acoma was particularly known for its high-quality white clay, which they traded to other pueblos to use as pottery slip (Parsons 1939:35; Shepard 1929:2).

Kaolin and other white clays were usually processed by being dissolved in water, then shaped into cones that were left to dry; examples of these cones are present in the ethnographic collections of the National Museum of Natural History. When the clay was needed as paint or whitewash, it could be rubbed down into a powder, reconstituted by adding water, and applied as a body paint, pottery slip, whitewash, or paint for ritual paraphernalia (Parsons 1964[1917] a:195; Stevenson 1904; White 1942:241, 242, 291). The symbolic power of the white clay was sometimes boosted by adding additional ingredients, such as "medicine-water" (Stephen 1936:644) or chewed squash blossoms and seeds (Stevenson 1904:574).

Freshly whitewashed walls were seen as a way for women to "make their houses beautiful for...the gods who are to come" (Stevenson 1904:236). The symbolism of mud plaster was intensified by the properties of wet clay, which was "the girls' prayer for rain," a tangible sign asking the rains to come and transform the dry washes into wet earth (Stephen 1936:198). The plasterers reinforced the symbolism by using the mud to make designs of lightning and clouds on the vigas, adding handprints to "signify the desire...to grasp at the clouds and bring rain" (Stephen 1936:198).

Although many of the white earthy paints used by Pueblo people would seem to be nearly identical in appearance, the Hopi people maintained separate terms for various kinds of white clay (Stephen 1936:1241, 1310) and reserved them for specific applications. One white clay, for example, was used to paint katsinas "because it smells sweet"; a different variety, used to whitewash houses, was considered inappropriate for ritual paraphernalia as it "smells offensive to the kachinas" (Stephen 1936:25).

### *Yellow*

At most pueblos, yellow was the color of the north, or the sunset at the summer solstice; for Tewa speakers, however, it was the color of the west. As the color of corn pollen and many flower petals, yellow was also a natural way to evoke the warm fertile realm of the Flower World (Hays-Gilpin et al. 2010) and to summon rain (Parsons in Dumarest 1919:181, note 1). Indeed, Pueblo people often used corn pollen and the dried, powdered petals of sunflowers as colorants; flowers were key ingredients in many recipes for yellow dyes (Colton 1965), including those used in making a yellow lake (Stephen 1898; White 1962:250; also White 1945:565).

In addition to literal flowers and pollen, people from Hopi used an iron oxide mineral, probably goethite, that creates a warm earthy yellow. As with red ochre, the Hopi apparently distinguished among different grades of yellow ochre, based in part on their source; one, which Stephen recorded as *Ko'honino sikya'chka (Kòonina sikyatsaq)*, or Havasupai yellow, came from the bottom of a spring at the place of Emergence in the Grand Canyon (Stephen 1936:1293–1294). Yellow ochre was ground and mixed with water to create a dull yellow paint or, if a more saturated color was desired, with water colored by boiling squash in it (Stephen 1936:521). This mixture could be used as body paint (Stephen 1898; 1936:521) or as a wash over the walls of kivas or other rooms (Harrington 1916:581; Stephen 1936:245).

Yellow ochre had another use, however, as a red paint on pottery. Yellow ochre is a hydrated iron oxide; when heated, some or all of the water is driven off, modifying the color (Houston et al. 2009:64; Rapp 2009:208). Potters took advantage of this change by using yellow ochre and iron-bearing clays to produce a range of warm red to reddish browns on their buff-to-yellow-firing vessels (Stephen 1936:1190; Stevenson 1904:375). The changes of clay and paint colors are important, as Hopi potters describe, because the "blush" of color indicates that the vessel has become animate (Charley and McChesney 2007).

When combined with black, yellow could evoke the colors of the mountain lion, the patron of the hunt and war; at the same time, those colors could also symbolize the "black... of rain clouds and the pollen of the fruits of the earth" (Stevenson 1904:198). Yellow was also used frequently in depictions of rainbows, along with red and blue (Lange 1990:53).

Like black and white, the pairing of turquoise and yellow was "a constant principle in almost all uses of pigment" (Parsons 1939:102). The juxtaposition of yellow and turquoise had strong gendered connotations, with yellow representing the female half of paired spirits or prayer sticks and blue-green the male (Parsons 1939:102; White 1932:67; White 1962:311). At Zuni notched sticks made by Shalako were painted blue for boys and yellow for girls (Parsons 1964[1933]:100). Yellow and blue-green could also represent the moon and the sun, respectively (Stevenson 1904:138, 537), although yellow, white, red, and turquoise were all colors associated with the sun (see Chapter 4).

### *Blue-Green*

Researchers working in the Southwest quickly realized that Pueblo languages glossed blues and greens as variations of a single color (White 1943:562). Although they initially found this confusing (Stephen 1936:1191), the mingling of blues and greens in Pueblo languages mirrors reality, for blues and greens in the Southwest came primarily from a diverse range of copper-bearing materials. These included sandstones or clays that have a naturally occurring dull green color (Stephen 1898:263; 1936:737, 878) and various minerals that co-occur in copper deposits (Gettens and Fitzhugh 1974). Thus, minerals that are distinctive on a chemical and structural level, such as turquoise, malachite (green), azurite (blue), and chrysocolla (greenish-blue; Rapp 2009:105, 113–115), were often treated as variations of the same material (Houston et al. 2009:56).

As with other pigments, Pueblo people could use copper-bearing clays and minerals to produce a simple paint by grinding them down and mixing them with water and other ingredients (Stephen 1898:108, 265). When preparing paint, men might chew seeds to generate saliva, then spit the mixture onto the ground minerals; while melon seeds were added to black paint, squash seeds were considered appropriate for green paint (Stephen 1936:899). In addition to choosing the right additives, individuals preparing blue-green paint had to be careful while grinding, as the color of both azurite and malachite changes depending on particle size (Gettens and Fitzhugh 1966, 1974). If the mineral was ground too fine, the color might become too pale to use.

The most elaborate paint recipe among the Pueblos was the one, described earlier, for making copper resinate paint by heating copper carbonate with piñon gum. The earliest known written description of that process for making resinate paint is a seventeenth-century recipe from Europe (Kühn 1970:30), but it seems likely that Pueblo people invented the method independently. Certainly, the ethnographic record is clear that copper resinate paint was produced at most of the pueblos in the late nineteenth century (Dumarest 1919:199; Lange and Riley 1966:215–216; Stephen 1936:1192–1193; Stevenson 1904:221; White 1942:33; 1962:31, 249–250). For the Hopi, the association between the ingredients of copper resinate paint goes back to the time of Emergence, when "the porcupine ate some piñon gum and after this his faeces were malachite" (Stephen 1936:1254).

Green copper resinate paint was used in ritually significant contexts for katsina faces, arm bands, anklets, and wristlets. It was not suitable for all purposes, though, for copper resinate could never be used for prayer sticks at Hopi. "'Cloud dislikes the smell of piñon gum,'" Stephen recorded (1936:1194), and "it would be evil to use ... any substance that has been boiled" on prayer sticks (Stephen 1898:265). Instead, prayer sticks were painted green with pulverized copper ore and a pinch of white bean meal mixed with spring water (Stephen 1898:108, 265).

In addition to being the color of vegetation (Stephen 1936:1191), blue-green was also associated with males and male beings such as Sun Father (Stevenson 1904:119). Turquoise itself, the quintessential blue-green material, was also masculine, a personified being who figured in the story of the origin of the Zuni Salt Lake. When evaluating individual pieces of turquoise, the Zuni referred to "the perfect blue" as male, and "the off-colored" ones as female (Stevenson 1904:58, note a). In addition to being used for jewelry, turquoise was ground at Zuni and used as a dry pigment for altars or as part of offerings (Stevenson 1904:334, 337, 428).

### *Pink*

The boundary between red, pink, purple, and maroon is rather vague; however, there are clear mentions in the ethnographic record of specific pink clays that were used for sacred body paint. *Palatsöqa*, the paint from Hopi made by mixing Grand Canyon hematite with white clay, was usually mixed to a pink tint when it was to be used as body paint for a katsina (Stephen 1936:1195). Clowns at Zuni used a pink clay body paint in similar fashion, to "identify themselves with their patron or prototype" (Parsons 1939:170). Sometimes the clowns painted their bodies with clay "applied so thin that the color is scarcely to be discerned" (Stevenson 1904:218), implying that the presence of the material was more important than a visible change in appearance. The clay, collected as part of a pilgrimage during summer solstice ceremonies was "greatly prized by the Zuñi, who believe that if the smallest portion should be parted with no rain would again fall upon the land" (Stevenson 1904:155).

## The Power of Color

Color was a profound aspect of the central organizing principles of Pueblo life, including the four directions, the layered worlds of Above and Below, and the many plants, animals, clouds, spirit beings, and sacred locations associated with them. Whether inherent or applied, color served many different purposes for Pueblo people, from the prosaic to the profound. Face and body paint could be used to designate the kiva affiliations of racers, to disguise hunters, or even to prevent sunburn (e.g., Judd 1954:284; Parsons 1939:28; Stephen 1936:264, 1023; Stevenson 1904:517). Most of all, colorful materials served as a kind of chromatic prayer, embodying katsinas, summoning rain clouds to parched fields, or causing harm those who mishandled them.

Pigments and dyes accomplished these feats in part because they were of the appropriate hue (red, blue-green, black, or any number of colors) through a process of mimetic symbolism, or like attracting like. Beyond superficial aspects of hue, though, colorants were powerful materials, obtained from significant locations: Yellow Earth Gap, Whitewash Mountain, even the sipapu at the place of Emergence. These special pigments and paints were part of the paraphernalia of religious societies (e.g., White 1942:123) and were often stored in special locations and heirloom containers, including pots recovered from ancestral sites (Parsons 1933:18, note 62; Stevenson 1904:419, 596, 599). In fact, Fewkes (1898:728) noted that Hopi priests specifically asked for pigments excavated from the ancestral site of Sikyatki because the old pigments were "particularly efficacious in coloring their ceremonial paraphernalia"; Judd (1954:284–285) records similar requests from Zuni workers in Chaco Canyon.

Harnessing color—using naturally occurring colorants and making them into paints and dyes—was a complicated process, requiring a great investment of time, skill, and materials. Supervised by kiva heads and other elders, painters mixed pigments with ingredients ranging from saliva and seeds to alum, clay, bear fat, or piñon gum. Some of these ingredients were immanently practical, serving as a base for a lake or helping to fix a colorant onto an object; others had more metaphysical roles, helping to deepen the symbolism and efficacy of a paint. Even the method of application could reinforce a paint's power, as spitting or spraying pigment helped to summon clouds by evoking droplets of rain. Indeed, the act of painting "signifies completion and 'making sacred'" (Odegaard and Hays-Gilpin 2002:307).

Colors are therefore deeply meaningful. Their diverse associations with directions, clouds, deities, sacred locations, and plants and animals mean that Pueblo people have a rich array of connotations to draw upon when choosing colors. Like the kiva murals discussed by Hays-Gilpin, Newsome, and Sekaquaptewa (2010:135), colors are neither codes to be broken nor a language to be translated and read like a book. Color is one expressive part of a rich symbolic world in which painting, dance, and song "are ways of bringing the spirit world and this world closer together…to ensure the continuation of relationships among the humans and ancestors, plants and animals, past and future" (Hays-Gilpin et al. 2010:137).

# 2

# Pigments and Paints in the Archaeological Record

Marit K. Munson

The ethnographic information discussed in Chapter 1 makes it clear that color was and is an important part of historic and contemporary Pueblo life. In addition, the literature highlights the fact that color is not abstract; rather, it has a physical, tangible nature. Prior to the mid-nineteenth century, anyone who wanted to apply color had to procure and process pigments and follow recipes to prepare paints that were appropriate for use in different contexts. Although archaeologists working in the Southwest have seldom focused directly on the technologies of color, a review of the literature shows that there are considerable records of pigments, paints, and the tools associated with processing, storing, and using these materials.

In this chapter, I build a picture of pigments and paints in the archaeological record, using published reports from across the Ancestral Pueblo Southwest, supplemented with observations on museum collections. In some respects, published accounts fall short of an ideal record. Researchers might mention the use of hematite or ochre in general terms (e.g., Hough 1914:12) but without any detail. In other cases, archaeologists encountered certain pigments, such as red ochre, so frequently that they ceased recording them. In his work in Chaco Canyon, for example, Neil Judd (1959:139) wrote that he found "only one piece of red paint worth cataloging" at Pueblo del Arroyo, clearly implying that he did not bother to save or record other examples.

The terms that archaeologists use also tend to vary considerably. Where Judd referred to "red paint," other researchers might record the same material as "ochre" (or "ocher"). In field notes from Pueblo Bonito, George Pepper used the term "ochre" for both red *and* yellow, specifying the color in some but not all cases. Even the term "hematite" is less precise than it may first seem, as the mineral comes in a variety of colors and forms (Figure 2.1). In similar fashion, some researchers distinguish between the distinct yet related minerals malachite and azurite, while others use the term "copper carbonate." The most problematic terms in the literature are "paint," "paint stick," and "paint stone," which can refer to a wide range of materials and colors; in some cases, "paint stone" even refers to ground stone used to grind pigments or paints (e.g., Smith et al. 1966:219).

When possible, I distinguish in this chapter between pigments, meaning minerals or other raw materials, and the prepared paints that were mixed from them; in practice, however, the distinction often breaks down. Absent other information, I accept each author's terminology at face value. Table 2.1 provides a simple tabulation of basic colors of pigments and paints as reported in the literature, without any attempt to discern the specific materials involved. Unfortunately, attempts to identify pigments or paint recipes using optical or chemical properties are relatively rare. With the exception of characterization of paint recipes for glaze ware pottery (e.g., Cordell and Habicht-Mauche 2012;

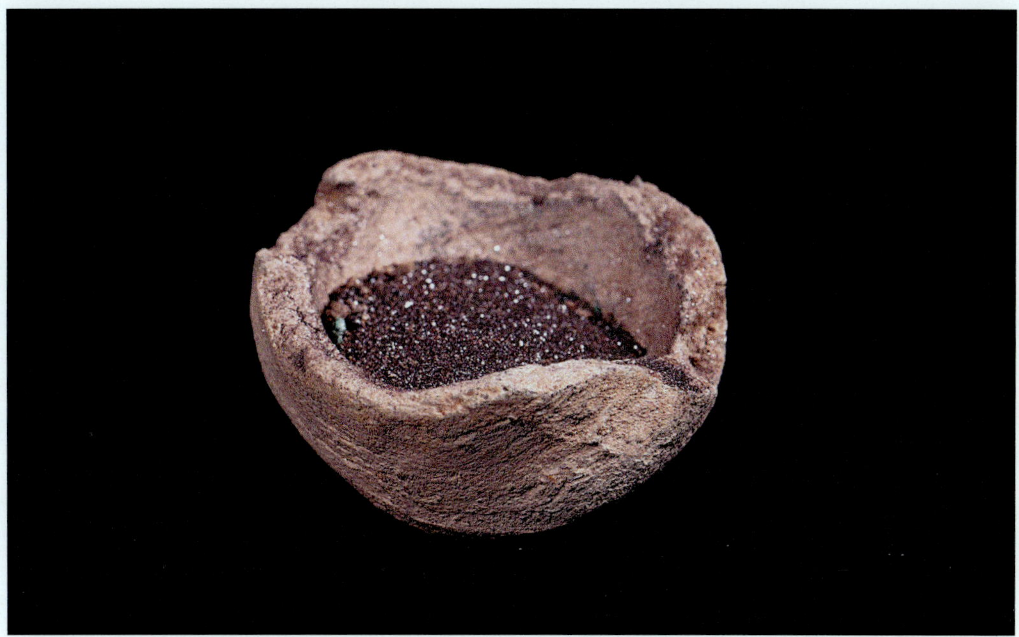

FIGURE 2.1. Although most hematite is red, the mineral also occurs in sparkling or metallic forms. This miniature pottery bowl from the Verde Valley holds ground specular hematite, a black sparkling pigment that was highly valued among many historic Pueblo groups. Tuzigoot National Monument, National Park Service. Catalog numbers TUZI 847 (hematite) and TUZI 689 (bowl). Photograph by Ryan Belnap and Monica Saaty. Courtesy of Northern Arizona University.

Herhahn 2006; Huntley et al. 2012; Huntley et al. 2007), the most detailed analyses of paint composition are in Watson Smith's (1952) study of the kiva murals at Awat'ovi and Kawàyka'a and the National Park Service publication of painted wooden objects from Chetro Ketl (Vivian et al. 1978). More recently, collaboration between archaeologists and conservators has led to additional work identifying pigments from Homol'ovi I and II, as well as other Southwestern sites (Meyers 2007; Odegaard and Hanson 2019).

I also compiled information regarding the prevalence of different colors at specific sites (Table 2.2). Note that the data reflected in both tables relate only to pigments and paints, not to items stained or colored with them. As much as possible, the numeric data in Table 2.2 excludes finished items, such as beads or other ornaments, that are made from materials that have potential as pigments. For example, stony forms of hematite were often shaped into beads, ornaments, effigies, mosaics, and even ax-heads (e.g., Judd 1954:103, 283; Morris 1919a:Figure 14b and c; Pepper 1920:134; Pippin 1987:77; Roberts 1929:142). Azurite, malachite, and occasionally limonite were also formed into finished objects (Judd 1954:103, 292–293; Mathien and Windes 1987a:Table 6.1; Young 1981:129). I have, however, included polished hematite cylinders in Table 2.2; they are sometimes interpreted as sources of pigment (Fewkes 1911:75; Hayes and Lancaster 1975:162; Judd 1954:287; Morris 1919a: 27), although their purposes are not entirely clear (Adams 2002:200).

The most obvious feature of Table 2.1 is that black and sparkling black pigments or paints are seldom mentioned in the literature in any location or time period. This may be because such materials are overlooked in excavation or because they are characterized as something other than pigments and paints. Galena, for example, has been reported from a variety of sites (Duff et al. 2017:771; Pepper 1920:37; Young

TABLE 2.1. Basic colors of pigments or paints present at select archaeological sites.

| Region/ Time Period | Site Name | Red | Yellow | Green | Blue | Black |
|---|---|---|---|---|---|---|
| Basketmaker | Broken Flute Cave & other Prayer Rock district sites | yes | yes | | yes | |
| Basketmaker | Woodchuck Cave | yes | yes | yes | yes | |
| Basketmaker | Broken Roof Cave & Cave 6 | | yes | | | |
| Basketmaker/ Pueblo I | Shabik'eschee | yes | yes | | yes | |
| Chaco | Pueblo Bonito | yes | yes | yes | yes | |
| Chaco | Pueblo del Arroyo | yes | yes | yes | yes | yes |
| Chaco | Pueblo Alto | yes | yes | yes | yes | |
| Chaco | Peñasco Blanco | yes | yes | | yes | |
| Chaco | Tsin Kletsin | yes | yes | | yes | |
| Chaco | Bc 51 | yes | yes | yes | yes | yes |
| Chaco | Tseh So (Bc 50) | yes | yes | yes | | |
| Chaco | Other small sites | yes | yes | yes | yes | |
| Pueblo III | Aztec | yes | | yes | | |
| Sinagua | Lizard Man Village | yes | yes | yes | yes | yes |
| Sinagua | Fitzmaurice Ruin & King's Ruin | yes | | yes | yes | |
| Sinagua | Nalakihu | yes | yes | yes | yes | |
| Mesa Verde | Badger House | yes | | yes | yes | |
| Mesa Verde | Big Juniper House | yes | yes | | | |
| Mesa Verde | Spruce Tree House & Cliff Palace | yes | | | | |
| Mesa Verde | Long House | yes | | yes | | yes |
| Mesa Verde | Mug House | yes | yes | | | yes |
| Mesa Verde | Other Mesa Verde sites | yes | | | | |
| Pueblo IV | Homol'ovi I | yes | yes | "blue-green" | | |
| Pueblo IV | Sikyatki | yes | yes | yes | | |
| Pueblo IV/Historic | Awat'ovi | yes | yes | yes | yes | yes |
| Pueblo IV/Historic | Hawikku | yes | yes | yes | yes | yes |
| Pueblo IV/Historic | Mound 7, Pueblo de las Humanas | yes | yes | yes | yes | yes |
| Pueblo IV/Historic | Pecos | yes | yes | yes | yes | |

| Sparkling Black | White | Other/ Comments | References |
|---|---|---|---|
| yes | yes | brown | Morris 1980:35, 43, 46, 80, 82, 91, Fig.51 |
| | yes | gray, pink | Lockett and Hargrave 1953:3, 7, 9–10 |
| | | | Guernsey 1931:73–74, 75; Guernsey and Kidder 1921:109 |
| | yes | | Chaco Research Archive (CRA); Roberts 1929:111, 141 |
| | yes | | Judd 1954:103, 285, 286, 292; Pepper 1920:Table 9 |
| | yes | | Judd 1959:11, 36, 139, 140 |
| | yes | | Mathien and Windes 1987a:Table 6.1 |
| | yes | | CRA |
| | | | CRA |
| | yes | | CRA; Kluckhohn and Reiter 1939:33, 54, Table 3 |
| | yes | | Brand, et al. 1937:90, 96, Plate XII |
| yes | yes | | CRA |
| | | red-brown | CRA; Morris 1924:151, 157, 190 |
| yes | yes | gray, pink | Kamp and Whittaker 1990:112; 1999:136, Table 71 |
| | | | Caywood 1936:113; Spicer 1936:69 |
| | yes | | King 1949:107 |
| | | Blue is from earlier Pueblo II context | Hayes and Lancaster 1975:162 |
| | | | Swannack Jr. 1969 |
| | | Also, “various colors” from Spruce Tree House | Fewkes 1909:41; 1911:75 |
| | yes | | Cattanach 1980:148, 280–281 |
| | | | Rohn 1971:93, 128 |
| | yes | | Nordenskiöld 1893:42, 82-83 |
| | yes | brown/ tan | Meyers 2007:152 |
| yes | yes | | Fewkes 1898:728, 729 |
| | yes | pink, brown, purple/ maroon, orange | Montgomery, et al. 1949:296; Smith 1952:23–24, 31–32, 56 |
| yes | yes | | Smith, et al. 1966:268–272 |
| yes? | yes | | Young 1981:130 |
| | | | Kidder 1932:111 |

TABLE 2.2. Prevalence of pigments and paints in the archaeological record.

| Sites | Red | Yellow | Green | Blue | Black | Sparkling black |
|---|---|---|---|---|---|---|
| Pueblo Alto | 135 | 136 | 155 | 102 | 3 | |
| | 7.2% | 7.2% | 8.2% | 5.4% | 0.2% | |
| Pueblo Bonito | 13 | 9 | 12 | 13 | | |
| | 17.3% | 12.0% | 16.0% | 17.3% | | |
| Pueblo Bonito | 44 | 60 | 40 | 46 | | |
| | 15.3% | 20.8% | 13.9% | 16.0% | | |
| Chaco small sites | 7 | 4 | 6 | | 1 | |
| | 22.6% | 12.9% | 19.4% | | 3.2% | |
| Aztec Ruin | 12 | | 2 | | | |
| | 50.0% | | 8.3% | | | |
| Long House | 16 | | 2 | | 1 | |
| | 80.0% | | 10.0% | | 5.0% | |
| Lizard Man Village | 117 | 13 | 51 | 6 | 1 | present |
| | 57.1% | 6.3% | 24.9% | 2.9% | 0.5% | |
| Lizard Man Village | 627.1 | 65.4 | 126.8 | 2 | 1.3 | present |
| | 70.3% | 7.3% | 14.2% | 0.2% | 0.1% | |
| Hawikku | 8 | 5 | 37 | 8 | 2 | 2 |
| | 11.6% | 7.2% | 53.6% | 11.6% | 2.9% | 2.9% |
| Homol'ovi I | 31 | 22 | 7 | | | |
| | 45.6% | 32.4% | 10.3% | | | |

1981:130). Although it is often assumed to have been a component of the glaze paints used on Pueblo IV pottery (e.g., Duff et al. 2017:771), it is not clear whether it was used as a pigment. In fact, experimental attempts to recreate galena-based glaze paints have raised questions about its viability as a source of lead paints (Blinman et al. 2012). Other potential sources of black pigment, such as charcoal, would not usually be recorded as such by archaeologists.

## Pigments and Paints in Time and Space

### *Basketmaker*

Researchers working on Basketmaker period cave sites have recorded a wide array of pigments. At Woodchuck Cave, a Basketmaker II burial site in Tsegi Canyon, archaeologists noted malachite and azurite, worked and unworked red hematite, yellow limonite, a white calcite-type pigment, a black manganese-bearing mineral, and an unidentified black pigment (Lockett and Hargrave 1953). They also mention gray and pink materials that consisted of a colored constituent mixed with a lighter base color, which suggests that these samples may have been prepared paints. While the range of colors present at Woodchuck Cave is impressive (Lockett and Hargrave 1953:30), similar colors are evident in other sites as raw pigments, on ground stone tools, and as offerings in burials (Guernsey 1931: 73–75; Guernsey and Kidder 1921:93, 108; Morris 1980:77, Table 6). One burial, from the Kayenta area, included a woven bag holding a piece of yellow ochre with distinctive wear patterns

| White | Other | Comments | References |
|---|---|---|---|
| 1355<br>71.8% | | Count of pigment/paint specimens | Mathien and Windes 1987a:Table 6.1 |
| 28<br>37.3% | | Number of rooms containing said color | Chaco Research Archive (CRA); Pepper 1920:Table 9 |
| 97<br>33.7% | 1<br>0.3% | Number of entries in CRA database | CRA |
| 13<br>41.9% | | Number of entries in CRA database | CRA |
| 9<br>37.5% | 1<br>4.2% | Number of entries in CRA database | CRA |
| 1<br>5.0% | | Number of pigment/paint specimens | Cattanach Jr. 1980:280–281 |
| 1<br>0.5% | 16<br>7.8% | Number of pigment/paint specimens. Other is gray; sparkling black is mentioned in the text, but was not reported as numeric data | Kamp and Whittaker 1999:Table 71 |
| 45.2<br>5.1% | 24.4<br>2.7% | Weight of pigment/paint specimens, in g. Other is gray; sparkling black is mentioned in the text, but was not reported as numeric data | Kamp and Whittaker 1999:Table 71 |
| 7<br>10.1% | | Number of burials including said color of pigment or paint. | Howell 1994:Table 4.8; also see Smith, et al. 1966:268–272 |
| 5<br>7.4% | 3<br>4.4% | Number of specimens of raw pigment. Blue-green is listed as one color; other is tan. | Meyers 2007:Table 4.4 |

(Guernsey and Kidder 1921:109), consistent with weavers' and basketmakers' practice of coloring weft by rubbing it with dry pigment during the weaving process (Kent 1983:37).

### *Chaco and Beyond*

Published sources, combined with information from the Chaco Research Archive (2018), show that many colors were present in Chaco Canyon sites during the Pueblo II period (Table 2.1). It is possible to estimate the prevalence of these colorants by using three different sources of information: counts of pigment pieces from National Park Service excavations at Pueblo Alto (Mathien and Windes 1987a:Table 6.1), the number of rooms at Pueblo Bonito containing specific pigments or paints (Pepper 1920: Table 9), and the number of entries for particular materials and sites in the Chaco Research Archive (CRA) database.

Based on these estimates (Table 2.2), white was the most common pigment or paint in Chaco Canyon. At Pueblo Alto gypsite and selenite collectively made up more than two-thirds of the pigments (Mathien and Windes 1987a: Table 6.1). White constituted about a third of the colorants at Pueblo Bonito, and a little more than 40% of those from Chacoan small sites. The observation that "white was the most desirable pigment" (Mathien and Windes 1987a:418) at Chaco may be explained in part because white minerals were versatile, with uses including slipping pottery, whitewashing walls, whitening textiles, and painting objects.

Red, green, and blue are present in roughly equal amounts in Pueblo Bonito, each constituting between 14% and 17% of the sample. The prevalence of yellow is less clear, with CRA data suggesting that it was about 20% of the Pueblo Bonito material, while Pepper's Table 9 indicates that it was about 12%. This discrepancy may be in part due to Pepper's tendency to use the term "ochre" interchangeably for both red and yellow.

The picture for Pueblo Alto differs somewhat, as malachite made up about 8% of the sample, hematite and limonite just over 7% each, and azurite about 5%. The data from Pueblo Alto may somewhat overstate the importance of malachite at the site, as most of that material was in the form of debris in a single deposit (Windes 1987b:483); nevertheless, Mathien and Windes (1987a:418) suggest that color preferences at Pueblo Alto were for white, "followed by green, then the red/brown/yellows, and blue."

Blue and green are interesting colors at Chaco. Turquoise, which varies continuously across a range of blue and green hues, is the signature mineral in the Chacoan world (see Chapter 6). If azurite and malachite are grouped together into a single blue-green category, they prove to be quite prominent in Chacoan sites, approaching and even surpassing the frequency of white pigments at Pueblo Bonito. Taken alone, blue azurite is the second or third most common pigment at Pueblo Bonito, yet is relatively rare at Pueblo Alto and is not recorded at any of the excavated small sites (although CRA data indicate that it was noted on surveys). The small sites contained relatively high proportions of red and green, with fewer occurrences of yellow and only a single recorded occurrence of black pigment (Table 2.2).

All together, these data suggest that white was ubiquitous at Chaco but that azurite was concentrated at Pueblo Bonito. In her survey of azurite and malachite in the Chacoan world, Lewis (2002) noted that sites outside Chaco Canyon, such as Aztec Ruin, Salmon, Guadalupe Ruin, and Casamero, have far less azurite and malachite than sites within Chaco Canyon itself. Indeed, data from the CRA suggest that half of the pigments from Aztec were red, a little more than a third were white, and less than a tenth were green; no azurite is recorded for the site. This could be due to some bias in excavation or reporting methods, yet Morris (1919a:27) stated that hematite "was not extensively used by the aborigines of the Aztec Region," perhaps indicating that residents did not use many pigments or paints of any color.

### *Sinagua*

In the Sinagua region, red, green, and blue are ubiquitous in the Pueblo III period (Table 2.1). The best data on the prevalence of different colors comes from Kamp and Whittaker's (1999: Table 71) report on more than 200 pieces of pigment recovered from excavations at Lizard Man Village, near Flagstaff. A geologist working with them helped to identify a variety of light red or pinkish pigments as various hematite-stained rocks and minerals, though the researchers noted that the reds seemed "fairly homogeneous, at least to the naked eye" (Kamp and Whittaker 1999:136); for the purposes of this chapter, I have grouped materials together into basic color categories. Whether considered by counts of the number of pieces or by the total weight, iron-based reds were by far the most common, constituting about half of the pieces and more than half by weight. The researchers also noted two pieces of specular hematite, as well as a few more red hematite pieces that contained "some small specular inclusions" (Kamp and Whittaker 1999:136).

Green was the second most common color at Lizard Man Village, though it was less than half the amount of hematite, both by count and by weight. Most of the green was malachite with a variety of inclusions, sometimes mixed with minerals such as chlorite, chrysocolla, azurite, hematite, and limonite (Kamp and Whittaker 1999:136). Yellow, identified as jarosite and limonite-stained limestone, made up another 6–7% of the colors. All of the remaining colors were quite rare, either present as a single piece of moderate weight or a handful of pieces that added up to an insignificant mass. Notably, azurite was among the rare colorants, represented by just six small pieces weighing less than 2 g in total (Kamp and Whittaker 1999:137). This is striking in comparison to other Sinagua sites, such as Fitzmaurice Ruin and King's Ruin, near Prescott, Arizona, where azurite seems to have figured prominently in burial assemblages (Caywood 1936:113; Spicer 1936:69).

### *Mesa Verde*

The colorful array of pigments in Chacoan and Sinagua sites forms a sharp contrast with the more limited range in the Mesa Verde world (Table 2.1). Early publications from the Mesa Verde region seldom mention pigments and paints beyond vague statements like J. Walter Fewkes's (1909:41) report that grinding slabs from Spruce Tree House were "found to be covered with pigments of various colors." While National Park Service publications from the 1970s and 1980s are more detailed, they do little to dispel the impression that pigments and paints were relatively rare in Mesa Verdean sites.

The most detailed account, from Long House, documents just 20 cases of pigments or paints (Cattanach 1980:280–281), including hematite cylinders, irregular "paint stones," and unmodified lumps of pigment. The vast majority were hematite, with just two examples of a green clay and one each of kaolinite and magnetite (Cattanach 1980:280–281). Reports from Mug House also document the presence of hematite in multiple forms, "ranging from soft, pinkish lumps through red and red-brown stones, to hard nodules with a metallic appearance" (Rohn 1971:128). Rohn (1971:128) suggests that the inhabitants of Mug House treated all of the hematite pigments the same, regardless of their form, consistency, or specific color, as "both shaped and unshaped lumps were normally found together." Researchers also recovered lumps of limonite and a single piece of black shale from Mug House (Rohn 1971:128) but did not find any green or blue pigments.

Indeed, the only substantial quantity of azurite recorded from a Mesa Verde site was from an earlier Pueblo II context at Badger House, where excavators found a Mancos Black-on-white canteen containing a squash seed and 158 g of azurite pebbles (Hayes and Lancaster 1975:162). Despite the lack of numerical data, then, it seems that hematite in various forms was by far the most common pigment in the Mesa Verde region, with green proving to be extremely rare.

### *Pueblo IV into the Early Historic Period*

Of all of the time periods, Pueblo IV and early historic sites have the most consistent reports of a full spectrum of colors, from the basics listed in Table 2.1 to pink, salmon, brown or tan, purple, maroon, and orange. Data from Homol'ovi I (Meyers 2007:Table 4.4) and from Mound 7 of Pueblo de las Humanas (Young 1981:130) suggest that red was the most common color by far, making up half of all colorants found. In his work on the Awat'ovi kiva murals, Smith documented a variety of different red or reddish colors, from an iron red to vermilion, salmon, orange, and pink. Although these were quite distinctive in appearance, all turned out to be based in hematite or clays or sandstones naturally containing iron oxide (Smith 1952:23). Similar reds seem to have been used for murals associated with the seventeenth-century Franciscan presence at Awat'ovi (Montgomery et al. 1949:295).

At the same time, Julia Meyers's (2007:149, 152) work at Homol'ovi I demonstrates that iron oxide-based reds that are similar in appearance may differ in their specific makeup; based on compositional data, she found that residents of the site preferentially used different pigments of the same color for mural painting than for other applications.

At Homol'ovi I, yellow made up another third of the pigment sample, followed by blue-green (10%), white (7%), and tan (4%; Meyers 2007:Table 4.4). At Pueblo de las Humanas (Young 1981:130), white gypsum was the second most common pigment, constituting about a quarter of the sample; yellow limonite was the third most common, followed by malachite, manganese, azurite, and a few cases of magnetite.

Smith's studies of Awat'ovi show that the yellow paints used in the kiva murals and found throughout the site consisted of iron oxides as well, probably in the form of limonite or goethite (Smith 1952:23), while white pigment or paint recovered from excavations at the pueblo included materials such as kaolin, chalk, and gypsum (Smith 1952:24). Most of the black that Smith tested consisted of carbon, typically from charcoal, or contained phosphates that suggested that the paint was bone black (Smith 1952:24). Gray paints used in the murals seemed to be mixtures of black and white (Smith 1952:24).

The prevalence and composition of greens and blues varied considerably across Pueblo IV sites. At Hawikku more than half of the burials that contained pigments included green malachite or a similar copper carbonate (Table 2.2). At Homol'ovi I, blue-green paints were relatively common but were rarely used in murals (Meyers 2007:Table 4.4); the Awat'ovi murals, in contrast, used a variety of greens and blues. Smith (1952:24) documented bright grass green paint made of malachite, as well as a dull gray-green that was probably a mixture of yellow iron oxide with carbon. Most of the blue in the murals, a dark gray-blue hue, proved to be a mixture of carbon with white clay or some similar material as a base (Smith 1952:23).

The additional colors that Smith described—pink, brown, maroon, and purple—were all variants of iron oxides, sometimes burned or mixed (naturally or by the human hand) with white clays, manganese, or carbon (Smith 1952:23). Curiously, lumps of brown pigment recovered during excavation differed in composition from the brown paints sampled from the murals (Smith 1952:23), perhaps suggesting that different browns were used for specific applications.

## Tools for Working Pigments and Paints

In addition to pigments and paints, the archaeological literature documents a wide range of tools used in grinding, mixing, and preparing colorants, although the prevalence of ground stone used for color work is difficult to address. Some publications suggest that the frequency of pigment staining on ground stone was quite low. Cattanach's (1980:278) report for Long House, in Mesa Verde, implies that just 7 of 505 pieces of ground stone showed signs of pigment staining or paint, or approximately 1% of the ground stone tools. Such low numbers could indicate limited use of pigments, or they could be the result of colors being washed off of the surfaces of tools during excavation or lab work (Mathien and Windes 1987a:364).

When researchers have explicitly addressed color on ground stone tools, the frequencies are sometimes considerably higher. The best example comes from Homol'ovi III (AD 1285–1375), where researchers examined 1,080 ground stone artifacts and documented pigments or paints on the surfaces of about 10% of the assemblage (Fratt 2001:229). Most of the stains were red, likely from hematite, with some yellow and black as well (Logan and Fratt 1993:418); curiously, there was little or no blue or green pigment at the site (Logan and Fratt 1993:418). In similar fashion, most of the ground stone with pigment or paint stains from Homol'ovi I was marked with red (65%), followed by black (17%) and yellow (7%). White, blue-green, and tan were each present on less than 5% of the pigmented ground stone (Meyers 2007:Table 4.4).

Ancestral Pueblo people in all parts of the Southwest used a range of informal tools for color work, such as grinding pigments on an unshaped or minimally shaped slab of stone or a flagstone floor (e.g., Judd 1959:31; Mathien and Windes 1987a:367; Meyers 2007:Table 4.4; Pepper 1920:53; Swannack 1969; Woodbury 1954:200). In other cases, people repurposed an artifact created for another purpose as a tool for grinding pigment (Adams 2002:22; Woodbury 1954:33). At Pueblo del Arroyo, for example, Judd (1959:21) recovered "half a sandstone doorslab on which yellow, then red, ocher had been ground for paint." Stained door slabs and jar covers used as grinding slabs were recovered from many other Chacoan sites (Brand et al. 1937:95; Judd 1954:127; Judd 1959:104, 139; Kluckhohn and Reiter 1939:62; Pepper 1920:91) and in Mesa Verde (Rohn 1971:235). Axes, "tchamahias" or hoes, and other hafted ground stone tools might also have been repurposed as grinding stones (Rohn 1971:248; Woodbury 1954:28, 33).

Manos and metates were sometimes used for the preparation of pigments and paints (Brand et al. 1937:91, 94; Guernsey and Kidder 1921:93; Judd 1930:53; Mathien and Windes 1987a:343; Smith et al. 1966:287; Young 1981:116, 122). At Lizard Man Village in the Sinagua area, researchers found that almost a fifth of the 60 whole or fragmentary metates were stained with hematite, including several examples of deep trough metates that were heavily stained up the sides of the trough (Kamp and Whittaker 1999: 101–102). There was no apparent link between metate form and hematite staining, suggesting that there was a range of strategies for grinding pigment, depending on its intended use (Kamp and Whittaker 1999:101). However, despite the large number of metates with staining, the excavators did not recover a single mano that showed any signs of hematite (Kamp and Whittaker 1999:102). The opposite situation occurred in Chaco Canyon, where approximately 7% of the manos from Pueblo Alto and neighboring sites showed signs of paint or pigment indicating that they were either used to grind minerals or as paint palettes (Mathien and Windes 1987a:324, 364). At the same time, researchers were only able to document three case of metates or metate fragments from within the canyon that showed any traces of pigment (Mathien and Windes 1987a:343).

Recognizing when artifacts such as jar covers or metates were used for color work can be a challenge for archaeologists prone to assuming that form equals function in ground stone tools. As Young (1981:122) points out regarding the ground stone from Pueblo de las Humanas, "were it not for the presence of pigments, we might not have recognized that these tools were used in paint grinding." It seems certain that the use of expedient and repurposed tools for preparing pigments and paints has been underreported in the archaeological literature (Rohn 1971:249).

In addition to expedient and repurposed tools, Ancestral Pueblo people created a variety of tools that were presumably intended to be used for processing pigments and preparing paints. These tools vary in the amount of labor invested in shaping the tool and in creating a grinding surface. Some, which Woodbury (1954:113) refers to as grinding slabs and tablets, were modest in form, with one or two smooth or concave surfaces resulting from grinding or rubbing. These tools were used for pigments and paints in all time periods across the Pueblo Southwest (Woodbury 1954:200). Mortars and palettes are more formal tools (Figures 2.2 and 2.3; see Plates 1 and 2), with mortars shaped into a deeper, more bowl-like form, and palettes having raised edges surrounding a central grinding surface (Adams 2002:127–136, 146–150). Woodbury (1954:115–116) believed that the form of mortars and palettes was specialized for working with liquid paint, with less concave grinding slabs reserved for use with dry pigments. However, Logan and Fratt's (1993) study of pigment-processing tools at Homol'ovi III shows that the form of ground stone tools is not enough to infer whether they were used for grinding, mixing, or both.

In contrast to the widespread use of grinding slabs, Woodbury (1954:200) argues that mortars were used in Basketmaker III contexts but then became uncommon until Pueblo III and later, despite examples from some Pueblo II contexts (Brand et al. 1937:95; Judd 1959:140, Plate 41i; Mathien and Windes 1987a:367, 369, Plate 5.9; Pepper 1920:58). He also believed that they were seldom present among the Eastern Pueblos (Woodbury 1954:119), although he acknowledged that this could be due to a lack of published information. Finally, Woodbury (1954:200–201) argued that raised border palettes, which he felt were originally inspired by examples from the Hohokam region, did not appear in the Pueblo region until the end of the Pueblo IV period, becoming common only in the Hopi area in the protohistoric period.

Although slabs, mortars, and palettes are relatively well documented, pebbles or pestles

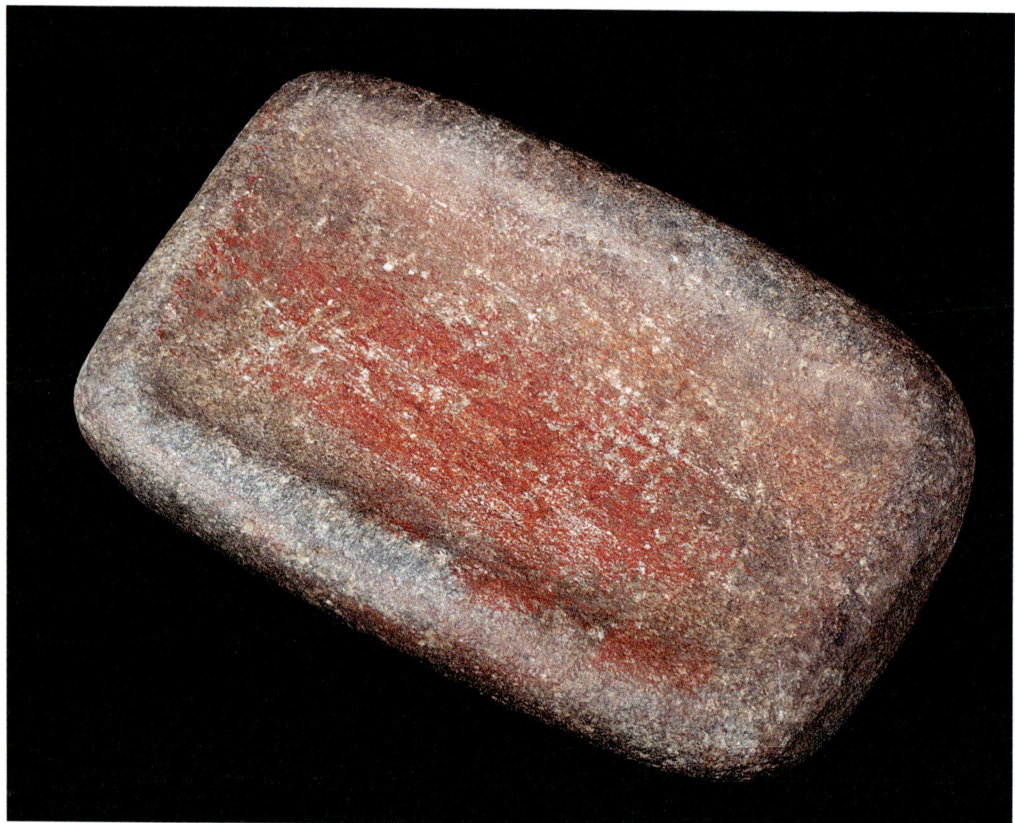

FIGURE 2.2. This simple rectangular stone palette with raised edges is smeared with red, probably from mixing paint from an iron oxide pigment. Wupatki National Monument, National Park Service. Catalog number WUPA 11509. Photograph by Ryan Belnap and Daniel Boone. Courtesy of Northern Arizona University.

used as hand stones are relatively rare in most time periods. At Pueblo Bonito, for example, Judd (1954:285) found so few pestle-like pebbles that he proposed "that the accepted practice in Chaco Canyon was to crush or rub bits of iron-stained minerals and other ores directly upon the stone palette." More specialized paint-grinding pestles take the form of small ovoid or conical stones with an almost flat, highly polished grinding surface on the base. These domed pestles, which Woodbury (1954:94–95) calls paint-grinding stones, are present in some Pueblo III contexts (Cattanach 1980:292, Figure 343a; Rohn 1971:208), but seem most common at Awat'ovi, where excavations uncovered 49 such items. Fifteen of these had paint, usually blue-green, remaining on the grinding surface or edges. Three of the pestles were found in situ as parts of sets, each with a piece of malachite or with green paint on a grinding slab (Woodbury 1954:113); these sets correspond well with descriptions of paint preparation at Hopi in the late 1800s (Chapter 1) and to ethnographic collections in the Smithsonian's National Museum of Natural History.

Woodbury (1954:200) argued that formal pestles were limited to the Pueblo IV, protohistoric, and historic time periods, and that such tools are common only in the Hopi area. Judd's experiences excavating at Chaco seem to support this idea; he felt that the Zuni at the turn of the twentieth century depended more on "tools and utensils" (Judd 1954:286) for preparing paints, preferring a stone mortar and a

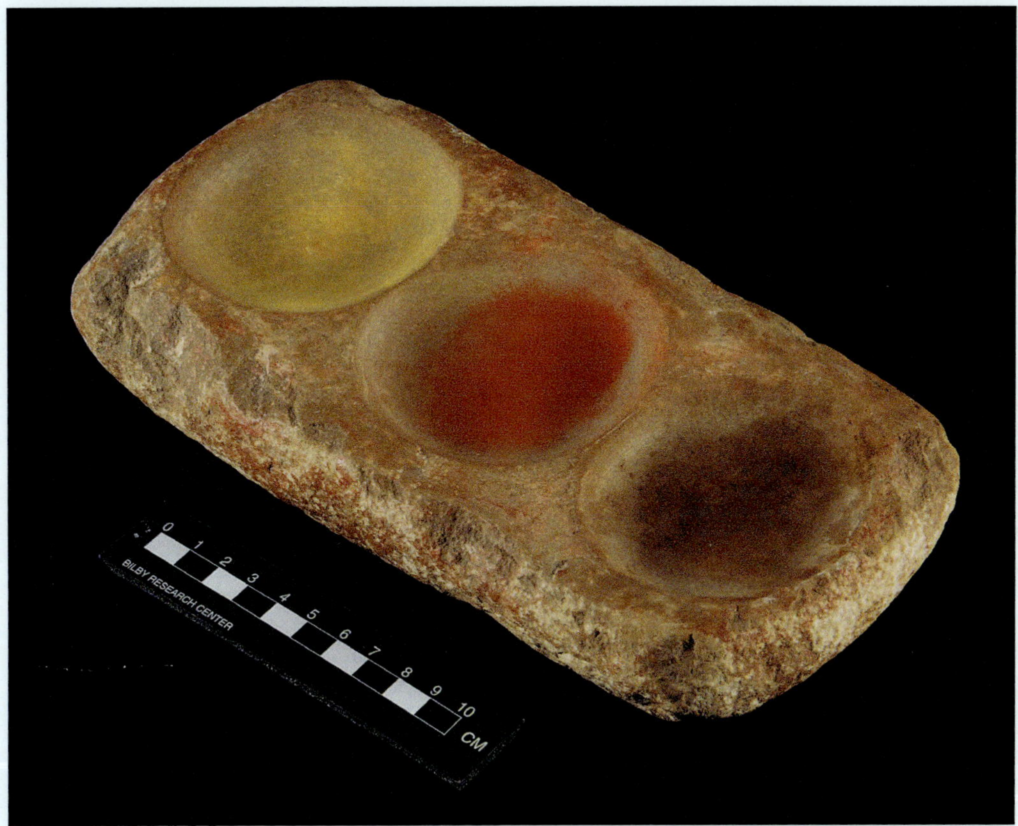


FIGURE 2.3. Paint palettes with multiple compartments are among the most formal tools used for color work. This triple palette has three shallow basins, each used for a different color: yellow at one end, red in the middle, and black (or possibly brown) at the other end. Wupatki National Monument, National Park Service. Catalog number WUPA 9509. Photograph by Ryan Belnap and Daniel Boone. Courtesy of Northern Arizona University.

small jar to hold ground paint, while Chacoans "were generally content to crush and mix their paints on any handy flat-surfaced object—a rough doorslab, a polished sandstone tablet, a jar cover, even a metate or mano. Rarely did they go to the trouble of making special mortars" (Judd 1954:285).

### Storing Pigments and Paints

The ethnographic records discussed in Chapter 1 document the varied ways that pigments and prepared paints might be stored before use, most of which have parallels in the archaeological record. Based on archaeological reports, bags and soft wrappings were frequently used as containers for pigments and sometimes for paint as well. In Basketmaker II and III, for example, individuals were often buried with green or blue pigments and paints contained in skin bags made from a small animal, such as a prairie dog, or from buckskin (Guernsey 1931:74; Guernsey and Kidder 1921:108; Lockett and Hargrave 1953:3). Skin or fiber bags or hides were occasionally used to hold other colorants, including red paint (Lockett and Hargrave 1953:9–10; Morris 1980:30), yellow ochre (Guernsey 1931:75), black "paint stone" (Guernsey 1931:73–74), gray paint (Lockett and Hargrave 1953:9), and a substance that may have been brown paint (Morris 1980:91). The quantity of colorants in these bags and wrappings seems to have been quite small, suggesting that the pigment or paint was significant in its own right, rather than serving as a functional supply of color.

Once they became available, ceramic vessels or sherds were often used as containers for holding pigments or prepared paints. At the Basketmaker to Pueblo I site of Shabik'eshchee, for example, excavators recovered a large bowl sherd holding "a cake" of red ochre that had been "worked up, probably to use as a paint" (Roberts 1929:141). In Pueblo II contexts at Pueblo Bonito, Pepper uncovered a large corrugated jar that contained "a thick layer of red paint" and some unspecified seeds (Pepper 1920:221) as well as "a fragment of pottery containing paint" (Pepper 1920:257). Judd (1959:140, 185, Plate 36b) found three cakes of kaolin from a single room at Pueblo del Arroyo, all molded by being poured into the same broken pitcher.

Chacoans also sometimes shaped earthy red or yellow paints while they were wet, including one example from Pueblo Bonito with marks indicating that it "had been placed in a bag, probably buckskin, when it was in a pasty condition" so that "the crimping of the skin left deep impressions" (Pepper 1920:37). Excavations at Aztec uncovered a cylinder of similar red paint, which had been wrapped in corn husks while still wet (Morris 1919a:Figure 15; Morris 1924: 157), as well as some small leather bags and pieces of tanned hide with traces of green pigment or red ochre staining (Morris 1919a:63).

Examples of containers used with green paints from Chacoan sites are quite rare. At Pueblo Bonito, National Geographic Society excavations recovered a white ware sherd that held a powdery green paint (see Crown and Wills 2003:Figure 4), while Pepper (1920:66) excavated an unusual white ware vessel consisting of three bowls joined into a cloverleaf shape that held green paint. The CRA (Pueblo Bonito, Kiva F) also reports a single example of a green clay-like material that may have been paint, which showed marks from having been wrapped in husks.

Handling of pigments and paints at Mesa Verde seems similar to that in earlier Chacoan sites. Researchers have noted various soft wrappings that were used to store pigments, from red ochre-stained hide strips at Mug House (Rohn 1971:124, 125) to cloth wrapped around pieces of white kaolin-type material at Ruin 9, Cliff Canyon (Nordenskiöld 1893:83). In addition, Nordenskiöld (1893:42, 82–83) found a similar white material at Step House, wrapped in corn husks and then tucked inside a ceramic jar. In addition to stored paints, sherds of pottery from Big Juniper House showed traces of hematite or limonite pigment, suggesting that they were used as palettes for mixing paint (Swannack 1969).

In Pueblo IV and later periods, containers of paint seem to have been quite common, although this impression may be due in part to the prevalence of such materials in burials at large villages, such as Sikyatki, Awat'ovi, and Hawikku, that were extensively excavated in the late nineteenth and early twentieth centuries. At Hawikku, for example, Frederick Hodge's expedition reported numerous cases of pigments and paints recovered from burials, usually of green (or occasionally white, black, or red) paint contained in a bag or some kind of soft wrappings (Smith et al. 1966:207, 212, 214, 254, 277–278, 290). At Sikyatki pottery bowls, shallow saucer-like vessels, and jars were often used to contain pigments placed in burials (Fewkes 1898:Plate 128). Pottery vessels were also used to hold pigments beyond burial contexts at Awat'ovi, as Smith (1952:22) mentions "lumps of varying colors found among the débris of the ruin, and sometimes in pottery bowls or caches where they had evidently been carefully stored." Unfortunately, the details of these deposits are not clear, though they apparently included "yellow and red ochres, malachite, azurite, and the like" (Smith 1952:22). Information about paint containers from the eastern Pueblo area is limited, but there is some evidence of sherds used as palettes for red ochre, yellow ochre, and gypsum at Mound 7, Pueblo de Las Humanas (Hayes et al. 1981:159–160).

In addition to containers of hide, cloth, and ceramic, Ancestral Pueblo people would presumably have used containers of other perishable materials, such as gourds, for storing or transporting paint, or, as documented at Sinagua sites, hollow reeds as containers for powdered azurite (McGregor 1943:290; Spicer 1936:69). Plant material would also have served as paint brushes and stir sticks, as shown by the discovery at Chetro Ketl of yucca or sotol leaf brushes and a variety of twigs used to stir and apply paint (Vivian et al. 1978:112–113, 128–130). The ends of the Chetro Ketl brushes and stir sticks are variously coated with green copper resinate, dull red, or dull black paint; one brush shows a small bit of red paint underneath the black (Vivian et al. 1978:112–113), suggesting that brushes were not reserved for particular colors. In addition, researchers have documented potential bone paint brushes from Pueblo Alto (stained with red; Mathien and Windes 1987b:659) and from Mound 7 at Pueblo de las Humanas, which dates to the Pueblo IV to early historic period and where a spongy piece of rib bone was "thoroughly impregnated with green paint, probably malachite" (Hayes et al. 1981:156).

## Pigments and Paints in Context

Pigments and paints are noted in virtually every imaginable context in the archaeological literature, including habitation rooms (Judd 1959:11, 13, 136; Kluckhohn and Reiter 1939:33; Smith 1952:23; Windes 1987a:72, 287), kivas (Rohn 1971:128, 235; Windes 1987a:328, 329), midden deposits (Rohn 1971:128; Windes 1987b:605), and fill (Cattanach 1980:281; Judd 1959:49; Smith 1952:23). At Pueblo Alto researchers even found an abundant deposit of malachite on a plaza surface (Windes 1987b:483).

Some of these contexts suggest specific activities centered around pigments and paints. In early Pueblo IV contexts at Arroyo Hondo, in the northern Rio Grande Valley, researchers noted that mineral pigments and polishing stones were more common in storage rooms than in living rooms (Phagan 1993:Table 32), suggesting "the short-term storage of ceramic-manufacturing equipment" (Phagan 1993:233).

A different kind of storage is suggested by special-purpose rooms at Pueblo Bonito, which contained a wide variety of artifacts and raw materials (e.g., Pepper 1920:98–111), including pigments, paint-grinding tools, informal paint palettes, mortars, and the triple paint pot with green malachite paint that was mentioned earlier (Pepper 1920:66, 97, 98, 105). These may have served as places for ritual specialists to prepare objects for use in ceremony or as storage rooms for ritual paraphernalia.

Pigments and paints at the Sinagua site of Lizard Man Village were concentrated in rooms adjacent to kivas or possible kivas, suggesting that the colors were used in ceremonies (Kamp and Whittaker 1999:137). Pigments may have been ground and prepared within kivas themselves in Mesa Verde (Rohn 1971:Figure 89), and at Pueblo de las Humanas, paint-grinding slabs seem to have been a regular fixture in several kivas, "buried flush with the floors flanking the hearths" (Young 1981:121). Indeed, the association of pigments and paints with ritual is demonstrated by shrines or caches of material in kivas at Long House (Cattanach 1980:110–111) and at Awat'ovi (Smith 1972:31, 32, 56).

### *Burials*

More than any other context, pigments and paints have been documented in association with burials from all time periods. Some of this may be due to archaeologists' detailed descriptions of burial assemblages, such that the presence of colorants is more likely to be reported. Nevertheless, there is ample evidence to show that pigments and paints were used as part of burial rituals and were considered appropriate materials to include in graves across the Ancestral Pueblo Southwest.

In some cases, the colorants played a role in the burial ceremony itself, being sprinkled into the grave or painted onto the body (Howell 1995:135; Kamp and Whittaker 1999:61, 167–168; Smith et al. 1966:254, 268–272). Face painting as part of burial rituals seems to have been most common in Chavez Pass sites (Fewkes 1904:34) and in the Sinagua area (Kamp and Whittaker

1999:137, 174–175; Spicer 1936:73), with some examples from Hawikku as well (Smith et al. 1966:254).

The most common use of pigments and paints in mortuary contexts was as offerings placed in graves. Basketmaker period burials of all ages and sexes in northeastern Arizona were often accompanied by yellow, green, red, or black pigments or paints (Guernsey 1931:73–74; Lockett and Hargrave 1953:7, 10). A burial of an individual at Shabik'eshchee Village, a site dating to the Basketmaker to early Pueblo I period at Chaco Canyon, included a bowl containing "three azurite crystals which show attempts at polishing and six pieces of red ocher which also show rubbing" (Roberts 1929:141). Most of the time, offerings in Basketmaker period burials included just one or two colors, placed in the grave with a variety of other goods and occasionally a grinding stone used for paint processing (Lockett and Hargrave 1953:11).

During the Pueblo II period, pigments and paints seem to be relatively rare in burial contexts. Of more than 270 individuals interred at small sites in Chaco Canyon, just 5 graves included pigments or paint: 2 with malachite, 1 with malachite and an unidentified red pigment, and 2 with hematite cylinders, which may have served as a source of pigment (Akins 1986:94, 124, Table B1; Brand et al. 1937:Plate 12; Kluckhohn and Reiter 1939:Table 3). The relative lack of pigments in the small sites is probably in part a reflection of the fact that burials at these sites have fewer artifacts overall than those in Pueblo Bonito (Akins 1986:126). However, pigments are scarce even in the Pueblo Bonito burials, and it appears that prepared paints were not included in burials at all.

Most of the known Great House burials from Chaco Canyon are from Pueblo Bonito (Akins 1986:112), where they occur primarily in two different clusters of rooms: a western crypt (Rooms 320, 326, 329, and 330) and a northern crypt (Rooms 32, 33, 53, and 56; Plog and Heitman 2010). The northern crypt included an "unusual complex distribution of human bones and materials," including "a wealth of cosmologically important substances (turquoise, shell, wood, cacao, sand, and ash)" deposited over a 300-year timespan (Plog and Heitman 2010:19624). Some colorants were present in Rooms 32 and 33, including malachite, gypsum, azurite, limonite, and yellow ochre (Akins 1986:116; Pepper 1920: 129–175), but in small quantities—especially when compared to the thousands of pieces of turquoise from the same rooms (Plog and Heitman 2010:19621).

Room 33 also contained caches in the corners of the room, which Plog and Heitman (2010:19625) have interpreted as "offerings to the four sacred directions, a microcosm of the Chacoan cosmos." The caches to northeast, northwest, and southeast consist mostly of turquoise, with some stone, jet, shell, and reed arrows; the southwest cache, in contrast, was composed solely of malachite, a bone bracelet, and fragments of shell bracelets (Akins 1986: 117)—a range of materials that, if green and blue are considered distinct, constitutes a different color palette and perhaps different symbolic meaning.

The western burial crypt at Pueblo Bonito is similar in that it consisted of a large number of individuals interred with varied materials, including malachite, azurite, fragments of hematite, yellow ochre, kaolin, and galena (Akins 1986:115–124, Table B1). As with the northern crypt, there is nothing in the excavators' notes to suggest that the quantities of pigments were substantial (Judd 1954), especially in comparison to turquoise and other materials. Thus, it seems that the pigments in Great House burials at Chaco Canyon may have been present as materials associated with or used to prepare ceremonial items, rather than as intentional offerings.

At Pueblo III sites in the Mesa Verde region, pigments were rarely placed in burials, although there are a few examples in the literature. One adult male was buried in the talus slope below Mug House with several pieces of pottery, a few arrow points, several pebbles, two hematite cylinders, and two amorphous chunks of hematite (Rohn 1971:93), more grave goods than buried with any other individual found at the site. Cattanach (1980:148) noted a similar pattern at Long House, where a young adult was buried in a midden deposit with a relatively large number of goods, including three hematite cylinders. In both cases, the excavators interpreted each of the burials as being of a "medicine man," even as Cattanach (1980:148) acknowledged that the young adult buried at Long House seemed to be unusually young to play such a role.

In the Pueblo IV world, the presence of pigments or paints in burials seems to have increased substantially. Fewkes (1898:728) wrote that mortuary vessels at Sikyatki often contained mineral fragments and "ground oxides and carbonates, of different colors," suggesting that "these substances were highly prized in ancient as in modern times." A copper-based green was the most common paint in Hopi-area burials, which also included red hematite-type paint, kaolin in solid masses and in powdered form, micaceous hematite, and a fragment of botryoidal hematite (Fewkes 1898:618, 656, 728–730). It was "not uncommon," Fewkes (1898:728) wrote, to find multiple small paint pots in a single grave. Indeed, one burial at Awat'ovi contained four separate black-on-white paint pots, each holding a single color (yellow, red, green, and micaceous hematite; Fewkes 1898:617–618).

### *Tool Kits*

While pigments and paints were clearly considered appropriate as offerings in their own right, there are also a few examples of colorants that are best interpreted as parts of tool kits. One Basketmaker period burial, at Woodchuck Cave in Tsegi Canyon, consisted of an old man buried with a yucca cord bag containing pieces of hematite, malachite, and a white calcite-type pigment, along with a possible grinding stone covered with green pigment, a large quantity of squash seeds, an acorn, some human hair, and "what appeared to be a small fiber brush" (Lockett and Hargrave 1953:9–10). Other materials in the same burial cist suggest that the man may have used an even more diverse set of pigments and tools, including limonite, an unidentified black pigment, prepared paints in gray, pink, and white, and a small mano used to grind paint (Lockett and Hargrave 1953:9); this part of the deposit had been disturbed, though, so the specific context of these materials remains unknown.

In addition, Guernsey (1931:110) reports a Pueblo III potter's kit found at Kayenta in the grave of a woman "well advanced in years"; it included reshaped sherds, scrapers, polishing stones, a few small ceramics, broken sherds, and lumps of unidentified paint (Guernsey 1931:111). Shafer (1985) documented a similar potter's tool kit from a late ninth- to early tenth-century woman's grave in the Mimbres area.

### *Ritual Leaders*

Beyond individual offerings and tool kits, some burials involved considerably more complicated and diverse arrays of grave goods, including distinctive deposits of pigments. Such burials are usually interpreted as those of ritual leaders by researchers, and often by Zuni or Hopi individuals as well.

The most famous example is of Burial 16 at Ridge Ruin, a Sinagua site near Flagstaff that includes some Chaco-style masonry and other evidence suggesting a connection to Chaco. The individual was an adult male, 35–40 years old, who was buried in the last half of twelfth century with a colorful array of ritual paraphernalia, ornaments, and pigments (Figure 2.4; see Plate 3), prompting archaeologists to refer to him as the "Magician of Ridge Ruin" (McGregor 1943). The burial assemblage included 25 pottery vessels, 420 projectile points, baskets, and numerous wooden wands, rods, and bows, as well as personal ornaments such as a beaded cap, *Conus* shell tinklers, a turquoise bead bracelet, a turquoise and argillite nose plug, and bone hairpins (see Chapter 6).

The grave also contained pigments and paints, from pieces of kaolin, a ball of yellow ochre, and several kinds of hematite to carefully ground and stored azurite and malachite (McGregor 1943:290–291). Many of these colorants were found in a coiled basket that contained a bundle of 20 reed tubes filled with ground and sorted azurite (McGregor 1943:290), a gourd holding blue paint, red paint in small skin bags, and pieces of hematite paint, among other items (McGregor 1943:Figure 3). Another cluster of artifacts included several pounds of malachite fragments and masses of specular iron laid out on shell fragments (McGregor 1943:290, Figure 3). McGregor (1943:284, 290) also mentions an additional gourd filled with ground azurite pigment, as well as several fragments of abalone shells that held unspecified "prepared pigments."

Red and blue were often paired in the burial assemblage, and copper-rich blue and green pigments were especially abundant; some of these materials were probably imported from about 60 kilometers south in the Verde Valley and may have had directional place-based symbolic meaning. Although most contemporary archaeologists shy away from the "magician" label, there is general consensus that this man was a ritual specialist, buried with the ceremonial paraphernalia of a religious society (Kamp and Whittaker 1999:183).

In addition to the well-known Ridge Ruin burial, there are similarly elaborate burials of likely ritual leaders from across the Southwest—and many of those include pigments and paints in the complex assemblages of materials interred with the individual. At Awat'ovi, for example, Fewkes (1898:617) identified an old man buried in the Western Mound as "apparently a priest," probably based on the presence of an unusual pottery vessel that consisted of "four globular paint pots, each full of pigment of characteristic color." He identified the paints as yellow ochre, red hematite, green copper carbonate, and micaceous hematite, adding that the latter was still in use by priests at Hopi (Fewkes 1898:618).

Burials of ritual leaders are especially well documented at Hawikku, where Zuni men working for Hodge's excavations identified several individuals as members of religious societies (in Smith et al. 1966:210–212, 216, 290). More recently, Howell (1994, 1995) reanalyzed the data, using statistical methods to try to identify burials that were distinctly different from others. Although Hodge's and Howell's results vary somewhat (e.g., on the status of Burial 816), the researchers concur that several burials at Hawikku were those of ritual leaders. These individuals were buried with items such as paint-grinding stones (Howell 1995:Table 3), yellow ochre (Smith et al. 1966:208–210), and a variety of green, red, and black pigments (Howell 1995:133).

In particular, Howell (1995:138) identified a group of males with paraphernalia, including pigments, that was likely associated with "a warfare-related leadership role and conduct of ritual activities." Zuni excavators working with Hodge specifically recognized one of the burials as that of a bow priest (Smith et al. 1966:210) and referred to glittering black pigments that occurred in other burials of male leaders as sacred (Smith et al. 1966:284). The female leaders that Howell (1995) identified tended to have a diverse range of relatively common items as grave goods, such as manos and metates, pottery, baskets, prayer sticks, and food. However, some of the burials also contained more unusual items, including paint-grinding stones, raw clay, and weaving tools, suggesting that some women's leadership roles involved an array of secular and sacred activities (Howell 1995:143).

## Conclusion

Archaeologists have been encountering pigments and paints throughout almost a century and a half of excavations of Ancestral Pueblo sites. The records of their work, however flawed, document a wide array of colorful materials, from pigments and the tools used to process them to prepared paints, stored for future use. These were then used to paint wooden objects and basketry, as well as on pottery (Chapter 3), wall paintings (Chapter 4), and rock paintings (Chapter 5). In addition, the colorants themselves were carried by individuals, cached in storage rooms, placed in ritual deposits, and provided to the dead as part of burial ceremonies. Clearly, pigments and paints were both practical and profoundly meaningful.

To a certain extent, the visibility of these colors in the archaeological record depends on the properties of the materials themselves, as well as how they were treated. Mineral pigments that are dense, hard, or well consolidated, such as hematite, specular hematite, limonite,

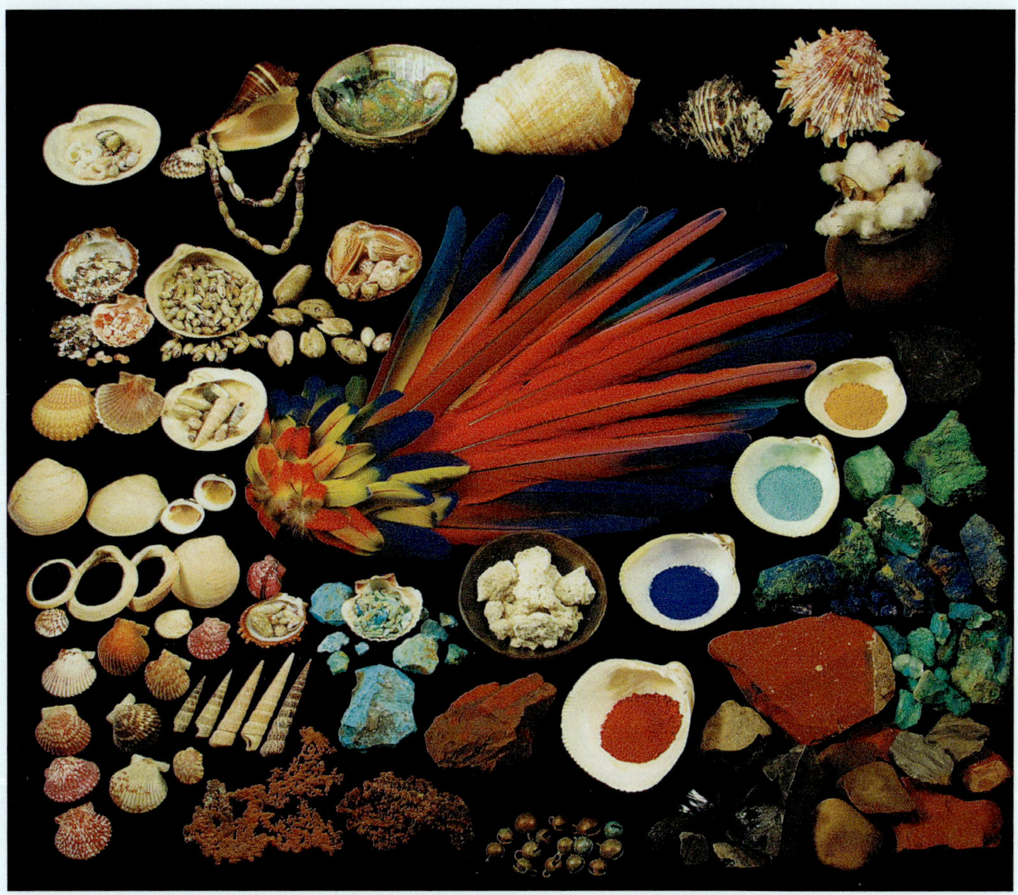

FIGURE 2.4. The "Magician" of Ridge Ruin was laid to rest with a stunning assemblage of colorful jewelry, paraphernalia, and raw materials. This illustration provides a sense of the visual impact of the materials placed in his grave by bringing together modern examples of similar shells, feathers, copper, cotton, and pigments. Photograph by Christian Downum, Ryan Belnap, and Daniel Boone. Courtesy of Northern Arizona University.

and some malachite and azurite, have excellent preservation potential. When reduced to finely ground powder, however, or mixed into paint, some colors become more difficult to detect. Azurite, despite its bright blue color, tends to absorb moisture once it is ground, eventually turning green (Rapp 2009:165). A dark green resinous copper carbonate used on painted wood at Chetro Ketl was also susceptible to change, weathering to a pale, powdery green (Vivian et al. 1978:123).

Unfortunately, the archaeological literature tends to be silent on colors such as black, pink, gray, and brown. Although a few researchers record a wide range of colors (e.g., Lockett and Hargrave 1953:9; Smith 1972:31), such pigments and paints are generally overlooked. This probably reflects researchers' general bias toward primary or basic colors, shaped by the hue-focused work of Berlin and Kay (see Introduction). This bias is particularly problematic for colors such as glittering black, which twentieth-century Pueblo people recognized as a particularly significant color (Smith et al. 1966:284).

Finally, despite archaeologists' assumptions that colors that look the same are identical in composition (e.g., Smith 1952:22), there is growing evidence that pigments from different sources may be used for different purposes (Meyers 2007:149) and that recipes for paints can vary considerably (Cordell and Habicht-Mauche 2012), whether based on learning networks or geography. This highlights the need for additional studies of pigment sources and paint composition in all parts of the Ancestral Pueblo world. The rich array of colors and their varied and meaningful uses have the potential to be visible to archaeologists, but only if we observe carefully and record material in detail.

# 3

# The Colors of Ancestral Pueblo Pottery

Kelley Hays-Gilpin and Jill E. Neitzel

Color is the most visually distinctive characteristic of Ancestral Pueblo pottery. Prehispanic potters made bowls, jars, effigies, ladles, and other forms in one, two, three, and sometimes four colors. Plain utility pottery was usually gray, brown, white, or red. For decorated wares, a great many—though not unlimited—color combinations were possible. Dual combinations were typically black on white, red, or orange; black or brown on yellow; white on red; and for glaze wares, green or black on white, buff, or red. Polychrome vessels were generally black and white on red or orange, black and red on orange, and sometimes white-outlined black or black-outlined red on yellow.

Complicated sets of choices determined a pot's color. Different geological materials and firing atmospheres and temperatures afforded some possibilities and constrained others. Cultural norms standardized the use of particular combinations, which were strongly patterned in both time and space. And a host of other social and ideological factors also came into play. As a result, any pottery color was never just a color—it signified many dimensions of Ancestral Pueblo life.

This chapter considers the overlapping sets of technical, social, and ideological characteristics that determined the colors of Ancestral Pueblo pottery. We begin with a brief review of the technical factors, and then summarize past and current archaeological thinking about temporal and spatial variation. Finally, we consider recent findings on how color intersects with vessel form and design, religious symbolism, and breaks in artistic conventions.

## What Causes Pottery Color?

Different colored plain pottery could be produced in several different ways—using distinctive clays for the vessel body, firing vessels made of the same clays under different conditions, or applying a slip (a fine clay slurry, often of a contrasting color) over the vessel surface. For decorated vessels, designs were painted on a smoothed, burnished, or slipped surface. The design colors were determined by the type of paint used and the firing conditions.

### *Raw Materials*

Potters almost always use locally available materials, and most Ancestral Pueblo pottery was made where suitable clays, tempers, and fuels were available. Many areas of the Colorado Plateau have plentiful clay deposits, but in a few, such as Mesa Verde, Black Mesa, the Hopi Mesas, and the San Juan Basin, the raw material is particularly high quality and thus does not need much processing.

For both raw and fired clay, the material's source and chemical composition are important determinants of its color (Rice 1987:333–334). Alluvial clays, which are available in and near many watercourses, often contain a lot of carbon and silt. The carbon can cause the raw clay to appear dark gray, but it usually fires red to orange to brown as the carbon burns out and the iron in the clay oxidizes.

Clays for making pottery are usually obtained from subsurface deposits rather than recent alluvial deposits. They vary in their mineral content, with the most important color determinants being the amounts of iron and carbon (Rice 1987:333–336; Shepard 1956:15–16). In its raw form, iron-rich clay can be red, yellow, orange, brown, green, purple, or dark gray. Under different firing conditions, the original color may remain or be transformed into red, orange, dark gray, or brown. Iron-poor clays, which are much less common, begin gray but can fire light orange, yellow, light gray, or white, again depending on the firing conditions.

A vessel's color may be altered by applying a slip made from another clay, such as a white slip on a gray body (Rice 1987:149–151). This is done before firing. Finer slips produce smoother surfaces, which take a polish better. Polishing gives the surface color a luster or sheen.

Painting designs on a pot's smoothed, burnished, or slipped surface adds other colors. Ancestral Pueblo people used a variety of paint types for pottery designs. Some were probably locally available, but others may have been transported or exchanged from long distances away. Carbon-rich organic paint, most likely local, was made by boiling down sugar-rich plants, such as tansy mustard or Rocky Mountain beeweed (Shepard 1956:33–35). Depending on firing conditions, this paint produced either a rich black to gray color or, if mis-fired with too much oxygen, a light orange "ghost" image. Not all slip clays will hold an organic paint, which must soak into the surface and bond with the clay minerals as it burns in firing.

Some pottery traditions added a little bit of mineral to a carbon-rich organic liquid to produce black and brown paint. For example, iron-manganese paint consisted of ground iron-manganese nodules, sometimes called "bog ore" and common in ancient wetland deposits, together with a plant-based binder (Shepard 1956: 40–42). Depending on the proportion of iron to manganese and firing conditions, this paint produces black to dark brown to reddish-brown (rust-colored) designs.

Some paint colors were made of clay. Red paint was usually an iron-rich clay, with a high content of limonite or goethite (yellow minerals that fire red) and hematite (Shepard 1956:104). White paint was composed of white kaolinite clay, which often flaked off, especially when applied to a polished surface as thin white outlines of black designs (Shepard 1956:42–43).

Glaze paints were made of ground pigments with high lead and sometimes copper content that were combined with a plant-based binder (Rice 1987:337–339; Shepard 1956:44–48). Suitable lead ore was mined at a number of sources in Arizona and New Mexico, most notably the Cerrillos, Socorro, and Magdalena deposits in the Rio Grande River valley (Huntley et al. 2012: 9; Nelson and Habicht-Mauche 2006). When fired, glaze colors in the Zuni and Rio Grande regions ranged from black to green with the edges of green glaze on a white slip often having purple margins (e.g., Pinnawa Glaze-on-white from the Zuni area).

Ground pigments, alone without a binder, were sometimes applied post-firing for red and occasionally green and blue designs. The results for red pigments were powdery and would wash off with water, which is why they are called fugitive paints. Green and blue pigments (malachite, azurite) were applied post-firing because they lose their colors when fired.

### *Firing*

Clay vessels cannot be used unless they are fired, a process that hardens the soft raw material by driving out water molecules and changing the clay's crystalline structure (Rice 1987:80). With the rare exception of post-1300 Hopi use of coal, Ancestral Pueblo people fired their vessels with wood as the fuel in pits, trenches, and aboveground bonfire-type settings. The firing conditions that affected the completed vessel's color were the amounts of oxygen and carbon in the firing atmosphere and the temperature and duration of firing (see Shepard 1956:103–104 for definitions of terms related to firing).

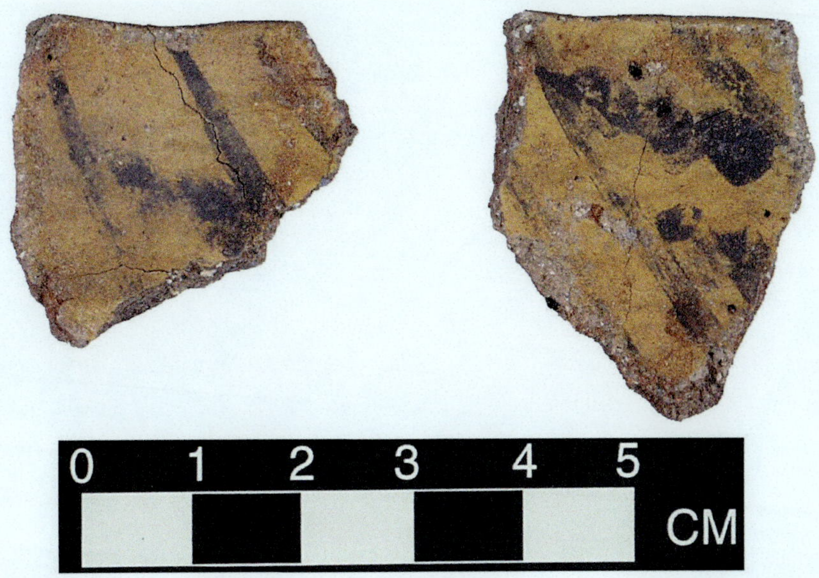


FIGURE 3.1. Two unfired sherds, Kayenta tradition, Tsegi Orange Ware, Tusayan Polychrome, from Long House, west of Kayenta, Arizona. Courtesy of Phil Geib.

Iron-rich clays offer a good illustration of the impacts of the amount of oxygen in the firing atmosphere. Originally red, yellow, orange, brown, green, purple, or dark gray, they fire red to orange in an oxygen-rich atmosphere (open firing), a range of brown hues with moderate oxygen, and gray in an oxygen-poor pit fire. Rarer iron-poor clays (originally gray) produce white in oxygen-poor atmospheres, buff with moderate oxygen, and cream to yellow with rich oxygen. Firing iron-poor clays with oxygen and high temperatures reached by coal fuel produces a brilliant yellow color. Yellow surfaces were always technologically possible, even though they did not appear frequently until after 1300.

Most raw clays of any composition or color can be transformed into an all-black vessel when fired in an atmosphere with plenty of free carbon. Known as "smudging," the process involves smothering vessels in a smoky fire, which can be produced by adding pine needles or, historically, powdered animal dung (Shepard 1956:88–90).

Firing conditions also affect paint colors. To produce black designs, both iron-based and organic black paints require pit-firing in a neutral to oxygen-poor firing atmosphere. Iron-based paints fire red in an oxygen-rich atmosphere, achieved in aboveground firings. Yellow clay paints such as goethite and limonite turn red when fired with oxygen.

Almost everywhere on the Colorado Plateau, the production of polychrome pottery required different materials and firing atmospheres than black-on-white pottery (one exception being the extremely low-iron clays of the Acoma area, which fire cream to white in any atmosphere). Tusayan Polychrome is an excellent example of the complicated color transformations of polychrome wares. In its raw form, it has a greenish surface with yellow slip or paint and black paint (Figure 3.1, see Plate 4). When fired with oxygen, the green turns orange, the yellow turns bright red, and the black stays black or turns slightly brown (Geib 2011:61–63). The resulting vessel has an orange background, a brilliant red slip or designs, and black designs (Figure 3.2, see Plate 5). Between about 1250 and 1300, designs on Tusayan Polychrome's successors, Kayenta Polychrome and Kiet Siel Polychrome, also had white outlining.

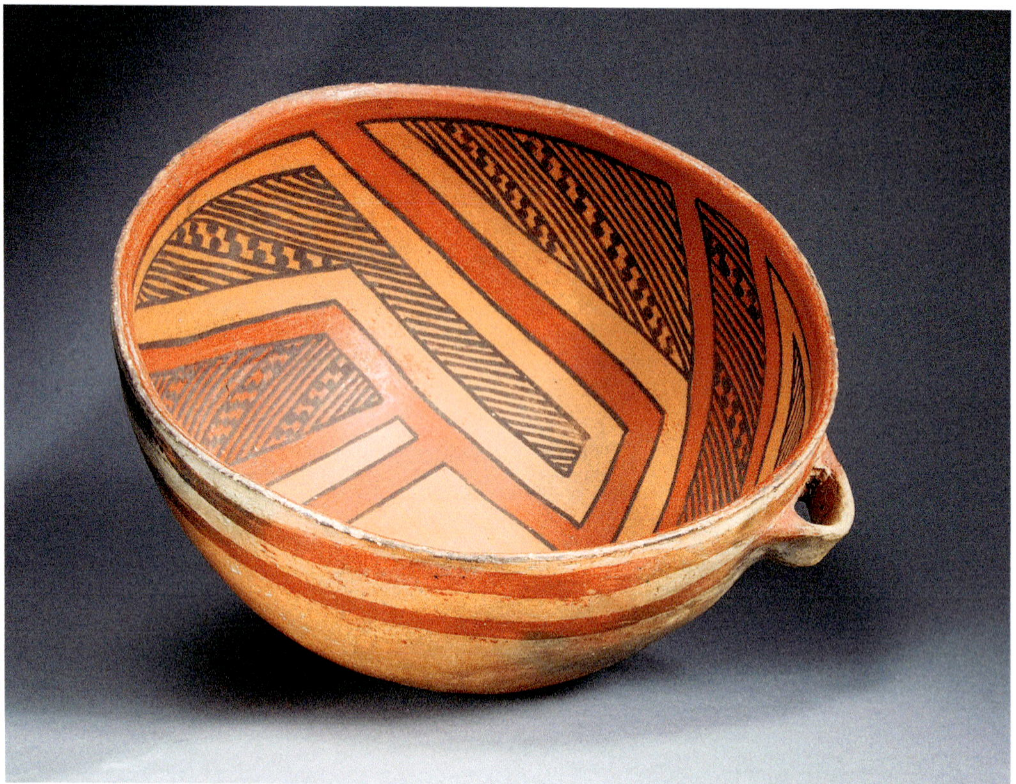

FIGURE 3.2. Kayenta tradition, Tsegi Orange Ware, Tusayan Polychrome bowl. Museum of Northern Arizona catalog number A-1077. Photo by Ryan Belnap and Daniel Boone. Courtesy of the Museum of Northern Arizona.

### *Technical Color Analyses*

Early researchers assumed pottery color to be a self-evident characteristic, but Harold Colton (1953) subsequently recommended using a color standard chart, particularly the Munsell color chart, to recognize and classify colors properly. He noted that "we are not interested in a particular rectangle [in the Munsell chart] but in a general class of colors" and linked each class to clues about clay sources and firing techniques (Colton 1953:33). Colton (1953:14–27) then conducted numerous experiments with clays, paints, fuels, and firing temperatures and atmospheres to explore the interacting forces that allowed potters to produce the range of pottery surface and paint colors.

Anna Shepard (1956:106–107) also conducted numerous experiments that incorporated her geological expertise to untangle the intersection of materials, firing conditions (atmosphere, temperature, and duration), and pottery color variation. Similar explorations of materials and methods continue today, for example, in "kiln conferences" at Crow Canyon Archaeological Center and around the Southwest, and in the work of contemporary potters like Clint Swink (2004), who has spent decades refining techniques for replicating Mesa Verde pottery.

Similar to Colton, ceramic analysts working in the northern Southwest today think about their color categories as modes in a spectrum. But they are also interested in how a natural spectrum of colors and their associated characteristics (hue, value, and saturation) can be consistently parsed. Furthermore, they use other attributes in combination with color to identify mis-fires, fire clouds, post-firing treatments, and other variations (Rice 1987:345). The goal is to work toward a nuanced understanding of what causes color and its variation.

### Temporal and Spatial Variation

Archaeologists' initial and most enduring preoccupation with pottery color has been classification. Early investigators assumed that color categories represented different cultural groups in a region-wide developmental sequence. Subsequent research focused explicitly on chronology building within smaller areas and at individual sites, resulting in refinements of the general sequence. New analytical approaches applied more recently have revealed the complexity of color variation in both time and space.

#### *Early Approaches*

The Southwest's first archaeologists viewed color as the primary criterion for classifying pottery. They assumed that their color categories, known as "wares," were associated with different cultural groups and that changes in color over time tracked the groups' cultural development from primitive to advanced or simple to complex (Holmes 1886; Stevenson 1883). For example, Alexander Stephen, working on the Hopi Mesas in the 1880s, described pottery as "advancing" from decorated black line to orange-colored, then to polychrome, and finally declining or decaying with cream-colored ware after Spanish Conquest (Wade and McChesney 1980). These so-called advances and subsequent decline were thought to reflect the evolutionary trajectory of Hopi groups of the Ancestral and historic periods.

Color continued to be the key characteristic for analyzing prehispanic pottery in the early twentieth century. In an effort to standardize their methods, archaeologists working throughout the Southwest proposed similar schemes for developing ceramic typologies, all of which began with color (Colton and Hargrave 1937; Ellis 1936; Gladwin and Gladwin 1930; Mera 1943). For example, in northern Arizona, Harold Colton and Lyndon Hargrave (1937:11, 37) recommended that any analysis begin with "major separations." First, a sherd should be sorted depending on whether its surface was altered (corrugated, incised, tooled) or not (smoothed, polished, painted). Then, within these two categories, it should be sorted based on its color: 1) gray or white or 2) brown, red, orange, yellow, or buff. Finer color distinctions would be made in subsequent steps (e.g., black on white, black on red).

The paramount goal of these typological analyses was chronology building, mostly from a culture historical perspective rather than the evolutionary emphasis seen in earlier research. Similar to their predecessors, early twentieth-century archaeologists viewed different wares as reflecting different cultural groups. But some area- and site-specific ceramic studies undermined this equation for locations in northern Arizona (Colton and Hargrave 1937), at the Ancestral Hopi site of Awat'ovi (Smith 1971), and in Tsegi Canyon (Beals et al. 1945), near Kayenta, Arizona. These researchers used new techniques of stratigraphy, seriation, and tree ring cross-dating to examine pottery sequences. In doing so, they confirmed the later parts of the previously defined regional sequence, in which red- and orange-based polychromes were followed by black-on-yellow and yellow- and buff-based polychromes. However, each project found that pottery from the early part of the sequence included co-occurring color combinations. In particular, they documented many black-on-white pottery types that were contemporaneous with black-on-red or black-on-orange types (see Hays-Gilpin et al. 2001 for additional evidence from Homol'ovi). Furthermore, Beals and others (1945:149–150) concluded that the same potters made both orange ware and white ware vessels at Kayenta sites and decorated them initially with similar designs and later with different designs.

#### *Refining the Sequence*

For the Ancestral Pueblo region as a whole, the general sequence that archaeologists defined by the mid-twentieth century remains fairly accurate—co-occurring black-on-white and black-on-orange/red in at least some areas early and then a gradual shift from black-on-white to red ware and then to yellow ware, accompanied by a concomitant increase in polychromes (Gilpin and Hays-Gilpin 2012). But when efforts are made to pin down dates and to compare sites and areas, the sequence appears to be oversimplified. It masks the different timing for when new colors and color combinations appeared in different places, understates how common and varied co-occurring combinations were, and ignores the colors of plainwares, which exhibit their own patterns of variability.

The first pottery vessels in the northern Southwest were plain utility wares. Their basic color sequence begins with an initial spread between AD 200 and 500 of brown to warm gray polished low-fired pottery known as the brown ware horizon (Wilson et al. 2000). This tradition was very similar to pottery to the south, well into Mexico, whence it probably spread. By the 600s, Colorado Plateau potters were producing sand-tempered gray pottery, and for the first time some vessels were decorated, with painted black designs and sometimes fugitive red pigment or red slip on bowl and jar exteriors.

The well-known black-on-white regional traditions emerged in most of the Pueblo region in the 700s. These white wares clearly developed out of earlier gray utility wares over a broad swath of the northern Southwest, from Durango and Mesa Verde in southwest Colorado through the Rio Grande and Chaco-Cibola regions of New Mexico and west to the Kayenta and Hopi Mesa areas of northern Arizona. Potters began to select finer temper, to polish and slip vessel surfaces, and to add painted designs using organic or mineral black paints. White wares developed a little later, in the 900s, in the Hopi Buttes and Rio Puerco of the West, and south into Mogollon Rim country. In southern New Mexico, Socorro Black-on-white appeared by AD 1000, and Mimbres Black-on-white pottery famously flowered around the same time, supplanting earlier red-on-white and red-on-brown pottery. Black-on-white vessels became increasingly elaborate in the 1000s and continued to develop distinct design variations through the 1200s.

In the Mogollon area, the roots of red wares date to as early as the 500s, when potters produced red-slipped brown wares, often with smudged black interiors (Stone 2018). To the north, red ware antecedents date to the 600s–800s, when gray ware vessel exteriors were sometimes slipped red (Tallahogan Red) or painted with fugitive red paint (Lino Fugitive Red). The fugitive red treatment persisted longer in the Virgin area, north and west of the Colorado River, than in eastern regions, where the red color dropped out for plain and corrugated exteriors a few centuries later.

Red-on-orange and then black-on-red pottery emerged in the 800s in southeast Utah. This San Juan Red Ware pottery was widely traded in the 900s and spread from southeast Utah to northern Arizona. In the 1000s, black-on-red pottery appeared in the Kayenta (Tsegi Orange Ware), Rio Puerco of the West (Puerco Valley Red Ware), and Cibola and White Mountain (White Mountain Red Ware) areas alongside increasingly elaborate black-on-white vessels.

Polychrome versions of red pottery appeared in the Kayenta, Hopi, Zuni, and White Mountain areas between AD 1125 and 1150, with the elaboration of black-on-red and polychrome pottery peaking in the late 1200s and 1300s. Black-and-red-on-orange polychrome appears with white outlining in the Kayenta area, after 1250, and black-on-red with white outlines appears in White Mountain Red Ware, with some use of solid white color fields and fill, in the 1300s. Zuni potters broke away from the White Mountain Red Ware traditions in the 1300s, producing green glaze and matte red designs on white slip (Kechipawan Polychrome).

Black-on-red and polychrome versions of red pottery were replaced by buff- and yellow-based polychromes between the 1300s and mid-1400s in many areas—after 1300 at Hopi and after 1400 at Zuni (Hays-Gilpin 2014; Hays-Gilpin and LeBlanc 2007; Schachner 2006). Red polychromes continued in the Acoma and Salado areas, and growing Pueblo communities along the Rio Grande produced a variety of red- and yellow-slipped glaze polychromes, as well as organic-painted white ware in some areas (Eckert 2006).

In the meantime, most plain utility wares remained gray in the north and brown in the Mogollon area until about 1300. Then warmer colors appeared—yellow corrugated and plain pottery on the Hopi Mesas, orange in the Homol'ovi area, and red in the Salado region.

### *New Perspectives on Time and Space*

Recent analyses have revealed the complex behaviors underlying co-occurring color combinations. For example, Hays-Gilpin (2008) has confirmed Beals and others' (1945) finding about the contemporaneity of red and orange wares and white wares in the southern Kayenta area. Here, color differences were not the result of available clay resources or separate communities of practice. Rather, the same potters combined the same materials and firing atmospheres in different ways to produce pottery with different color combinations (as well as gray utility ware pots). Elsewhere, potters produced different colored pots in other ways. In the White Mountain and Cibola traditions, they manipulated the color of the same clay body with different slips and firing atmospheres.

Sometimes potters emulated other ceramic traditions, manipulating their local materials and techniques to produce vessels similar to those made in other regions. Their products added to the variety of colors in their communities' pottery assemblages. In one extreme case of local versatility, potters in the Rio Puerco of the West used local brownish clay with crushed sherd temper between about AD 1050 and 1200 to produce 1) polished smudged brown wares, some with a thin red slip, similar to vessels from the Mogollon highlands to the south; 2) warm gray corrugated pottery similar to that to the north and east; 3) slipped black-on-white pottery similar to that made in the Cibola tradition to the east; and 4) organic-painted black-on-red pottery that appears to be stylistically unique to this region (Hays-Gilpin and van Hartesveldt 1998).

In addition to local potters' color preferences and technical skills, trade and site function also contributed to the co-occurrence of pottery with different color combinations. At early Pueblo I period sites in southeast Utah, Allison (2008) found a great deal of variation in the proportions of contemporaneous red and white wares, which he attributed to participation in different exchange networks, but no differential association of red wares at sites with ritual structures. In contrast, at Pueblo II period sites on Black Mesa in the Kayenta area, Plog (1989) found higher frequencies of red wares at sites with ritual structures (also see Blinman 1989). This change suggests that color was perhaps secondary to factors related to trade early on and then to religion. Both trade and religion may have become even more important in later time periods.

Another new approach to the relationship between pottery color and time has taken a micro-perspective, examining the sequence in which white, red, and black paints were added to polychrome vessels from different areas. The results have shown that color order was often conventional within pottery traditions. For example, Salado polychrome bowl interiors and some jar exteriors were typically slipped white, then red was applied, and finally black (Crown 1994:44–45).

However, color order varied among traditions and could change through time. Bowl interiors of Wingate Polychrome, the earliest polychrome White Mountain Red Ware, had a red slip that was then painted with black; the exteriors were left white or slipped with a cream color and then painted with red. In contrast, most later White Mountain Red Ware polychromes were slipped red inside and out and then painted with black elements, some of which were subsequently outlined in white. Tsegi Orange Ware polychrome bowl interiors have a similar sequence: red applied first, then black, and then white outlines. The exteriors often have broad red ribbons on plain orange surfaces. In studies of color patterns and brushstroke order on Fourmile Polychrome bowls from different sites, Van Keuren (2006) has demonstrated how these details can help identify communities of practice and their trade networks.

### Other Dimensions of Variability

Much recent research on pottery and color has moved beyond temporal and spatial variation to other issues. Some investigators have looked for patterns between color and vessel form and design. Others have explored color symbolism as a means of studying religious ideologies. Finally, rare vessels that seem to break the color "rules" have piqued interest for what they signify about the complexity of pottery color choices.

### *Form and Design*

Apart from its color, a pottery vessel's other most visible characteristics are its form and, if decorated, its design. Form is usually taken as a proxy for function and in turn people's activities (see Braun 1983, who describes "pots as tools"). Designs reflect identity and interaction at the community, regional, and interregional scales. Considering color in conjunction with form and design offers further insights into the behavioral correlates of all three characteristics.

Comparing the forms of contemporaneous vessels with different color combinations, Hays-Gilpin (2008) found a strong tendency for jars to be predominantly black and white and for bowls to be predominantly black-on-red and polychrome. This pattern, which appears to be strongest in the Kayenta area, spans the Western Pueblo region from the early 1100s to the mid-1200s and disappears by 1300.

Feinman and others (1981) included form in comparisons of the relative frequency of different color combinations at different kinds of contemporaneous sites. They found that polychrome bowls predominated at the largest sites with public architecture, while black-on-white and plainware pottery was more common at smaller sites that lacked public structures. Feinman and his colleagues attributed this pattern to status differences that restricted access to polychrome bowls, which were most costly due to three painted colors on two surfaces.

During the late Pueblo I period in southwest Colorado, Blinman (1989) found that red ware bowls occurred more frequently at sites with ritual structures, which suggested an association of both bowls and red wares with communal ritual activities and feasting. While contemporaneous black-on-white pottery was locally made, the red ware bowls were manufactured in southeast Utah. Blinman hypothesized that the bowls' exotic origin, rather than any meaning inherent in their color, may have made them attractive for status display in feasting and ritual contexts.

Mills (2007a, 2007b) has linked shifts in the colors and designs of large red ware bowls to broader demographic and other societal changes. Throughout the Pueblo III period in the Mogollon Rim and Zuni regions, these bowls were presumably used for feasts. But as communities grew by aggregation into plaza-oriented villages, several related changes occurred: 1) the plazas became the locations of community feasts, 2) more (and more diverse) people began to participate in these feasts, and 3) potters began to decorate bowl exteriors, which would be seen by hosts and guests, with bold, highly visible designs—first red on white (Wingate Polychrome), then white on red (St. Johns Polychrome), and then black with white outlines on red (Pinedale Polychrome).

The relationship between color and design is quite complicated. Rarely is one ware associated exclusively with a single design style. Rather, one color combination could be decorated in several styles, and many styles decorated more than one ware. Further complicating the color and design relationship is that a few styles were executed in just one ware, but the ware could be decorated with other styles. For example, the Tusayan Polychrome style appears only on Tsegi Orange Ware, but Tsegi Orange Ware vessels are also often decorated with Dogoszhi-style designs (a type called Tusayan Black-on-red) and rarely with Sosi-style designs (for which no type has been defined). Typology, therefore, is helpful for defining chronologies but leaves out more interesting patterns of variation.

The most long-standing pattern was for design styles to cross contemporaneous, locally made wares (colors). Examples of this pervasive, cross-cutting pattern, in which the same designs appeared on both black-on-white and black-on-red types, include the Puerco and Escavada styles in the Pueblo II period Chaco world, followed by the Reserve-Tularosa style in the Cibola and White Mountain area in the 1100s–1200s. The Reserve-Tularosa style emerged out of earlier eleventh-century Mimbres Style III and also appeared on twelfth-to thirteenth-century polychrome types such as St. Johns Polychrome. During the 1200s, the Pinedale style appeared in the Cibola and White Mountain areas on both bichrome and polychrome vessels and spread to other wares in the Ancestral Hopi and Zuni areas.

As discussed previously, the relationship between color and design underwent a change in the Kayenta area. The cross-cutting pattern characterized the 1000s when the same potters were making Pueblo II white wares and orange wares, both of which they decorated with somewhat similar designs (Beals et al. 1945:149–150). This pervasive design system shifted to a partitive pattern in the late 1100s and 1200s when potters continued to make both wares but now decorated them with different designs (Hays-Gilpin 2008). The later red ware designs seem to mimic local plaited "sifter" basket designs. The later white ware designs resembled those on contemporaneous cotton textiles, some of which were imported from the south along with Hohokam weaving techniques (see Hays-Gilpin 2008).

The contrast between the pervasive (or cross-cutting) and partitive patterns of color and design style raises questions about the signaling of community and regional identities. When a style was executed with just one color combination, a distinct identity was being signaled within the much larger region associated with that combination. An example is early Pueblo III period Kayenta potters, who executed the Tusayan Polychrome style exclusively in orange polychrome. However, when a style was executed with more than one color combination, as the Reserve-Tularosa and Pinedale styles in the White Mountain and Cibola regions, its meanings in terms of identity and interaction were independent of those associated with the colors.

### Color Symbolism

Efforts to investigate color meanings have used ethnographic data to study religious symbolism (see for example Crown 1994:171). The religions of Native peoples throughout North America in the historic period ascribe colors and other meanings to directions (see Chapter 1). Details vary—emphasis on cardinal versus intercardinal directions, four directions versus six (including zenith and nadir), and the specific colors associated with each direction. But when cultural patterns are so widespread, we can assume they are very old (DeBoer 2005).

For historic and Ancestral Pueblo people, cultural continuity in religious beliefs and rituals is well documented, with color playing an integral role in both (see Chapter 1). For the historic Hopi, all of the colors of their ancestors' pots were imbued with a multiplicity of symbolic meanings. As with other Native American groups, these colors were associated with directions, here defined by horizon points of summer and winter solstice sunsets and sunrises (intercardinal directions). The colors also signified sacred places, crops, flowering plants, birds, butterflies, and mammals, all of which had their own symbolic and cosmological associations that in turn were indirectly associated with the color. On prehispanic pottery, this symbolic content would have been compounded when two colors were combined, as in black with white, black with red or orange, and black with yellow, and would have been further amplified when three colors were used, as in black, white, and red polychromes, or after about 1375, yellow, black, and red polychromes.

Color symbolism may have been complemented and amplified by the meanings associated with different pottery designs. Just as no ceramic color was ever just a color, most if not all pottery designs represented complicated metaphorical relationships. Figurative designs, such as flowers, animals, and human figures, are most easily recognized. But stylized linear and geometric designs were also symbolic, such as zigzag lines representing lightning, stepped designs representing clouds, and scrolls that might represent water waves or snakes, according to the interpretations of historical and contemporary Pueblo potters. Each reference had its own set of symbolic meanings, and when a vessel was painted with multiple motifs in two or three colors, its symbolic content was strengthened.

Some pottery designs may have represented colors. Plog (2003) has suggested that

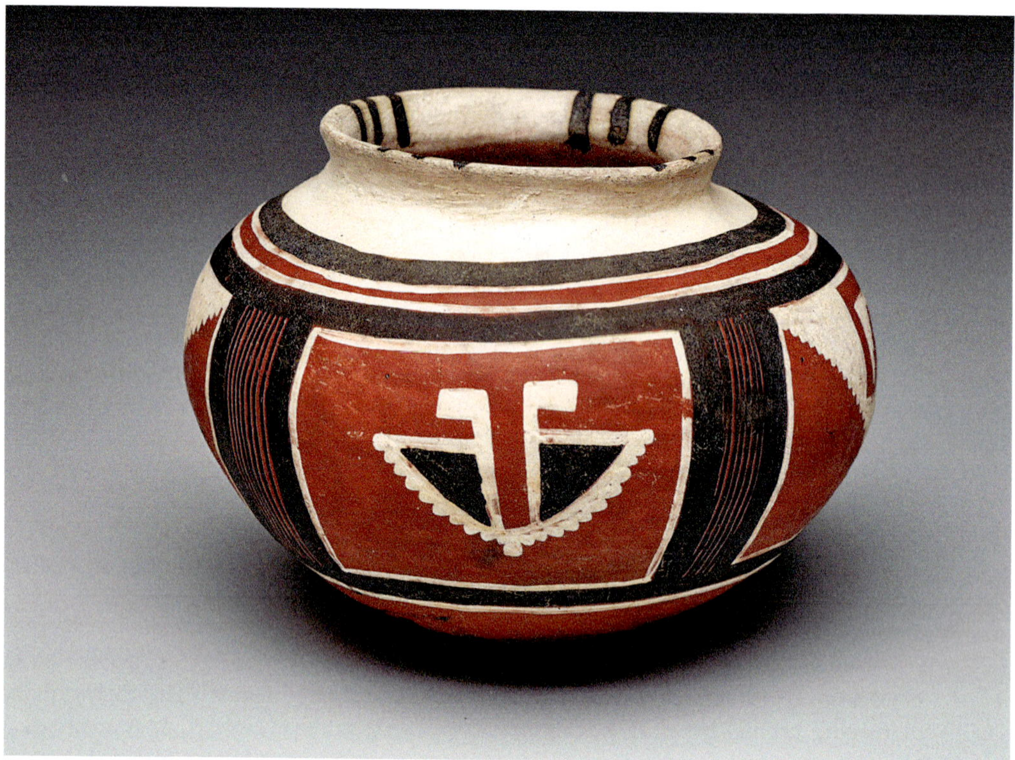

FIGURE 3.3. Cibola–White Mountain tradition, White Mountain Red Ware, Showlow Polychrome jar, ca. AD 1300–1400. Note butterfly motif. Ceramic and slips; 5½ × 7¾ × 7¾ in. Unknown provenience. Dallas Museum of Art, Foundation for the Arts Collection, anonymous gift. Catalog number 1991.402.FA.

the hatched, black-on-white designs of the Chacoans' Dogoszhi-style pottery represented the color blue-green and consequently were imbued with the symbolic meanings associated with that color. This raises the questions of whether hatching on vessels with both hatched and solid black-on-white designs also represented the color blue-green and, if so, whether the solid designs represented other colors (see Russell et al. 2018).

For pots with multiple color combinations, each color's location may have had more general cosmological significance. For example, in the late 1200s, Pinto and Gila polychrome bowls had black-on-white interiors and red exteriors, and Kwakina Polychrome had black-on-white interiors and white-on-red exteriors. These different interior and exterior color schemes not only referred simultaneously to the ancestral black-on-white and black-on-red pottery traditions and the specific symbolism of the individual colors and their combinations, they also might have been metaphors for the earth (the bowl exterior) and sky (the bowl interior). In addition, red could reference other earth imagery, such as soil, maize, and women's work, and white other sky imagery, such as cotton, clouds, rain, and men's work (Hays-Gilpin and VanPool 2009). The metaphorical significance of color placement is also suggested by Showlow Polychrome jars of the 1300s. Their black-on-white necks and shoulders and red polychrome bodies evoke white cumulus clouds with dark bases full of moisture hovering over red soil and fields (Figure 3.3; see Plate 6).

Cross-media design comparisons suggest that different colored pottery designs may have also had broader metaphorical significance. For example, in the Kayenta area, the Pueblo III period black-on-white pottery designs in the 1100s and 1200s that resembled contemporaneous cotton textiles (Figure 3.4) were part of

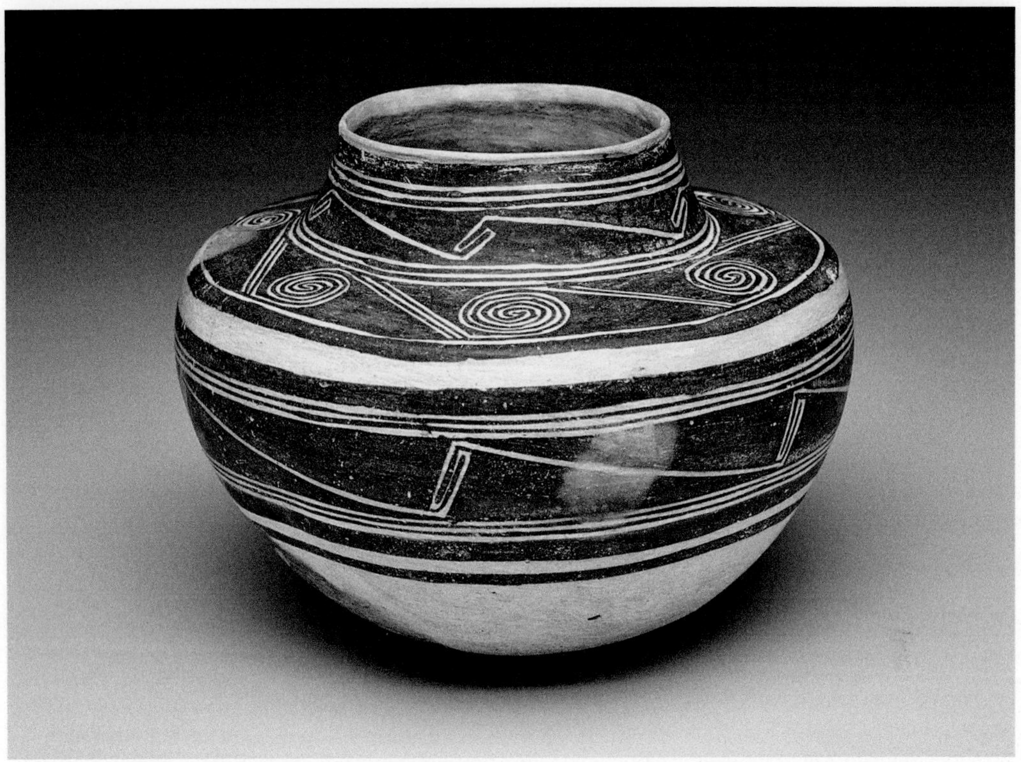

FIGURE 3.4. Kayenta tradition, Tusayan White Ware, ca. AD 1250–1300. Ceramic, slip, and paint; 6½ × 9½ × 9½ in. Unknown provenience. Dallas Museum of Art, Foundation for the Arts Collection, anonymous gift. Catalog number 1991.345.FA.

a style horizon that extended far to the south, encompassing the Sinagua and Hohokam areas and much of northern Mexico.

From a broader perspective, the symbolism of pottery colors and designs added to the sacred meanings and mythological associations of the raw materials that were used to create a pot and their transformation into a finished vessel, which was viewed as an animate being (Charley and McChesney 2007:89; Cushing 1886; VanPool and Newsome 2012). For historic period Pueblo potters, clay is the flesh of Mother Earth, and a potter enters into a relationship of respect and reciprocity when gathering clay. Potters are expected to take what they need, to leave an offering, and to make Mother Earth beautiful in their creations (Trimble 2004:10).

Making a pot is akin to procreation, not just in the shaping of the vessel but in the transformation of raw clay into a finished pot and its successful emergence from ashes that occurs during the firing process (Charley and McChesney 2007). This metamorphosis corresponds to the themes of fertility and transformation that are central to Pueblo religions (Hays-Gilpin 2011). For the Hopi, color plays a central role in the transformation of raw clay into finished pot—during firing, gray clay becomes yellow, sometimes with anomalous patches of orange mottling or "blush," which reveal the pot's "animate quality" and the presence of a "heart" (Charley and McChesney 2007). A probably similarly meaningful metamorphosis in Ancestral Pueblo pottery was the transformation of yellow paint to red during the firing of Kayenta vessels.

Late period Ancestral Puebloans may have also viewed at least one paint material as having sacred associations. The raw materials for some glaze paint were processed from lead ore mined at several sources, most notably Cerrillos, New Mexico, which was also the location of prolific prehispanic turquoise mines (Nelson and

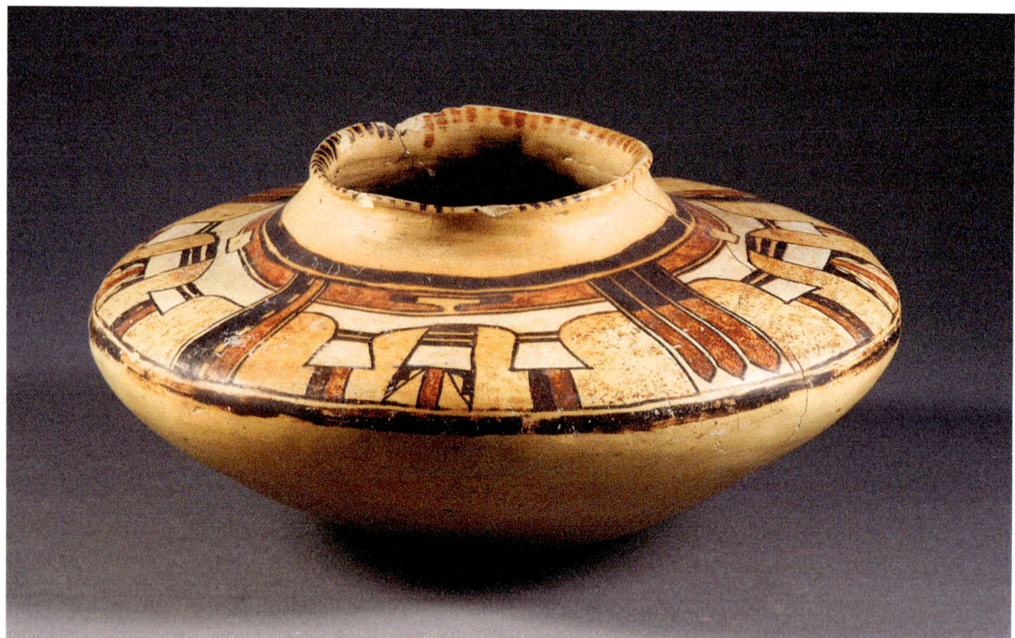

FIGURE 3.5. Jeddito Yellow Ware, late style Sikyatki Polychrome jar from the Hopi Mesas. Harold Colton and other early pottery typologists defined this vessel as the type specimen for Kawaioku Polychrome, a late variant of Sikyatki Polychrome with the addition of white paint. Today, ceramic analysts recognize that defining a type for every color combination produced in the Pueblo IV era is a futile exercise. Potters of this era exercised their skills to produce myriad colors, textures, and patterns. This vessel features feather designs, and spattered paint that may represent moisture and clouds. Museum of Northern Arizona catalog number OC1820. Photo by Ryan Belnap and Daniel Boone. Courtesy of the Museum of Northern Arizona.

Habicht-Mauche 2006:213–214). Because potters obtained the glaze paint ingredients either through long-distance travel or trade, glaze raw materials may have been considered pieces of sacred places (Bradley 2000; Huntley et al. 2012: 16). When applied to pottery vessels, they may have added to the color's sacred symbolism, along with glaze paint's shiny, glassy surface, which may have evoked the appearance of water (e.g., Doyel 2015:164).

Ancestral Hopi Sikyatki Polychrome (1375–1629) pottery with its yellow background and red and black designs is an excellent example of the layers of symbolic meanings that could imbue an Ancestral Pueblo pot (Figure 3.5; see Plate 7). The vessel itself was probably viewed as an animate object. Shaped originally from light to dark gray clay, it was transformed into yellow during firing. This yellow background had a series of associated symbolic meanings related to directions, places, clouds, plants, and animals. It was also the quintessential flowery color in Hopi language, especially katsina songs (Hays-Gilpin and Sekaquaptewa 2006:15–16). The red and black paints had their own diverse symbolic meanings. Images of flowers, birds, butterflies, and katsinas evoked the common themes of the summer agricultural season, katsina dances, and fertility. Flowers are harbingers of good harvests—they bloom in spring after a moist winter and after the summer rains come and the plants start to mature. This symbolism is part of a much broader "Flower World" cosmology that encompassed much of the Southwest and Mesoamerica (Hays-Gilpin and Sekaquaptewa 2006; Hill and Hays-Gilpin 1999).

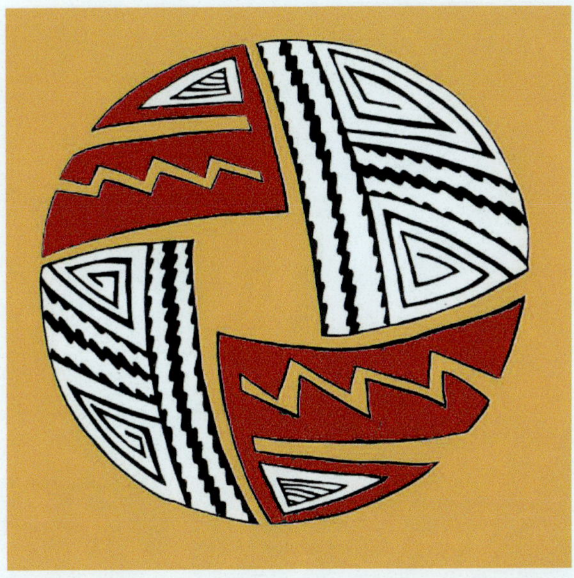

FIGURE 3.6. Kayenta tradition, drawing of Tsegi Orange Ware bowl with anomalous design, half Tusayan Polychrome, half Flagstaff Black-on-white. Artist's rendering: Victor Leshyk and Daniel Boone. Courtesy of Northern Arizona University. Original bowl (funerary object) University of California, Los Angeles catalog number RB568-462.

### *Breaking the Rules*

Archaeologists are good at recognizing patterns such as color preferences and thus good at knowing what to expect in a given assemblage from a particular time and place. But interesting anomalies remind us that potters were creative individuals. The most extreme examples of artistic license involve color, rather than design, choices.

Two examples are bowls whose interiors display both black-on-white and polychrome designs. These anomalies dramatically refute the idea that color combinations were determined solely by technology or tradition or habit. The bowls date to the late 1200s, a time of demographic upheavals, when white wares were dropping out of most areas. Under these conditions, a few potters were able to play with the rules about how colors should be combined. They maintained the standard pairings but in combination with each other.

One of these rarities is a Tsegi Orange Ware bowl from the Kayenta area (Figure 3.6; see Plate 8). It was recovered from an adult female burial (50) at the site of RB568 during the Rainbow Bridge–Monument Valley Expedition and is currently in that project's collections at the University of California, Los Angeles (UCLA catalog number RB568-462; see Beals et al. 1945: 131–133; Crotty 1983:49). The bowl's exterior is orange with stripes of white paint instead of the usual red, and its interior is decorated with four alternating black-on-white and orange polychrome design panels. Each color combination has its own distinctive design motif. The black-on-white panels contain identical layouts of a perpendicular set of zigzag lines with an angular scroll on either side, typical of Flagstaff Black-on-white. The polychrome panels each have broad-line red zigzags outlined in black and a hatched black-on-orange triangle, typical of contemporaneous Tusayan Polychrome bowls.

The second example is a Pinedale Polychrome bowl of unknown provenience in the collections of the Dallas Museum of Art (Figure 3.7; see Plate 9). The exterior has broad black

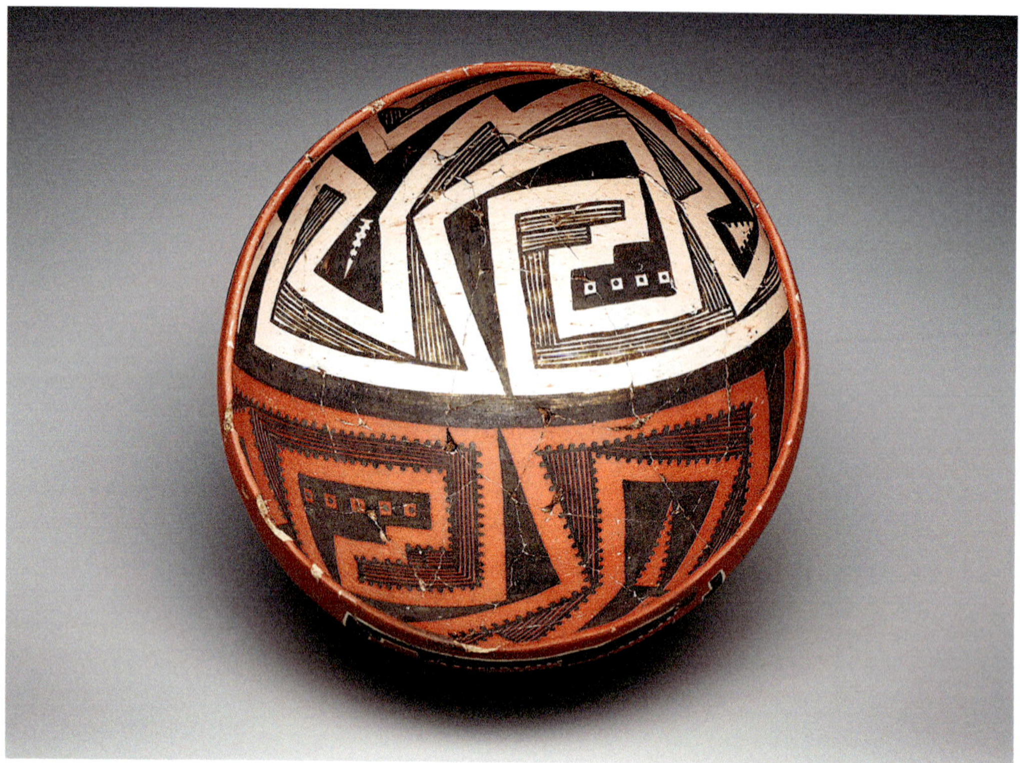

FIGURE 3.7. Cibola–White Mountain tradition, White Mountain Red Ware, Pinedale Polychrome bowl with Pinedale style interior, half black-on-red and half black-on-white, ca. AD 1275–1300. Ceramic, slip, and paint; 5⅛ × 10⅝ × 11 in. Unknown provenience. Dallas Museum of Art, Foundation for the Arts Collection, anonymous gift. Catalog number 1988.88.FA.

line rectilinear design units outlined with white, completely typical for Pinedale Polychrome bowls. The interior is divided in two, one side black-on-white and the other black-on-red. Both depict the same design motif—geometric interlocking hatched and solid triangles and stepped motifs with four dot-in-square elements inside. Divided by a broad black line, the two halves are identical except the black-on-red design has tick marks and the black-on-white design does not. A few details of one triangular unit also differ. The two motifs are positioned in rotational symmetry, the most common symmetry used in Ancestral Pueblo pottery prior to the mid-1300s.

These unusual bowls must have been even more eye-catching for the Ancestral Puebloans than for us today. The presence of both black-on-white and polychrome designs compounded the colors' symbolism and cosmological metaphors, which were further strengthened by the designs' meanings. But the co-occurrence of the two color combinations must have also conveyed something more—about the potter, as well as the time, place, and context.

Rare color anomalies such as these were not restricted to bowls. One notable example, also from the Dallas Museum of Art, is a black-on-white bird effigy jar with post-firing addition of red and blue paints (Figure 3.8, see Plate 10). The jar has no provenience, but its technology is Cibola White Ware, and its design conforms to thirteenth-century Pinedale and Kayenta styles, with broad lines separating fine-line designs reminiscent of cotton textiles with brocade decorations. Sometime after firing, its central

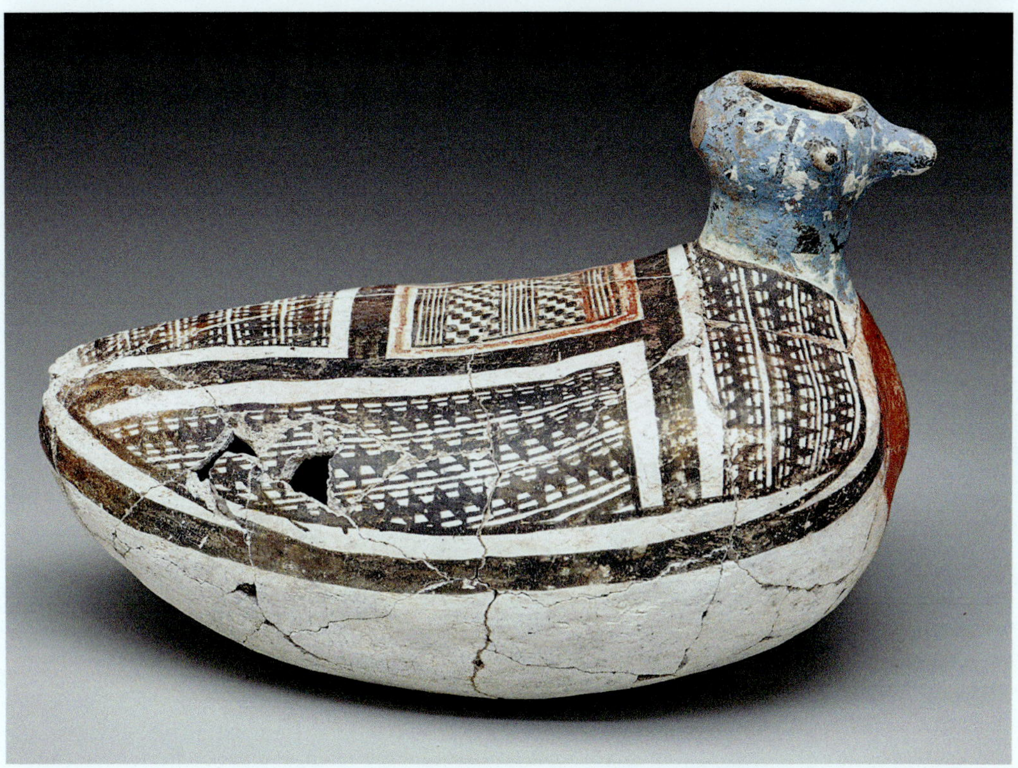

FIGURE 3.8. Cibola–White Mountain tradition, Cibola White Ware, Tularosa Black-on-white bird effigy jar with post-firing addition of fugitive red and blue pigments, ca. AD 1250–1300. Ceramic, slip, and fugitive paints; 5¾ × 9 × 6½ in. Unknown provenience. Dallas Museum of Art, Foundation for the Arts Collection, anonymous gift. Catalog number 1988.102.FA.

panel was outlined in fugitive red paint (probably hematite), the chest was painted red, and the head was painted blue (probably azurite). This vessel would have been imbued with all of the symbolic meanings that Ancestral Puebloans associated with birds, the colors white, black, red, and blue, and designs echoing cotton textiles and thus clouds and rain. Broken stubs of a strap handle reaching from head to tail indicate that it originally was a pitcher, perhaps used for pouring water.

At Pueblo sites dating from the 1100s to recent times, painted wood and stone artifacts show layers of bright colored paint. Ethnographic evidence indicates that the addition of paint to ritual objects, such as prayer sticks, consecrates and animates them, enlisting their help in communicating prayers to the spirit world (Chapter 1; Lewis 2002; Odegaard and Hays-Gilpin 2002). Adding colored paint to a black-on-white bird-shaped vessel used to pour water in a ritual context might have served a similar animating function.

## Conclusion

Because the colors of Ancestral Pueblo pots signified overlapping sets of technical, social, and ideological characteristics, the colors on a single pot could convey information about the individuals who made and used it. The same was true for pottery assemblages at successively larger spatial scales, extending from individual communities to the locality, region, and entire Colorado Plateau. These patterns in turn changed through time at variable rates and to variable degrees. Thus, the intersection of technical, social, and ideological characteristics made color, the most visible pottery characteristic, a portal into many dimensions of Ancestral Pueblo life.

While technical factors associated with clays, paints, and firing techniques were essential determinants of a particular pot's color or colors, they were not the only ones. This is best demonstrated by the Kayenta communities in which the same potters made both black-on-white and black-on-orange vessels and by the rare anomalous bowls whose interiors were decorated with both black-on-white and polychrome designs. In these cases, and probably more generally, technical knowledge was not restricted. Instead, using their vast knowledge, potters chose the combination of clays, paints, and firing conditions that would produce their desired outcome.

These choices were complicated, given the absence of an automatic, one-to-one relationship between particular technical characteristics and colors. Rather, the interaction of minimally two characteristics could produce varied results. For example, under different firing conditions, the same clays could be transformed into different colored vessels, and different clays could be transformed into same-colored vessels. For decorated vessels, these correspondences were even more complex, as slips and painted designs were added prior to firing.

Potters' technical decisions about color were strongly influenced by a variety of social factors. Women grew up in communities in which pots of certain colors were ubiquitous, learned pottery production, including how to produce the group's characteristic colors, from family and community members, and undertook this production with others. In these social contexts, color preferences were maintained over generations and became part of potters' ingrained production habits. For both potters and consumers, these preferences in turn came to have social significance, representing their community, local, and regional identities.

Social factors also influenced the coexistence of different color combinations, shifts in their popularity through time, and the adoption of new colors and color combinations through interaction with groups from other areas. Other social factors included the group setting in which a vessel was to be used, such as by family members in the home, in community-wide events, or for trade, all of which could affect a vessel's function and in turn its color. Technical and social factors may have sometimes intersected in how potters were able to access their raw materials, either locally or through trade.

Religious symbolism pervaded pottery colors during all stages of a pot's production and its subsequent use-life. Color transformations during the firing process must have been especially powerful. These meanings were reinforced by those associated with other characteristics, including raw materials sources, vessel function, design symbolism, and use context. Most fundamentally, pots were viewed as animate objects, and their colors contributed both directly and indirectly to their status as living beings.

For early researchers, pottery colors represented social groups and, as such, were the first step in classification both in time and space. While much of this is still true today, we now recognize that the relationship between color and groups is extremely complicated and that color can signify many other aspects of Ancestral Pueblo life. A vessel's shades of gray, white, black, red, orange, yellow, brown, green, and occasionally blue were imbued with powerful meanings related to community and regional identities, religious beliefs and practices, and ancestral heritage—all important topics for future research.

# 4

# Painted Kivas, Painted Rooms

Polly Schaafsma

Graphic images painted on the walls of kivas and other rooms offer an ample opportunity to explore the use of color by Ancestral Pueblo people. In Ancestral Pueblo sites, the walls of rooms and circular and rectangular kivas were frequently mud-plastered and then renewed as needs dictated. (See Lomawywesa and Coochsiwukioma 2010:187 and Figure 8.4 for a cross-section of layers from a painted kiva at Awat'ovi.) In the course of renewal, while most layers were left undecorated, others were painted with varied abstract patterns and life forms (Smith 1952:Tables 1 and 2). As for the terminology used in describing these wall paintings, although "mural" may be broadly acceptable, I refer to the earlier and less complex pre–AD 1300 paintings dominated by geometric patterns as "wall decorations" and reserve the term "mural" for the complex abstractions and integrated ceremonial scenes that distinguish the later Pueblo IV work. The latter comprise the apex of prehispanic Pueblo painting.

While walls provided smooth, wide "canvases" for Pueblo painters, centuries later the fragility of these walls and the paintings on them have posed a significant challenge to archaeologists. In open sites, such as the large pueblos in the Rio Grande Valley, erosion and moisture have often destroyed the tops of the walls, and the upper registers of paintings have been lost. Preservation is sometimes better in sites protected by rockshelters on the Colorado Plateau. In all cases, however, the thin layers of plaster and their colors have proven vulnerable to deterioration when exposed to the open air in the course of excavations. There is, nevertheless, a significant body of data with which to examine Pueblo wall paintings and color usage through time. A multitude of murals have been documented from both the pre-migration period before AD 1300 in the Four Corners region and from Pueblo IV (ca. AD 1300–1625+) at Hopi and in the Rio Grande region. A few wall paintings have been found in Pueblo II sites (ca. AD 900–1130; Cole 2006:96), although they occur increasingly through Pueblo III (ca. AD 1130–1300). The post-migration Pueblo IV era marks a florescence in this art, as color diversity was amplified in tandem with a new iconographic repertoire that marked accompanying ideological shifts that occurred at this time.

## The Colorado Plateau before AD 1300

Prior to AD 1300, the Ancestral Pueblo people in the San Juan drainage enhanced the interior walls of circular kivas, rectangular rooms, and occasionally towers with simple designs. Rarely, paintings on the outside walls of cliff dwellings have been preserved under protective overhangs of deep rockshelters. Barring a few notable exceptions, these early Plateau Pueblo paintings combine various tan or reddish earth tones with white or cream-colored clay washes, all natural earth pigments easily obtained from nearby sources. Numerous sites with wall paintings are known in the greater Mesa Verde region (Brew

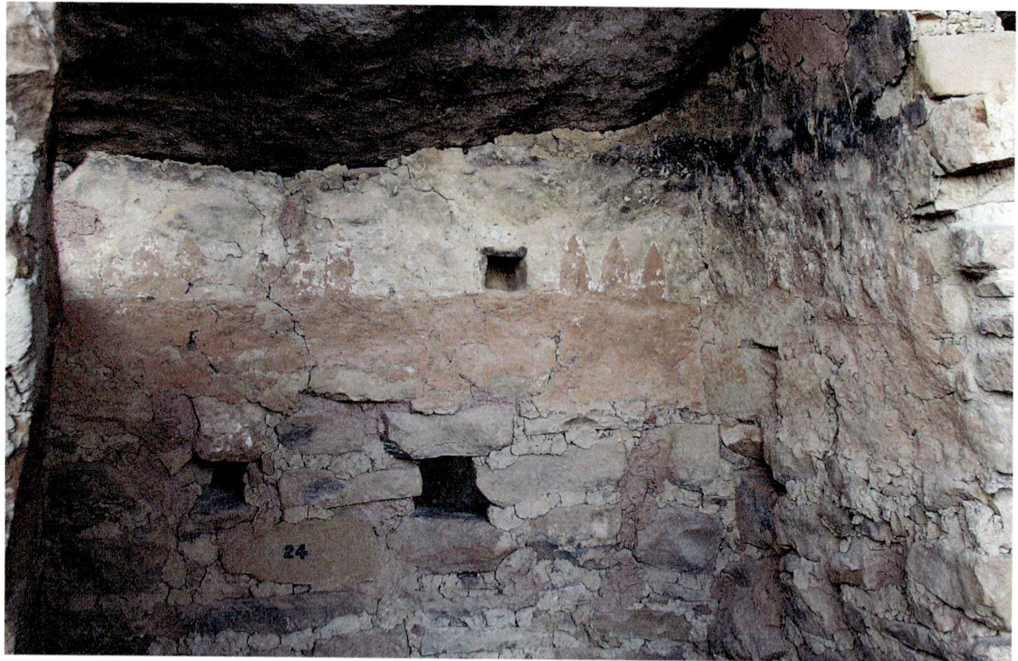


FIGURE 4.1. Balcony House, Room 24b, Mesa Verde National Park. This was a special use room (Fiero 1999:23). The walls were painted with a band of reddish clay topped with sets of three elongated triangular elements that project into a white background. Photograph by Polly Schaafsma.

1946:41, Figures 87b, d; Brody 1991:59–68; Cole 2006; Jackson 1876:373, Plate 3; Morris 1919b: Plates 34c, 35; Prudden 1914:48–49; Rohn 1971: 70–71; Silver 1982; Smith 1952:55–68). East of the San Juan drainage, the largely black-on-white wall paintings of the Gallina Culture in the upper Chama Valley also date from the 1200s (Bellorado 2017). Like other aspects of the Gallina culture, the wall paintings deviate from the mainstream Pueblo paintings in that they have their own limited repertoire of designs including pennants, a branching plant that is seemingly a sunflower, and, more rarely, birds.

During Pueblo III in the northern San Juan, most wall paintings fall into two major design categories: 1) the triangle-dot complex (Figure 4.1; Brody 1991:Figure 51); and 2) decorative horizontal bands that commonly feature geometric designs similar to those found in weaving and on pottery (Figures 4.2a and b). The triangle-dot complex is painted in earth tones on a light background above a broad horizontal band along the base of the wall, called a dado. Within kivas the decorative bands were usually painted on the vertical faces of the bench and pilasters where they function as accents to the structural elements of the architecture (Cole 2006:Figure 11.1; Newsome 2010:Figure 4.1). These two classes of wall paintings, popular throughout the Mesa Verde region, rarely occur in the same sites, much less in the same room (Cole 2006: 94). Various small, usually crudely painted life forms may be added to this repertoire, seeming to float randomly in space above the dado-triangle designs or occurring independently. Beyond the usual variations on earth tones including tan, browns, reddish browns, reds, and various shades of white, additional colors are extremely rare and were used sparingly. There was, nevertheless, an increase in color use after AD 1150 in the central Mesa Verde region (Cole 2006:94) that includes shades of green, green-blue, yellow, red, and red-black, but with the exception of red, these hues occur only sporadically and are very rarely dominant. The most unusual examples are an extensive use of yellow

a

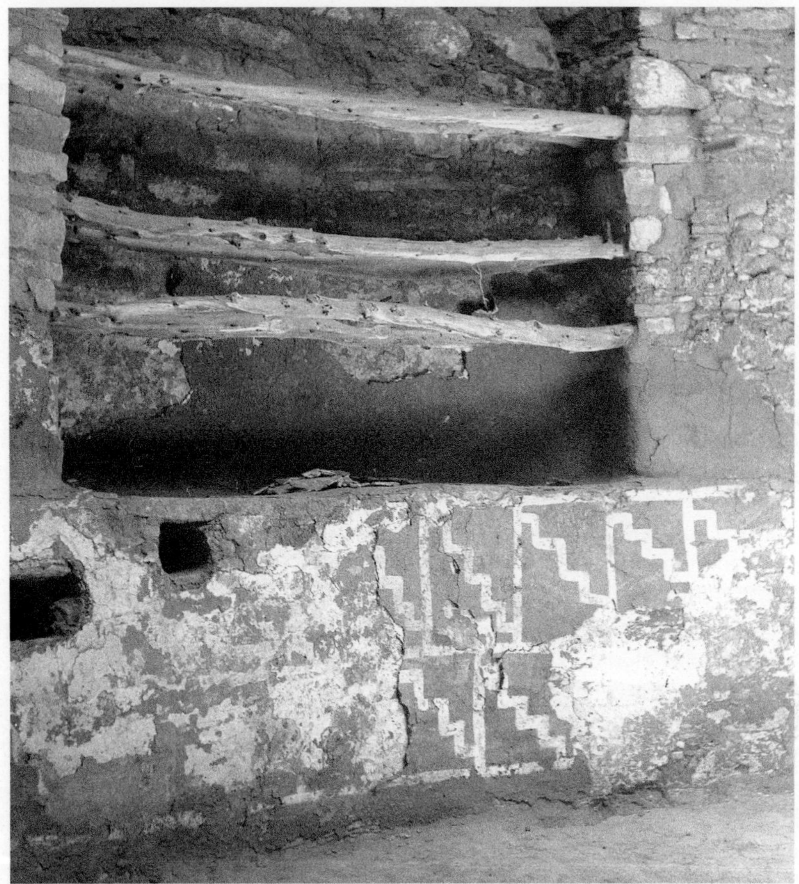

b

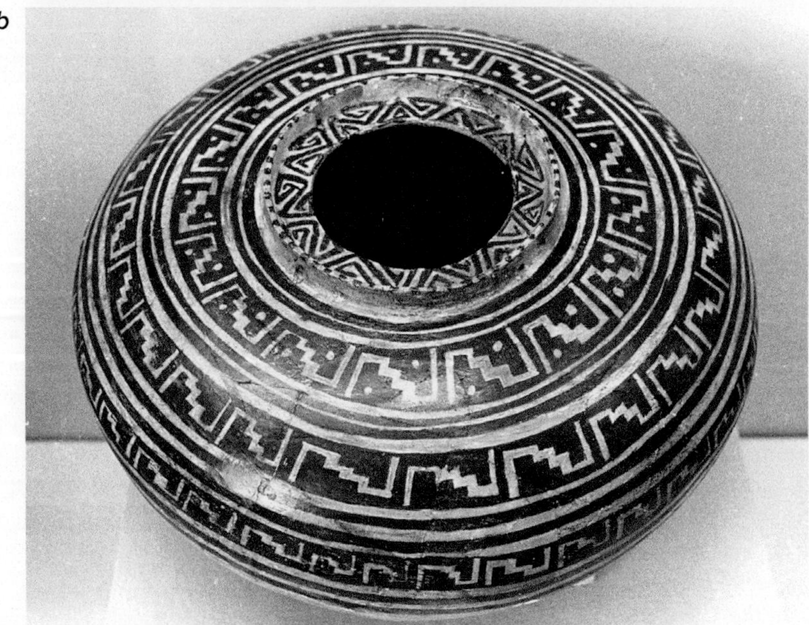

FIGURE 4.2. (*a*) Wall painting in Mesa Verde style kiva, Lowry Ruin, Colorado. Photograph by Curtis Schaafsma. (*b*) Mesa Verde kiva jar with banded design similar to geometric bands from Mesa Verde kiva paintings. Photograph courtesy of David Noble.

on a room wall (Ben Bellorado, personal communication 2016), and bright green paint employed for a variation on the band/triangle/dot complex on the outer walls of a cliff dwelling on Cedar Mesa (Cole 2009:Figure 84b). In addition to aesthetic considerations, these surprises may be attributable to the local availability of these pigments. In the same section of Cedar Mesa, a much older painting of Basketmaker II origin also utilized a similar bright green paint.

### *The Dado-Triangle-Dot Motif*

Mud washes in contrasting, although muted, earth tones commonly divide the walls of rooms and kivas. In these examples, the upper wall is typically plastered in some shade of white, contrasting with the tan or reddish-brown dado or lower wall, the upper edge of which is elaborated with triangular elements of the same color. Projecting into the white space of the upper wall, these triangles, sometimes varied in contour, are pictured in various arrangements, and a row of earth-toned dots may run above the triangles and the dado (Brody 1991:Figure 51). There are numerous variations on this basic scheme. The triangles may extend upward from a narrow band or be suspended below. In other instances a baseline or band for the triangles may be lacking (Cole 2006:95). In some cases, a limited number of life forms are added at random in the upper field.

There are at least 17 known sites in the northern San Juan region with these wall designs (Cole 2006:94–95), found throughout the Mesa Verde region. In 1893 Nordenskiöld described paintings of this genre from Painted Kiva House and Cliff Palace on Mesa Verde (Cole 2006:Figure 11.4 and Plate 21). Additional sites with these wall decorations include Spruce Tree House (Fewkes 1909:20), New Fire Temple (Fewkes 1916:106, Figure 2, Plate 7; Schaafsma 1980:Figure 101), Balcony House (Figure 4.1 and Fiero 1999:125); and Mug House (Rohn 1971:Figures 75–77), all in Mesa Verde National Park itself, as well as Eagle's Nest on southern Mesa Verde in the Ute Mountain Tribal Park. Although Eagle's Nest was described by Smith (1952:56) as Pueblo II, subsequently, 41 tree ring samples have demonstrated that all of the standing architecture at this cliff dwelling was constructed between AD 1206 and 1220 (Nickens 1981:16).

Rohn (1971:24–25, 70–71, Figures 75–77) provides an excellent description of the treatment of kiva plaster and decoration in thirteenth-century Mug House. In these Mesa Verde kivas, as elsewhere, plaster consisted of several layers of thin coats of earth-colored adobe varying from reddish-brown to tan, obtained from a neighboring rockshelter or from nearby sources such as mesa-top loess. Plasters in earth shades varied from monochrome to two to three colors. Kivas A and C had figures and designs. Kiva C is described in detail. On the top layer "a deep red covers the lower two feet of the wall, allowing the natural tan color of the underlying plaster to show through for the upper portion. Where these two colors meet, a 0.2-foot-wide band of white almost completely encircles the kiva.... Numerous white triangles project from the top edge of the white band like mountains" (Rohn 1971:70 and Figure 75). These occur in groups ranging from two to as many as 34 triangles. Earlier layers of plaster had similar designs (Rohn 1971:Figure 77).

Moving eastward, a brick red dado with triangles against a gypsum whitewash was recorded on the wall of a second-story room at Aztec Ruins north of the San Juan in New Mexico. The room is said to have been remodeled by Mesa Verde immigrants (Lister and Lister 1987: 43). A similar pattern was found on wall plaster at Salmon Ruin on the north bank of San Juan River (Brody 1991:Figure 51).

Significantly fewer wall paintings are known from Chaco and the immediate vicinity. Pueblo II wall paintings from Kiva 6 in site Bc 51 (AD 950–1025) at Chaco consist of a group of crudely painted life forms in white that include hunters and animals (Brody 1991:Figure 47). Also from Chaco, simple, painted designs in one room at Chetro Ketl and another in Kin Kletso may date from the Bonito Phase (ca. AD 1025–1130), which overlaps Pueblo III (Lekson 1983; Vivian and Mathews 1973:50–54 and Figure 30). Near Chaco Canyon, at site LA17360, a kiva painting in red and white, dated by archaeomagnetism to around AD 1190, includes flute players floating in space above a dado marked with triangles, similar to those in the Mesa Verde region (McAnany 1982; Silver 1982:715). This postdates the Bonito Phase by around six decades and could indicate work by later Mesa Verde migrants into the Chaco vicinity. (Other citations to the painting at LA17360 have erroneously referred to it as "eleventh century" [Brody 1991:Figure 49] or as one of "the earliest examples" of a wall painting [Newsome 2010:65.])

Several wall paintings in the dado-triangle-dot category also occur south of the San Juan River, in Canyon del Muerto, including designs in white at Antelope House (Loendorf 2010:49–51, Figures 3.4, 3.5). Other paintings in a mealing room at Antelope House break from these conventions, consisting of horizontal lines below which is painted a series of parallel lines forming a meandering rectangle motif along with a white anthropomorph (Loendorf 2010:Figure 3.5).

### *Geometric Bands: Textile and Pottery Designs*

The other major type of pre–AD 1300 wall painting consists of bands of geometric elements that closely resemble those found on Mesa Verde Black-on-white pottery and on textiles (Figures 4.2a and 4.2b; Newsome 2010:Figures 4.1, 4.3). In kivas this patterning commonly enhances the face of the bench, and decorative elements, usually painted in white on an earth-colored background, may extend to the pilasters characteristic of Mesa Verde kiva architecture. A kiva from Lowry Ruin (ca. AD 1080–1150) north of Mesa Verde itself provides what is probably an early Pueblo III example of this type of kiva decoration (Figure 4.2a; also see Cole 2006:Figure 11.1). Here, white stepped designs were painted at floor level against a brown plaster backdrop on the bench of a Mesa Verde–style kiva. In contrast to the usual white design against a tan background, a kiva bench in Mummy Cave in Canyon del Muerto is probably the most complex Pueblo III kiva painting known to date. Here a band divided into panels of finely rendered, opposed, nested triangles and other patterns—all in white—is featured against a varied background of red and tan (Figure 4.3; see Plates 11 and 12). The decorative band is bordered by solid bands in red and white and pink.

Patterns in the Chaco region are less clear. In Kin Kletso's Kiva D, plain red and yellow bands, lacking geometric elements, are painted on a white background, gracing the bench and pilasters of a Mesa Verde style kiva (Vivian and Mathews 1973:50–54, and Figure 30). The kiva, which dates in the late 1100s (ca. AD 1178), is contemporary with the dado-triangle Pueblo III paintings in LA17360. Meanwhile, simple paintings on a white plastered wall in Room 106 in Chetro Ketl defy categorization. Consisting of a short series of squares joined at the corners, they follow a diagonal trajectory against a white plastered background (Lekson 1983:Figure II:2, 3, 6). Two squares are an azurite blue, while two are very dark blue or black. The original hues of the others are indeterminable and today appear tan. Other wall markings from Chetro Ketl and elsewhere in Chaco consist of colorless incised designs.

### *Life Forms and Miscellaneous Motifs*

In addition to the two major types of wall paintings described, miscellaneous life forms and a few self-contained geometric designs add to the pre–AD 1300 inventory (Grant 1978:Figure 4.50; Schaafsma 1980:Figure 102). In Mesa Verde's Cliff Palace tower, an apparent textile and a set of long ticked lines are painted in red against a white background (Newsome 2010:64–67). At Mesa Verde and elsewhere, life forms are depicted as simple monochromatic silhouettes in white, red, or more rarely in yellow, or bluish tones. Lacking in detail, they float casually placed against earth-toned backdrops or light-colored plaster, often above a dado. Had details been significant, contrasting colors could easily have been employed to delineate them. Human stick figures, hunters, flute players, bighorn sheep, and birds resemble their rock art analogs (Cattanach 1980:84 and Figure 81; Rohn 1971; Schaafsma 1980:Figure 101; Silver 1982). Finally, at Moon House on Cedar Mesa in the western Mesa Verde region, a crescent and full moon (or

a

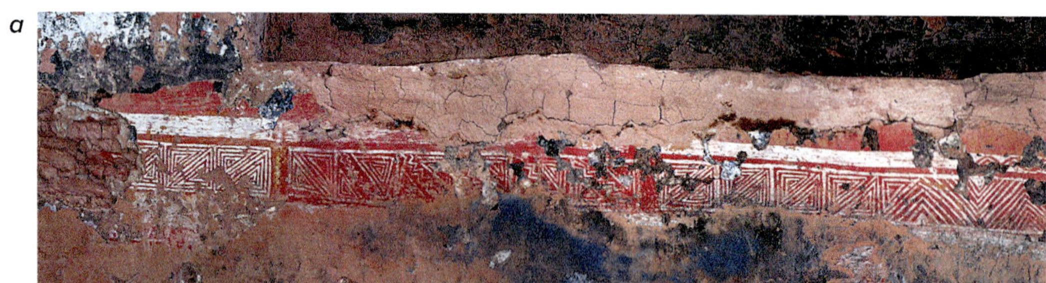

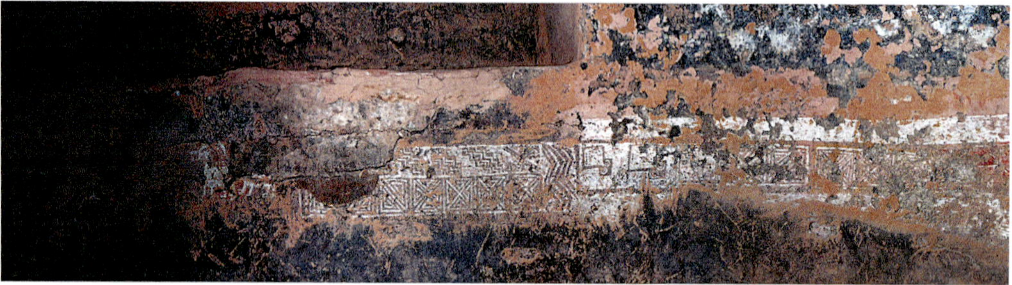

b

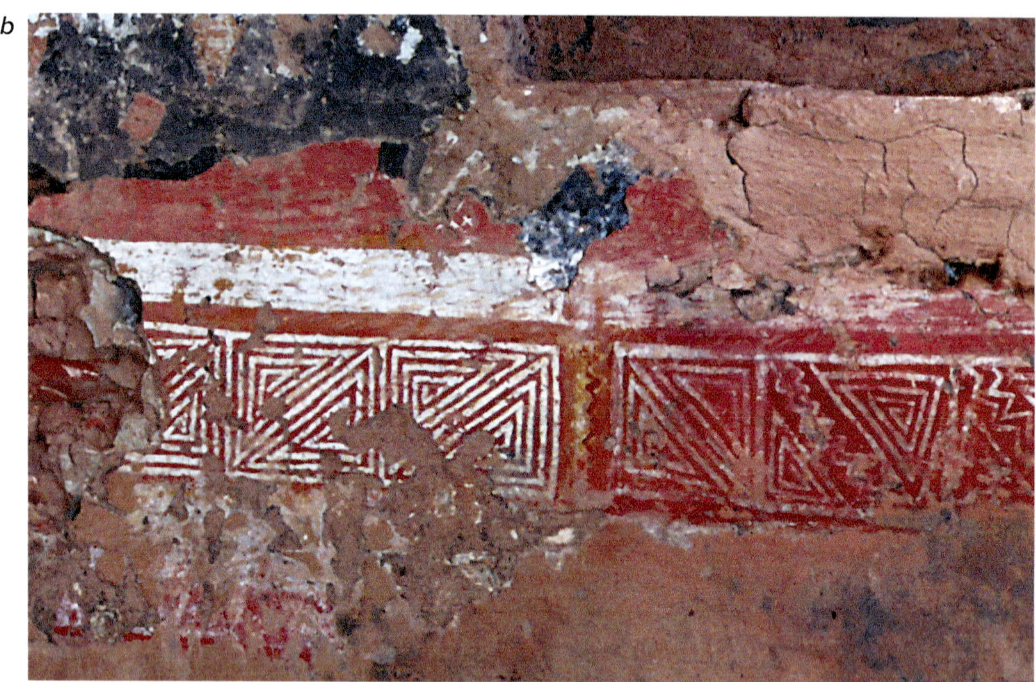

FIGURE 4.3. (*a*) Sections of a detailed band of opposed nested triangles in red and white and other elements encircling a kiva wall, Mummy Cave, Canyon del Muerto. (*b*) Detail, color enhanced. Photographs courtesy of Robert Mark, Rupestrian Cyber Services.

was the latter meant to be the sun?) are rendered negatively as unpainted shapes within wide white bands on adobe-colored plaster (Cole 2009:Figure 84c).

### Color and Content

In pre–AD 1300 wall paintings, earth tones and white predominated, and altogether they were low in contrast and visual impact. As described earlier, many of the banded geometrics are painted in white against the tan adobe hues of the background plaster. As a pigment easily obtained from a variety of potential sources in the Southwestern landscape, whether white paint conveyed any symbolic meaning in the early kiva decorations is not really known. Based on ethnographic information, however, it may have been the most appropriate color for a variety of stepped designs featured in these wall paintings—designs that symbolize clouds (Newsome 2010:Figures 4.1, 4.3; Ortman 2006: Figure 12.7; Schaafsma 2013). In a parallel case, Hays-Gilpin and VanPool (2009) propose convincingly that between AD 1100 and the late 1200s, Tusayan White Ware pots bearing similar cotton textile-like designs have symbolic connections to clouds. Further, there is a strong likeness between the banded wall paintings and designs on Mesa Verde Black-on-white pottery (Figure 4.2a and 4.2b). Hopi cultural expert Emory Sekaquaptewa interpreted a similar band of interlocking frets on a Jeddito Black-on-yellow bowl as clouds moving along and building (Sekaquaptewa and Washburn 2010: Figure 7.30).

Referencing Ortman (2000, 2008), Newsome (2010:64) describes an "overlapping formal language between textiles, ceramics, and mural decorations." These associations are manifest in various ways. As for textiles, it is probably not coincidental that the role of cotton among the Plateau Pueblos increased after AD 1100 when the upright loom appeared on the Colorado Plateau (Schaafsma 2013; Teague 1998). At that point depictions of large cotton textiles with frets and stepped elements make their appearances in Ancestral Pueblo rock art as well as on kiva walls as described here. I have proposed that these petroglyphs under the open sky are petitions for rain (Schaafsma 2013).

Cotton itself, being white and fluffy, is likened to clouds, and today it plays a vital role in rainmaking rites (Bunzel 1932b:799; Parsons 1939:397–398, 705; Stephen 1936). Its use in ritual contexts is essential, from the string used on prayer sticks to the sashes, kilts, and leggings used in ceremonial attire, all related to appeals for rain (Schaafsma 2013; Schaafsma 2015:24–28). Accordingly, ritual offerings consisting of cotton in pots cached in caves (Haury and Huckell 1993) link clouds with their underground origins in lakes and springs, with which pottery vessels themselves have symbolic associations (Benedict 1931:62; Schaafsma 2002, 2013; Stephen 1936:483, 618; Stevenson 1894:315). The kiva itself has been likened to a bowl (Newsome 2010). In summary, the white kiva paintings were another medium through which cloud symbolism could be expressed, simultaneously recalling the shared symbolic referents between designs on black-on-white pottery, the vessels themselves and textiles. Though white clays are common in the Southwest, Ancestral Pueblo painters might have chosen specific clays from sacred sources for these designs, contributing to their efficacy and symbolic import (e.g., Bunzel 1932b:859–861; Young 1988:191–192).

As for the dado-triangle-dot complex, a number of researchers subscribe to the idea that these paintings represent the horizons of surrounding landscapes in which mountain peaks occur at varied intervals (Brody 1991; Cole 2006; Newsome 2010:64–67; Newsome and Hays-Gilpin 2011:158; Ortman 2008). Ortman (2000) suggests that these paintings constitute the metaphorical integration of architecture with the cosmic order. One might also argue that the horizon hypothesis is questionable, given that the so-called mountains are highly abstracted, and the inverted triangles and lines of dots in this complex are not representational. In fact, these paintings occur within a visual system that lacks any definitively identified landscapes as subjects. On the other hand, it might be argued that the landscape interpretation is supported by the rare crescent and full moons (or

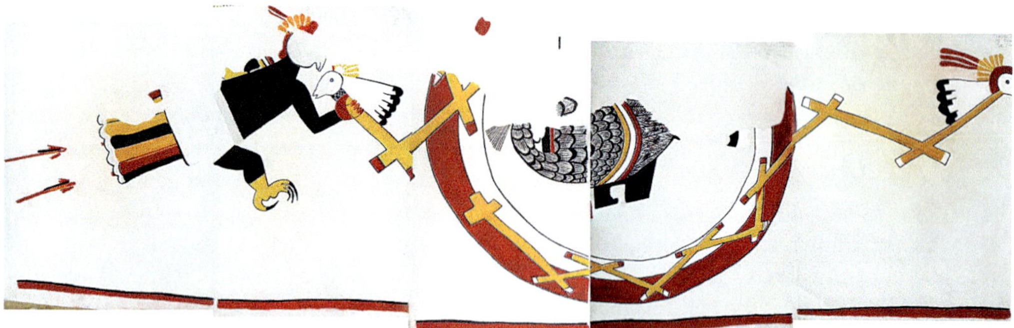

FIGURE 4.4. Ceremonial scene with composite birdman and lightning, Kiva 8, Layer 1, south wall, Pottery Mound. Drawing by Patricia Vivian (Vivian 1961:Figure 101).

sun) pictured in the negative within the upper painted bands at Moon House on Cedar Mesa. On balance, the proposal that the wide painted bands signified layers of the cosmos remains plausible without reference to "landscapes" as such. The symbolic use of color, if any, in this scheme is not clear.

Assessing the wall paintings from securely dated rooms and kivas at the end of the Pueblo III occupation of the Colorado Plateau, researchers (especially Smith 1952) have been challenged to look for evidence in the latest works of a transition to the elaborate murals that characterize the Hopi and Rio Grande kivas of the Pueblo IV period. At one point, Smith proposes that the appearance of crudely drawn representational figures in mural art on the Colorado Plateau was the "genesis of a style of mural decoration that was destined to ramify itself flamboyantly during Pueblo IV and later" (Smith 1952:59); nine pages later he roundly rejects this proposal, saying, "*When we have reviewed the flamboyance of the handiwork of the mural painters during Pueblo IV, we will be the more puzzled at the paucity of the evidence for a developing tradition behind this Renaissance*" (Smith 1952:68, emphasis added).

## Pueblo IV and the Advent of Color in the Fourteenth Century

One is compelled to ask, "Is this a 'rebirth' or something new?" In what ways do Pueblo IV murals differ from the pre–AD 1300 wall paintings (e.g., Newsome and Hays-Gilpin 2011)? Following the Ancestral Pueblo migrations away from the Four Corners region at the end of the AD 1200s, Pueblo society was reconfigured in a multitude of ways. Among the changes that ensued, wall art underwent revolutionary developments, and within it, the explosion of color might be described as "celebratory." Within a new stylistic framework, a full-blown new iconographic system was pictured, and the communication potential of the complex content of these murals was greatly enabled by a rich palette of many contrasting colors and shades (Figures 4.4 and 4.5; see Plates 13 and 14; Crotty 1995; Dutton 1963; Hays-Gilpin and Schaafsma 2010; Hibben 1975; P. Schaafsma 2007b; Smith 1952; Vivian 1961).

Color was used for definition, emphasis, and, selectively, for its symbolic connotations. Dado colors vary, rainbow stripes in red, white, and yellow frame ceremonial scenes and outlines provide clarity, all on a variety of new background colors. Murals from Awat'ovi, Kawàyka'a, and Pottery Mound, crowded with imagery and detail, draw upon color to enable "readability" within the complexity of the representations and abstractions. These paintings include a vast inventory of elaborately costumed ritual participants, animals, birds, and other life forms of symbolic importance. In ceremonial scenes, human figures hold or are surrounded by diverse paraphernalia and are laden with other details, all designed to unite the ritualists with the cosmos (Figures 4.6 and 4.7; see Plates 15 and 16). In these murals, depicting both human and spiritual actors (Newsome and Hays-Gilpin

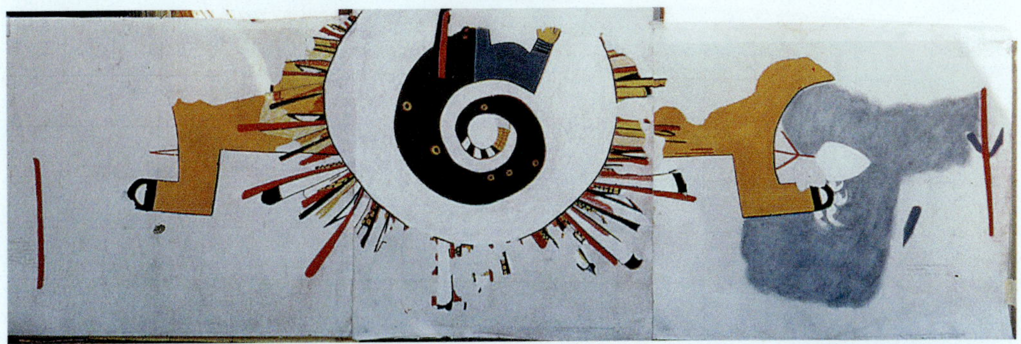

FIGURE 4.5. Orange mountain lions with black feet and white claws emerge from a white sun shield bristling with feathers, Kiva 8, Layer 5, south wall, Pottery Mound. Centered on the shield is a snake person in dark brown and blue-gray with a human head, hair, and hand. Drawing by Patricia Vivian (Vivian 1961:Figure 104).

2011:156), dynamic engagement with the cosmos is a dominant theme.

All of the wall paintings discussed from this time period are from kivas dated between the fourteenth and early seventeenth centuries, widely distributed from the Hopi Mesas in Arizona to the Rio Grande Valley in New Mexico. Fourteenth-century dates for the earliest murals include those from Atsinna, a site located in the El Morro Valley east of Zuni in west central New Mexico, the Western Mound at Awat'ovi (Smith 1952), and possibly Picuris Kivas B and C, although the Picuris dating is somewhat uncertain (Dick et al. 1999:Table 4.3). Less well known is an additional kiva with paintings of large human figures from Homol'ovi II, near Winslow, Arizona, with pottery dating to AD 1375–1400 (Adams 1994:41; Pond 1966). At Atsinna, founded late in the thirteenth century with a final tree ring date of AD 1349 (Kintigh 2007:376, note 10), colorful geometric patterns in red, yellow, black, and white painted on the last coat of plaster of a rectangular kiva probably date to the last decades of the site's occupation. At Awat'ovi's Western Mound, the murals from Rooms 218, 229, and 240 depict geometrics similar to those from Atsinna along with a widely varied repertoire of other images (Smith 1952: Figure 40–46a and c). Pottery assemblages from these particular rooms date between AD 1320 and 1400 (Smith 1952:316), indicating that the paintings may overlap in time with those from Atsinna, although the most recent overall estimates for the Antelope Mesa murals from Awat'ovi and Kawàyka'a are between circa AD 1375 and 1625+ (Hays-Gilpin and LeBlanc 2007:110). Likewise at Pottery Mound, based on pottery data at the site, the earliest murals are thought to date from circa AD 1370 (C. Schaafsma 2007).

In the 1930s archaeologists working in a square kiva at the site of Kuaua (ca. AD 1575–1610), along the Rio Grande north of Albuquerque, were the first to discover and record Pueblo IV murals (Bliss 1948; Dutton 1963). The total number of plaster layers in Kuaua's Kiva III is uncertain, although according to Brody (2007:3) "both Dutton (1963:38) and Bliss (1948:219) give the count as 85, including 17 that they unequivocally considered to have had pictures painted on them." At Kuaua, archaeologists employed techniques that preserved the murals layer by layer (Bliss 1935, 1948; see also Brody 2007; P. Schaafsma 2007a; Smith 1952:38–52). The most complex Pueblo IV murals are those from Awat'ovi and Kawàyka'a on Antelope Mesa in the Hopi Jeddito region (Smith 1952) and from Pottery Mound (ca. AD 1370–1475), south of Albuquerque (Crotty 2007; Hibben 1975; P. Schaafsma 2007b; Vivian 1961, 1994, 2007). Additional painted kivas are known from elsewhere in the Rio Grande Valley and neighboring regions (Crotty 1999; Schaafsma 1965; Schaafsma and Wiseman 1992). In addition to the archaeological evidence, Spanish accounts indicate that wall paintings were once commonplace, especially in the southern regions of the

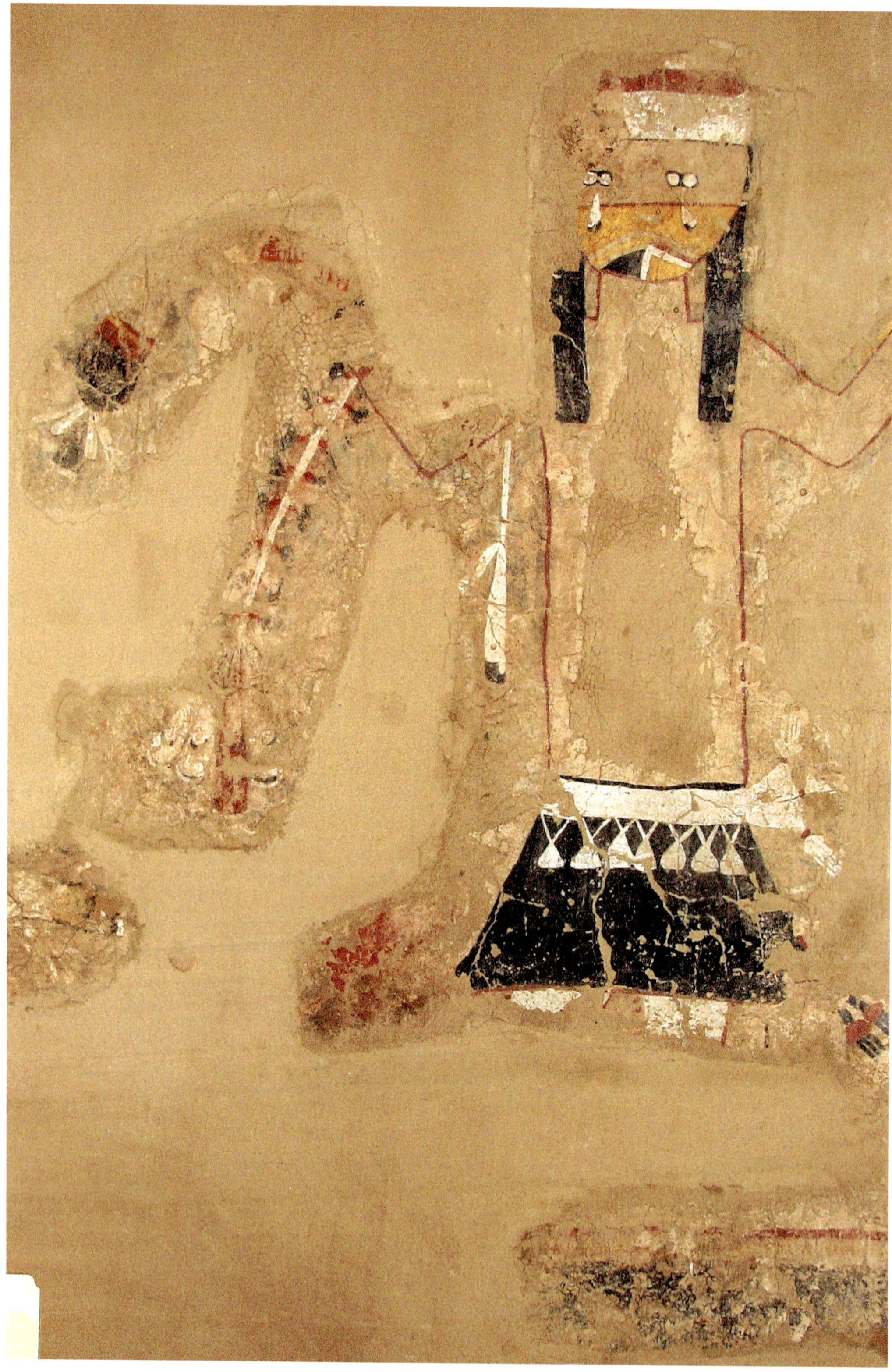

FIGURE 4.6. One of four ritually attired figures participating in rain-bringing rites, Kiva III, Layer G-26, Figure 52, Kuaua Pueblo, Coronado State Monument, New Mexico. The participants stand on a black dado bordered with a rainbow, a portion of which is visible at lower right. Elsewhere in the same scene, black ollas situated on the dado spout rain and lightning (Dutton 1963:Plate 15). Photograph courtesy of Curtis Schaafsma.

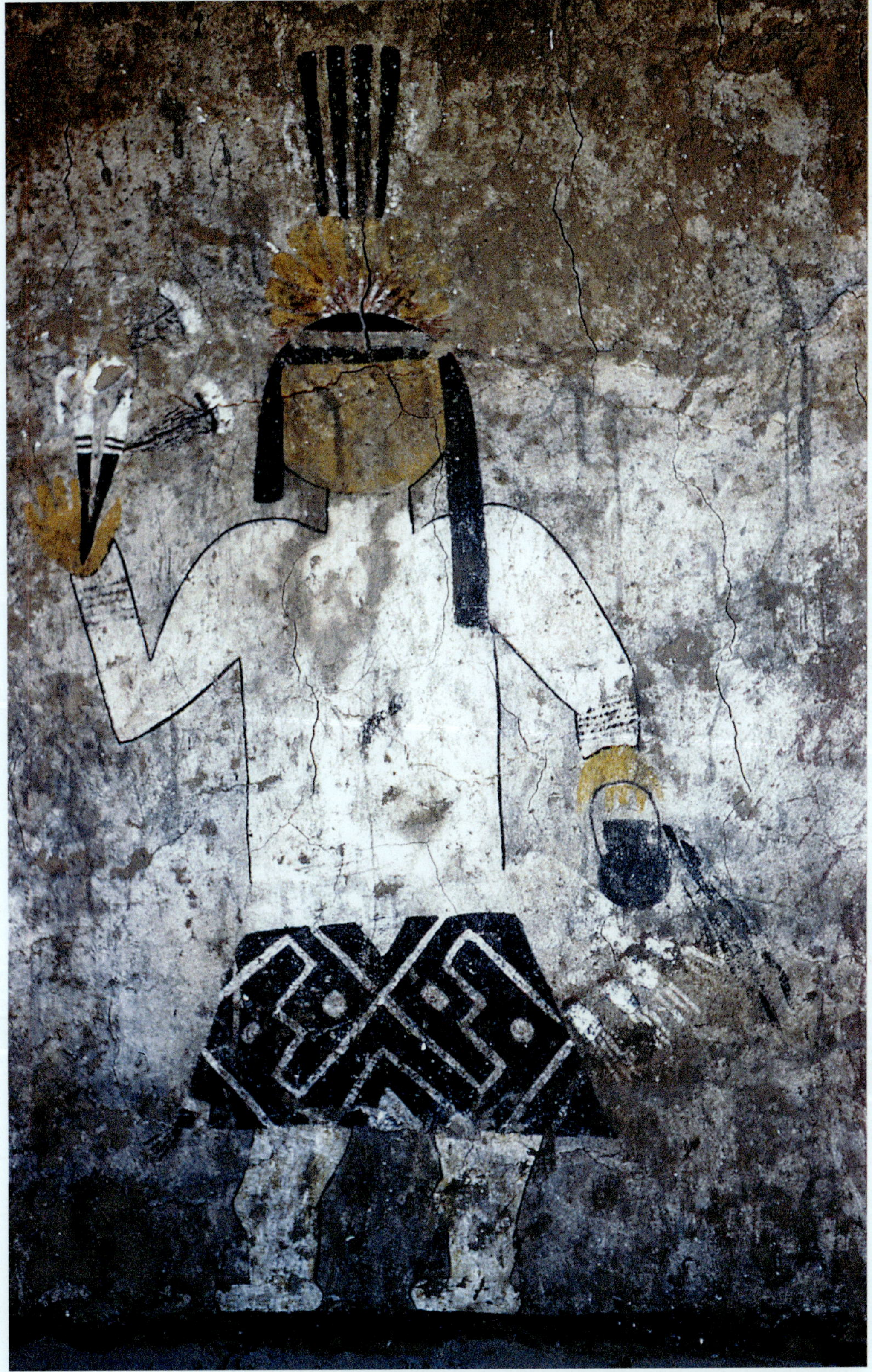

FIGURE 4.7. Ceremonial figure, Kiva 8, Layer 1, Pottery Mound. The black and white emphasis in this painting is likely to pertain to rain cloud symbolism. Note the black pot spilling moisture, a rain-inducing rite. Photograph courtesy of Patricia Vivian (Vivian 1961:Frontispiece).

Pueblo province (Dutton 1963:8–12). East of the Rio Grande Valley, paintings from Gran Quivira portrayed colorful ceremonial participants similar to those in the regional rock paintings (Hayes et al. 1981; Peckham 1981).

### *The Paintings Revealed: Color, Techniques, and Observations from the Field*

Reds, orange, yellow, blue-gray, green, and maroon are among the many colors described for these murals; beyond the expanded palette, the murals are also notable for the distinctive ways in which colors are employed. Figures are defined by flat areas of color bordered by outlines in contrasting hues. The judicious use of black and white for outlines and fine details as well as for flat areas, used in tandem with a variety of colors, provides sharp contrasts to create visually complex and aesthetically compelling fields of imagery.

Techniques for paint application at Awat'ovi and Kawàyka'a include the use of fingertips, spattering, outlining, and over-painting (Smith 1952:113–117). From Pottery Mound, Patricia Vivian (1961) provides detailed on-site observations on color and its subtleties, as well as several modes of pigment application for generating special effects. Her firsthand account of uncovering and recording these murals provides a valuable bridge between today's archaeologists and the mural painters:

> Often the walls looked very muted or grayed in overall appearance when they were first uncovered. But usually we found that this was due to a general disintegration of the colors on the surfaces, or of a dirty film covering the initial brilliancy. Sometimes colors faded as soon as they were exposed to the sun and air. This was especially true of reds and yellows.
>
> Black and white were used extensively. Sometimes the black had a bluish tone which gave the otherwise flat color a quality of depth. The application of white varied from an extremely thick impasto consistency to a thin, rather transparent wash. In some instances the white was a brilliant gleaming color, while in others it had a blue-gray, or brownish tinge, indicating that it had probably been impure, or mixed with a few other particles of another color.
>
> There were other very interesting features concerning the technique of color application. Sometimes it was difficult to determine the original color precisely because it had been superimposed over another color area. This gave the effect of vibration, depth and transparency....
>
> In other cases, areas of the neutral wall surface, or background were left unpainted, and were integrated into the positive design itself, their forms being defined by the surrounding shapes and colors. This type of area would sometimes be played against an off-white, or white color, making rather subtle and sophisticated combinations. [Vivian 1961:75–77]

As for painting techniques, she explains,

> at Pottery Mound there are instances of not only flat, opaque color application with the usual brush dipped in fluid paint, but effects from other techniques as well. Some of these appear to be dry and wet brush stroking, stippling, smudging, spattering, finger painting, dripping, scraping, and incising. It also seems that they used pigment in all forms from raw lumps to thin washes, resulting in many different effects such as impasto and various transparencies. [Vivian 1961:78]

She also notes that the tools used to apply the paint included a variety of brushes with which paint was applied in both wet and dry strokes. Other tools for creating desired surface textures may have included "knives, scrapers, and the fingers or whole hand" (Vivian 1994:83–84; see also Vivian 2007:81).

An in-depth analysis of one figure provides some idea of the complexity of the painting process (Figure 4.8; see Plate 17):

> This figure is drawn within part of the confines of a circle, the background of which is painted with an extremely thick white bluish tinge. Perhaps the dry pigment was mixed

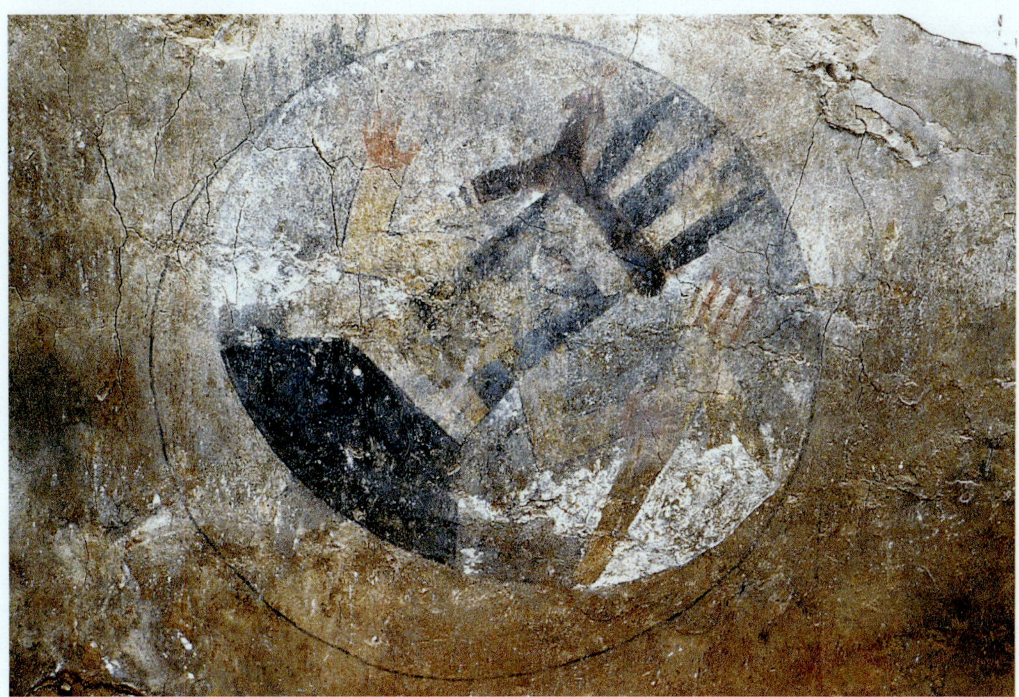

FIGURE 4.8. Warrior in shield-like circle, Kiva 8, Layer 1, east wall, Pottery Mound. Photograph courtesy of Patricia Vivian (Vivian 1961:Figure 113).

> with a smaller degree of fluid to form more of a paste, and smoothed on the wall with some instrument other than a brush, the latter being used only to apply the white next to the very outline of the figure itself. The remaining part of the circle, where the figure stops, forms a crescent moon shape, and appears to have been left the natural color of the adobe-plastered background. The shape of this portion is established by the drawing of the thin black line. [The headdress,]... constructed of various feathers rising from a rattlesnake skin crown...is painted first with a coat of red ochre, then with a layer of black. The black seems to have been applied with a raw lump of pigment, coloring only the higher spots of the rough-textured wall, thus leaving openings for the red underneath to show through. The effect is one of a beautiful velvety texture. [Vivian 1961:81]

Similarly at Kuaua, pigments of different colors seem to have been mixed on the wall while wet to create a greater sense of depth and variation in textures (Dutton 1963:Plate X, Figures 92, 95), and green was overpainted with black on serpents and a "sun" (Dutton 1963:Figures 77, 100).

Mural artists were clearly concerned about the visual impact of their paintings above and beyond being satisfied with a mere depiction. Carefully chosen, color increased the meaning of the paintings as well as effectively achieving a variety of aesthetic effects. The time-consuming care with which these murals were created indicates that they had an unprecedented and significant role in Pueblo kiva ritual and ceremony during the Pueblo IV era.

### *Paint: Colors and Sources*

Although direct evidence is lacking, it is, nevertheless, not unreasonable to suggest that the preparation of mineral and clay pigments for use in wall paintings may have followed ritual protocols such as those described for ritual paraphernalia at Zuni (Bunzel 1932a). Among the Pueblos, paint pigments for use in ritual contexts are often obtained from landscape locations associated with the times and places of origin (see Chapter 1). Hence, they are regarded as sacred and inherently powerful (Young 1988:191–192). In Ancestral Pueblo times as well, it is very likely that similar understandings prevailed. Thus paint alone may have added a symbolic dimension to the mural figures, rendering them more meaningful and intrinsically efficacious, blurring the boundaries between a sacred source and the paintings themselves, conveying efficacy to the paintings (e.g., Schaafsma 2018). Unfortunately, at the present time, the sources of pigments procured for use in Pueblo IV murals remain unknown.

Their chemical components, however, have been variously addressed and analyzed. The most extensive study is that of Watson Smith (1952:22–39) for the Jeddito murals (see also Schaafsma and Wiseman 1992 for the Fox Place; and Watchman 1997 for Kuaua). As for colors, Smith (1952:22–23) lists yellow, red, blue, green, red, vermilion, pink, orange, salmon, brown, purple, maroon, black, gray, and white, with the observation that these all occur in varying shades and intensities. Chemical analyses revealed that all were mineral in origin, except for black, the source of which was determined to be charcoal. Charcoal was also used for various admixtures to produce other tones, including some blues. Bright blue, on the other hand, had its origin in copper carbonate. A similar suite of paint sources is reported from Pottery Mound, although the chemical analysis—said to have been carried out by the "late Professor John Clark"—reads as plagiarism from Smith (Hibben 1975:36–49). A highly complex palette at Pottery Mound, however, is indisputable, and it is probable that similar mineral components were involved (Vivian 1961:75–77, Appendix II; Vivian 1994:83; Vivian 2007:81; see also Chapter 1).

### *Content, Color Choices, and Symbolism*

Just how color was used in Pueblo IV mural painting is a complex issue. What determined color choices? I propose that color choices were made on the basis of three considerations: their representational value, their symbolic value, and aesthetic values, all used in combination. These considerations are not clear-cut or necessarily separate from one another, factors that make this discussion somewhat difficult. There were no hard rules. As for aesthetics, black and white paint used for both outlines as well as designs assumed a major role as accents that provide sharp value differences, heightening the visual qualities of these murals. The use of many colors and the juxtaposing of flat areas of color, combined with contrasting outlines, contributed to the pictorial clarity of lively panoramas, often staged against a contrasting background.

The significance of color usage must be assessed in accordance with the context in which it appears. White, for example, functions in Sikyatki designs to establish aesthetic contrasts but without any apparent symbolic intentions. White is also used to portray the sun, representing its brightness but again without any apparent symbolic significance, or so it seems. Within Pueblo IV murals, color used symbolically may manifest varying degrees of consistency. In some instances, the natural color of an object is a determining factor, establishing its symbolic associations and thus ritual use. As previously discussed, white has a major role to play in rain-related contexts where it is used to symbolize clouds (Stephen 1936). White cotton is used ethnographically in rain rituals due to its color in that it appeals to white rain clouds (Parsons 1939:397–398; Schaafsma 2013), and in the Hopi murals ceremonial figures wear white embroidered kilts just as they do today (Smith 1952:Figures 71, 81). A single color can send a more extensive message. Hays-Gilpin and colleagues (2010:123) note that yellow flowers can stand for "all flowers, sacred pollen, and summer weather and the growing season." The variety of colored pigments and clays employed in these paintings worked in harmony with the images to convey the meanings the cosmos held and still holds for Pueblo communities (e.g., Hays-Gilpin et al. 2010).

While aesthetic considerations seem to have been a major factor in color choice, subject and context are critical in evaluating the symbolic use of color in the murals or whether color

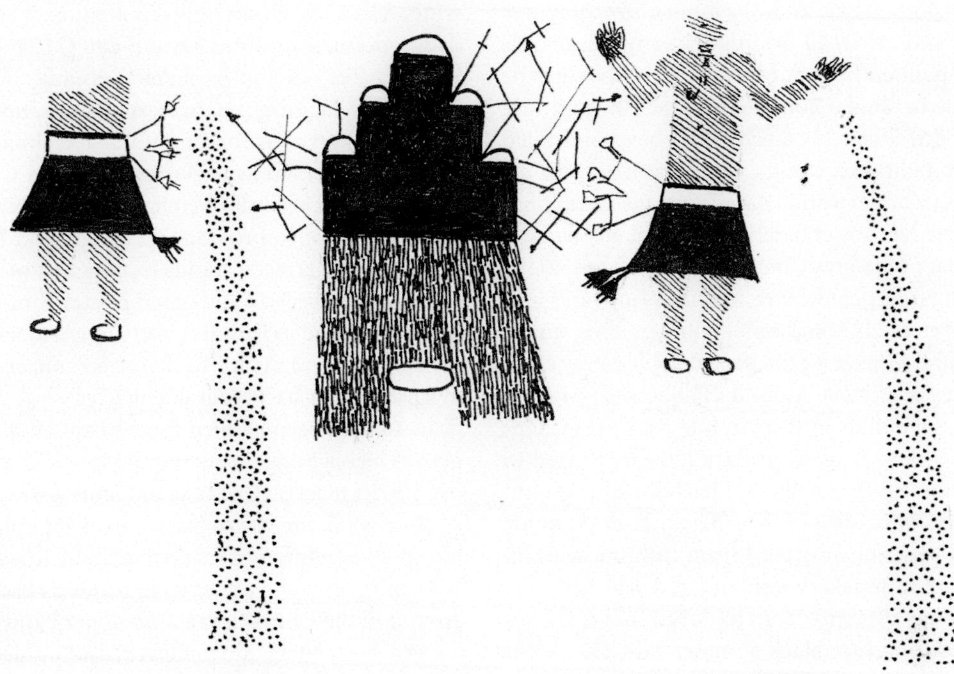

FIGURE 4.9. Black and white rain clouds above the kiva niche with black rain falling, Kiva III, Layer F-23, Kuaua Pueblo. Drawing by Polly Schaafsma.

symbolism was used at all. Murals from the Tiwa sites of Kuaua in the south and Picuris in the north share a strong emphasis on terraced clouds, lightning, and birds, all with regard to rain-bringing symbolism, but use differing solutions with regard to color (Crotty 1999; Dutton 1963). Although yellow, orange, red, white, and, sparsely, even green, add to the color complexity of the Kuaua paintings, there is a prodigious use of black paint that, along with white, is associated with rain clouds (Figure 4.9).

Rainmaking themes with ritual participants wearing black attire and white sashes dominate the majority of the 17 painted plaster layers from Kiva III at Kuaua (P. Schaafsma 2007a, 2009). Here and at Pottery Mound and Awat'ovi as well, black kilts and mantas with white tie-dyed patterns signifying corn (Webster et al. 2006) seem to amplify the symbolism in this ceremonial attire, as they suggest corn kernels in a context propitious for fertility and growth (Hays-Gilpin et al. 2004; Hibben 1975:Figures 99–100). Although the yellow color of the bodies of the ceremonial participants in these scenes may associate them with rain-dependent maize, the relationship between black and dark summer thunderheads, warmth, and fertility (Ortiz 1969:94) explains the predominant use of black paint in the context of rain symbolism and metaphor at Kuaua. Large, black, terraced clouds, sometimes with hemispherical white caps on the terraces, feature prominently on several painted layers. Black birds fly around, and black, red, yellow, or white lightning shoots from the clouds, while black ollas on, or slightly above, a black dado spout rain and lightning. On layers H-31, G-26, D-17 and D-14, and C-11, black dados represent the earth or underworld (Dutton 1963:Plates 14, 15, 16, 22, 23). The black ollas are symbolic of springs that, along with lakes, are regarded as the chthonic sources of rain and homes of rainmaking spirits (Ortiz 1969:107; Schaafsma 2002:57; Schaafsma 2009:684–685; Stevenson 1904:146).

In Hopi murals, black domed features are similarly interpreted as representing the earth

(Sekaquaptewa and Washburn 2010:Figures 7.6 and 7.10). In addition, many basebands are painted in dark blue-gray clays having the same or similar connotations. Smith (1952:Figure 60) illustrates a wide dark baseband filled with lightning, clouds, and creatures from the watery underworld. Karl Taube (2010:102) has likened narrower basebands, frequently painted in dark blue-gray (Smith 1952:Figure 68), to the horned serpent who resides in springs and is in charge of chthonic water sources. This supernatural serpent is represented in blue-gray earth tones at Pottery Mound (Hibben 1975:Figure 34), as well as in Rio Grande rock art (Chapter 5). Just as black or dark hues were used to symbolize the earth that harbors springs and lakes, ethnographically blackish dark muds and pigments procured from chthonic sources where rainmakers reside (e.g., Laski 1958:139; Parsons 1939:397) are employed in ritual contexts to attract black summer rain clouds. At Hopi dancers' chins are sometimes painted with dark clay to emulate the dark rain clouds, enabling the ritual performer to identify with and hence attract and hasten the arrival of rain (Stephen 1936:713, 853). I suggest that the black kilts of the Kuaua ceremonialists may well have functioned similarly as chromatic rain prayers, while, as previously mentioned, the white cotton embroidered kilts worn by ritual figures in the Hopi murals may have had the same function (e.g., Schaafsma 2013).

The Pueblo IV circular kivas in the Tiwa village of Picuris, north of Santa Fe, also featured rain-bringing themes, but in contrast with Kuaua, the Picuris cloud terraces, lightning, birds, plants (including corn), and rainbows are all painted in bright colors. Ceremonial figures are lacking. With the exception of Kiva B, black is notably restricted. The Picuris terraces are painted in as many as five hues including blue, gray, red, yellow, green, white, black, and peach. Inside the elongated, terraced clouds, vertical bands of color follow the outer contours, but within, their patterns are varied to create asymmetrical designs that lend dynamism to the whole (Crotty 1999:Figures 9.6–9.9). Simple, wide, black baselines replace Kuaua's black dados, occurring only in Kivas B and C (Crotty 1999:Figures 9.8 and 9.9). As at Kuaua, they probably symbolize the earth. At Picuris, however, wide horizontal background bands higher on the wall served as backdrops. In Kiva C, a pale blue band against which lightning and birds are depicted, also provided a background for multicolored terraced clouds resting on a black base line. Above is a band of tan plaster. Similar banding existed in Kiva B (Crotty 1999:156, Figures 9.8 and 9.9). As for background concerns, in Kiva sub-A, a background "patch" of white appears to have been painted for the explicit purpose of highlighting the superimposed red figure of a scarlet macaw (Crotty 1999:Figure 9.6).

In Kiva B, the use of black comes into play, but in a very different manner than at Kuaua. In keeping with the use of wide bands as background in the Picuris murals, an upper band of tan gives way to a wide midlevel band in black that appears to represent a dark and rainy sky into which white lightning shoots. Below, light-colored stepped clouds and rainbows in pale hues of green, reddish-tan, white, and gray are painted against a whitish backdrop, projecting into the black zone (Crotty 1999:Figure 9.8). Below, clouds are situated on a black base line that again may represent the earth. Overall, the muted and rather eerie "scene" suggests a dark summer afternoon or night storm, with pale rainbows, although one cannot be certain that this was the original intent.

Whether differences in color choices for the same themes between Kuaua and Picuris were due to pigment availability, random choice, or other social or ritual dictates, remains an unanswered question. At this point it is certain only that the systematic choice of black for rain clouds at Kuaua, while symbolic, was not a rigid prescription for representing clouds elsewhere (see Chapter 5). At Picuris the predominant choice of bright colors may allude to bright summer landscapes.

At Pottery Mound and Awat'ovi, large paintings of whole textiles with Sikyatki-style designs were represented, and at Pottery Mound limited renderings of these elements are depicted on clothing, shield-like objects, or employed as background for other elements (Figures 4.10a and 4.10b; see Plate 18; and see Crotty 2007; Hays-Gilpin and LeBlanc 2007; Hibben 1975; Smith 1952). From nine Pottery Mound kivas, Sikyatki designs were recorded from at least 23 layers of plaster. The designs are painted in combinations of black, white, red, yellow, yellow-orange, and orange, with limited use of blue, blue-gray, gray, and green. Given that this dynamic complex combines stylized representations of flowers, dragonflies, birds, clouds, feathers, and corn with a plethora of moving, curving abstract motifs (see Hibben 1975:Figures 38 and 62), it is highly likely that the colors employed also make reference to the desired flowery, sunny world of summer marked by water, fertility, and growth.

Color ambiguity pertaining to symbolism prevails, however. Ethnographically, color associations with seasonality among the Tewa are explicit in that green, yellow, and black indicate warmth and summer, while red and white allude to cold and winter. These associations are described by Ortiz (1969:40) for Ohkay Owingeh, where this symbolic use of color is apparent among the Summer and Winter moieties dancers' regalia. Color symbolism is not exclusive, however, and it may be used differently depending on the context. Red, for example, is related to warfare and hunting and, by extension, to winter (Ortiz 1969:34; Young 1988:134). Yet as a directional color, red is assigned to the south, macaws, and warmth. At Pottery Mound, scarlet macaws are usually pictured in murals with fertility themes (Hibben 1975:45), while red-tailed hawk feathers are found exclusively in association with war-related iconography (Hibben 1975:Figure 25, 57, 59). At Pottery Mound, however, a scarlet macaw on a perch sits next to a bird warrior wielding an ax (Hibben 1975:Figure 46). Is its red color meaningful in this context? In the Hopi murals, scarlet macaws also perch on the rims of sun shields carried by warriors in ritual combat (Smith 1952:Figure 56a). The circumference of sun shields is commonly enhanced with red, sometimes spattered to suggest radiance (Smith 1952:Figures 56a, 70c, 72a, 84b, 89a and c). Likewise, long red macaw feathers are frequently paired with eagle feathers in both the murals and in contemporary ritual attire. Both macaws and eagles have symbolic reference to the sun, the macaw by virtue of its color, the golden eagle, whose tail feathers are black and white, primarily by virtue of its relationships to war and the sun's role therein, without any references to color (Tyler 1979:18, 78–79).

While there are no hard boundaries between realistic and symbolic color in cases where the object portrayed may have acquired its symbolic status by virtue of its normal color, there are examples for which a repeated color choice deviates from natural appearances. As in Rio Grande rock art, suns in murals may be painted not as white but green (Smith 1952:Figures 70c, 84b). Green suns in the Kawàyka'a murals may be substitutes for the turquoise suns found in Rio Grande rock art of this period (see Chapter 5), suggesting parallels with the turquoise sun and shield iconography prevalent in Postclassic central Mexico (Izeki 2016; Townsend 1979). The supernatural blue-gray serpent described earlier also seems to lack a reference in the natural world; its coloration appears to be linked instead to sacred muds and clays in the bottom of springs. Another case in point is blue-gray portrayals of spotted felines, possibly jaguars (Hibben 1975:Figure 77; Smith 1952:Figures 63b, 71a). The reasoning behind this color choice remains unexplained, although the use of blue-gray occurs repeatedly, suggesting that it may have had symbolic connotations. A small percentage of jaguars have a melanistic blue-black hue (Will Russell, personal communication 2018).

Only rarely detectable in the murals, directional color symbolism exerts important roles within the Pueblo ritual structure today and undoubtedly in the past, although the colors associated with the directions are somewhat inconsistent between communities (see Chapter 1). At Pottery Mound, it seems likely that directional symbolism played a role in choosing

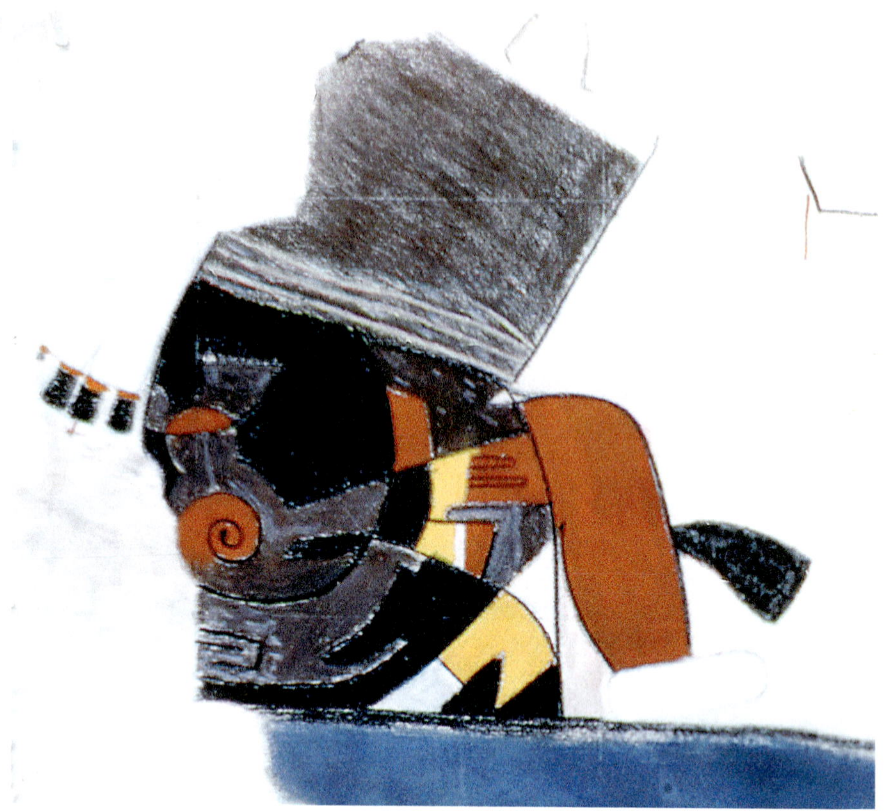

*b*

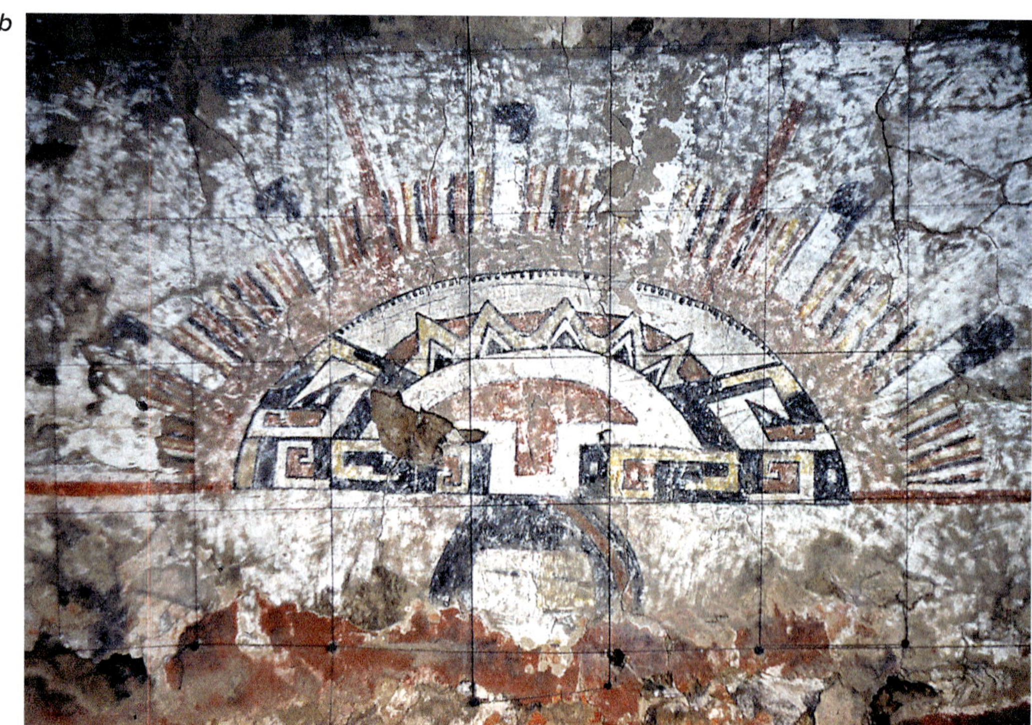

FIGURE 4.10. (*a*) A ceremonial figure seated on a blue dado, wearing kilt with Sikyatki designs, Kiva 7, Layer 10, Pottery Mound. Photograph courtesy of Patricia Vivian (Vivian 1961:Figure 52). (*b*) Flamboyant headdress based on Sikyatki designs, Kiva 9, Layer 1, Pottery Mound. Note the black outlines used in the details to create contrast and clarity. Photograph courtesy of Patricia Vivian (Vivian 1961:Figure 151).

the locations of scarlet macaws, with the west being favored. According to the sample reported by Hibben, images of scarlet macaws occurred on five west walls, two south walls, and two southwest corners. On an east wall they are pictured only once, and none appear on a north wall (Hibben 1975:Figures 16, 18, 38, 39, 44–46, 64, 65, 76, 96). At Hopi, the Antelope Mesa kivas themselves lack consistent directional orientation (Smith 1952:6), so wall direction is not a relevant consideration.

On the other hand, concerns with directionality in the Hopi murals may be present on a metaphorical level. According to Sekaquaptewa and Washburn (2010:Figure 7.29), a pyramid of corn represented in Room 3, Layer 9 at Awat'ovi represents corn in the four directional colors. They elaborate: "The colored cobs also acknowledge the clouds of the same colors that represent the Four Directional Cloud leaders who coordinate the life-sustaining rains that come from the four directions" (Sekaquaptewa and Washburn 2010:174). In other words, the graphic depiction of one set of images may trigger a whole set of associations, beyond what is represented. In this case, color directional symbolism is inherent in the painting of the colored corn.

In summary, many factors are latent in the color choices made by the mural artists, only a few of which have been considered here, and many remain unknown. It appears that there were no strict codes, and often the colors selected seem to have been up to the judgment of the individual artist—at least within certain bounds. It is nevertheless apparent that color usage was determined by its representational significance, which was often loosely calculated as to its symbolic meanings and, above all, its successful engagement toward aesthetic ends. As mentioned, a color may evoke a suite of connected meanings empowered and amplified by their very ambiguity. And the message evoked may supersede the icons employed. These murals, bolstered by their extensive and varied use of color, were powerful agents in promoting Pueblo ideology, and their messages were complex.

## *Color and Complexity: Some History and Some Social Implications*

At the end of the 1200s, Ancestral Pueblo people migrated out of the Four Corners region, pushed by a cultural crisis, or possibly a series of crises. Although there is some disagreement on the nature of what transpired, there is general consensus that stress caused by drought and hostilities led to the exodus from the north into the Hopi region and as far south as southern Arizona, as well as southeastward into the Rio Grande Valley. The new communities established in the wake of these migrations consisted of large, aggregated pueblos that would have necessitated changes in social organization (Cordell and McBrinn 2012:223–277).

For these pueblos to function, there was a need to establish social institutions that would integrate larger populations (Adams 1991; Schaafsma and Schaafsma 1974). Times of social disruption are commonly followed by revitalization movements characterized by the adoption of new ideologies, promoted through pan-community activities and the arts (Burger 1988; Newsome and Hays-Gilpin 2011:154; Schaafsma 2000:163–164). Spielmann (1998), for example, proposes that black and white pottery traditions in the Rio Grande were replaced at that time by colorful glaze wares, the sizes and shapes of which indicate their use for communal feasting linked to community-wide events. The katsina and formalized warrior societies evident in the visual arts are also testimony to the presence of organizations that, based on ethnographic data, drew their memberships from across kinship lines, thus filling those demands (Adams 1991; Schaafsma and Schaafsma 1974). The simultaneous and vast increase in rock art and mural production indicates that images related to Pueblo religion and cosmology had a powerful societal role in promoting new beliefs and information vital to the reorganization of Pueblo society in the post-migration years. Graphic imagery, combined with the use of color, facilitated these endeavors. The kiva murals defined and validated a new cosmological outlook and sociopolitical order. Within the kiva, knowledge conveyed through a combination of oral traditions, pictorial means, and ritual performance would have promoted societal consolidation at a time when it seems likely that the newly organized communities were comprised of populations from diverse Pueblo origins and language groups (Hays-Gilpin and LeBlanc 2007). Graphic imagery was an agent of change, and color was an asset.

In order to achieve these ends, the demanding investments in planning, time, and labor behind the production of these finely executed murals have numerous and wider social implications. Nelson and Habicht-Mauche (2006), in their study of mineral sources for decorating lead-glaze pottery, point out that there were specialized patterns of acquisition with concomitant social and symbolic significance. They conclude that these exchanges defined "complementary and cross-cutting social relationships and identities on a local, regional, and interregional scale" (Nelson and Habicht-Mauche 2006:214). The acquisition of paint pigments from diverse sources for use in the murals would have undoubtedly involved similar social entanglements and procuring expeditions of one kind or another. Once acquired, subsequent preparation of the pigments in ritually prescribed ways is labor intensive (see Chapter 1). Ingredients such as seeds and flower petals may have been ground and added for ritual efficacy of the murals just as they contributed to the paint used for ritual objects (e.g., Bunzel 1932:852–862; Stephen 1936:852–853). With paint in hand, the execution of these large and complicated murals would have required well-developed skills. The practiced rendering of outlines in black, red, or white plus the painting of many fine details demanded careful attention and would have been a painstaking and time-consuming enterprise by specialists.

Exactly how these murals functioned within their kiva contexts is a final factor for consideration. Smith (1952:320) suggests the possibility that formerly these paintings served as upright altars, noting that today slat altars are sometimes replaced by "painted screens used in the same position." He surmised that wall paintings may have had a similar function but that this practice declined over the years. When wall paintings were present on only a single wall, as in the rectangular Hopi kivas, this would make sense, but murals were also found on more than one wall in rectangular kivas or painted continuously around the walls of circular ones (Crotty 1999; Dick et al. 1965:74). In the rectangular kivas at Pottery Mound and in Kuaua's Kiva III, integrated scenes on the west wall, often around the kiva niche, were extended to encompass the south and north walls as well. In a similar manner in Kivas B and C at Picuris, a series of repeated motifs extended throughout. In these cases, the wall imagery would have literally surrounded those present, and ceremonial participants would have found themselves within colorful, all-encompassing scenes. As Newsome and Hays-Gilpin (2011:155) discuss, "in ritual performance and observation, sight and viewership take place within a state of perceptual awareness heightened by attention to a dynamic interplay of sensations and bodily impressions, from scent to sound, the touch of ritual objects, ceremonial gestures and choreography." The murals would have been colorful complements to these events and a means of unifying the community.

## Conclusions

In replacing the more abstract and typically bichrome wall paintings that seem to have mapped out a general idea of a layered cosmology, Pueblo IV murals are filled with engaging polychrome content featuring dynamic ceremonial scenes with ritual participants and paraphernalia, and symbolically rendered natural phenomena central to Puebloan cosmology, all in unprecedented detail. The imagery itself represents a major break from the Pueblo world of prior centuries, and the katsina complex that is part of this new religious system contributed to social integration of newly aggregated towns. The vital roles these paintings must have played within a revamped social organization cannot be overestimated, as their aesthetic appeal would have substantially enhanced their roles in promoting what appears to be a new Pueblo cosmology, while consolidating and strengthening social ties among community or society members. The veritable explosion of brightly colored and detailed paintings was related to new needs in communicating, verifying, and solidifying both religious beliefs and society. As background for kiva "dramas," they would have served to reinforce cosmological precepts and metaphorical relationships as they added to the enjoyment of the proceedings. In short, the new ideology promoted in color displays fostered its acceptance. These murals represent the apex of Pueblo graphic arts, cut short by the Spanish Conquest, which in turn initiated another crisis and new cultural adjustments. But without losing the knowledge that these paintings harbor, Pueblo religion today maintains its close connections with this colorfully pictured religious iconography from former days.

# 5

# Complexities of Color in Pueblo Rock Paintings, circa AD 1000–1600

Polly Schaafsma

Protected under rocky overhangs and within sandstone shelters, colorful paintings are found throughout the arid and semi-arid landscapes of the American Southwest. Unlike petroglyphs, defined by the removal of accumulated dark surface patina to reveal a lighter unvarnished surface beneath, painted figures are created by the addition of liquid media made primarily from mineral sources—materials that may have been selected for aesthetic reasons. Painted pigments may also contribute layers of meaning to imagery if chosen for their symbolic properties or efficacy, especially when pigments were procured from sacred sources (Young 1988:178).

Among the oldest rock paintings in the Southwest are those attributable to Archaic hunter-gatherers.[1] On the Colorado Plateau, the Barrier Canyon and Esplanade Styles are among the most detailed and labor-intensive paintings known from any period; they may date back several thousand years (Christensen et al. 2013: 62–79; Cole 2009; Schaafsma 1980:61–72). Between circa AD 1 and 500, the earliest farmers in the Four Corners region, the Basketmaker II people, adorned the expansive arching walls of sandstone alcoves with large human figures and polychromatic panels of stamped handprints (Christensen et al. 2013; Grant 1978; Loendorf 2010). Throughout the millennia, the subjects, color choices, and painting techniques of the Archaic and early Basketmaker rock paintings are variable and notably complex, deserving their own investigation. This chapter, however, addresses the use of color in Ancestral Pueblo rock paintings between circa AD 1000 and the early seventeenth century on the Colorado Plateau and in the Rio Grande Valley. Following Spanish settlement and missionizing efforts, between AD 1598 and 1610, rock art production was severely curtailed.

Painting on stone can be accomplished via a variety of techniques. Brushes served well for detailed work, while smearing or daubing paint with one's fingers or hand or a paint-dipped cornhusk were useful strategies for covering broad areas. Dotting with one's fingertips was a useful way of applying decorative details, often in a contrasting hue. Spraying paint—or spurting by mouth or through a cane or bone tube, often around a hand stencil—were additional means. Further enhancements may include scratching or pecking, and several techniques used in combination produce visually compelling results. Some modes of applying paint may have had more to do with meaningful ritual gestures than obtaining a desired aesthetic effect. Stamping one's paint-covered hand against a rock in a sacred location may, for example, have been a means of identification, facilitating communication with the spirit realm (Young 1988:178–180).

Following the suggestion of Jane Young's (1988:178) observations at Zuni, Ancestral Pueblo painted sites may have had more sacred connotations than petroglyph sites.[2] This proposal is most valid for the Pueblo IV period (ca. AD 1325–1600), for which there is close continuity with the ethnographic record. While there is occasional evidence that some petroglyphs were originally painted, and thus their efficacy enhanced, these examples are scarce. Enclosed within the spatial limits of rockshelters, painted sites may have functioned as landscape localities for ritual activities. The subjects represented in such rockshelters have more coherency than do the images at petroglyph locations, and the clays and other pigments employed for these images may have been regarded as sacred and empowering in themselves, adding meaning to imagery beyond representation. Today pigments intended for use on ritual paraphernalia, katsina faces, and as body paint are subject to prescriptive ritual preparation, from the gathering of pigments to their application (Bunzel 1932b:859–861; Parsons 1932:320–321; Parsons 1939:286–287, 403; Young 1988:191–192). Similarly, if paint for rock art use was procured from localities named in oral traditions as linked to the times of origin and other sacred events, and subjected to ritual gathering and preparations procedures, the paint itself would have granted spiritual agency to the resulting painted imagery (see Chapter 1). That pigments alone are invested with power is exemplified by the Zuni practice of carrying red and black pigments as amulets that are honored by prayers and songs (Bunzel 1932a:491). At Isleta red and black pigments are offered to the sun and the five directions (Parsons 1932:281, 319). Color itself has meaning and symbolic associations that are expressed in ceremony and ritual, and some of these relationships are aids to understanding colors used in Ancestral Pueblo rock art, especially during Pueblo IV times. On the most fundamental level, colors are associated with different aspects of the structured cosmology. This includes the six directions and, by extension, maize, birds, animals, and flowers linked to the directions by virtue of being "clothed" in the appropriate directional colors (Hays-Gilpin et al. 2010:127–129; Riley 1963). Colors also have seasonal implications, and Rio Grande Pueblo moieties that are affiliated with the winter (cold) and summer (warm) parts of the year are symbolized by the colors appropriate to these dualities (Ortiz 1969). Other categories that take on color symbolism are those related to rain, warfare, fertility, and gender. Details of traditional clothing of ceremonial participants incorporate color symbolism, as do body paint and ritual paraphernalia (see Chapter 1). In public ceremonies, structured color choices reinforce these associations through ritual and performance.

A number of variables, however, complicate addressing color symbolism in the past, posing challenges to the search for its meaning in Ancestral Pueblo rock paintings. A lack of standardization between communities and the recognition that color associations may change through time are factors to be considered. As well, color use may be inconsistent or multivalent, and the original reason for color selection is not necessarily clear. In many cases, practical considerations may also have determined color usage. Among these was the availability of pigments or clays, as well as the desired size of the images to be produced—the two go hand-in-hand. Thus availability may have overridden the concerns for the symbolic use of color in many paintings.

On the Colorado Plateau prior to the 1300s, figures rendered in white or in red often dominate painted panels, since white is readily available in clays and mineral sources, along with red ochres. Yellow ochres were used more sparingly (see Baker 2009). After the mid-fourteenth century, in concert with a new and more complex iconography, color choices appear to have been driven more by the need for contrast and symbolic import. The overall palette was significantly expanded, and color variation added a meaningful symbolic dimension to the visual vocabulary.

## Pueblo II–III (ca. AD 900–1300)

On the Colorado Plateau, extensive displays of Basketmaker handprints in red, pink, yellow, green, and white grace the walls of alcoves, stamped alongside imposing human figures wearing necklaces and fancy headgear. Within some of these same shelters but in contrast with

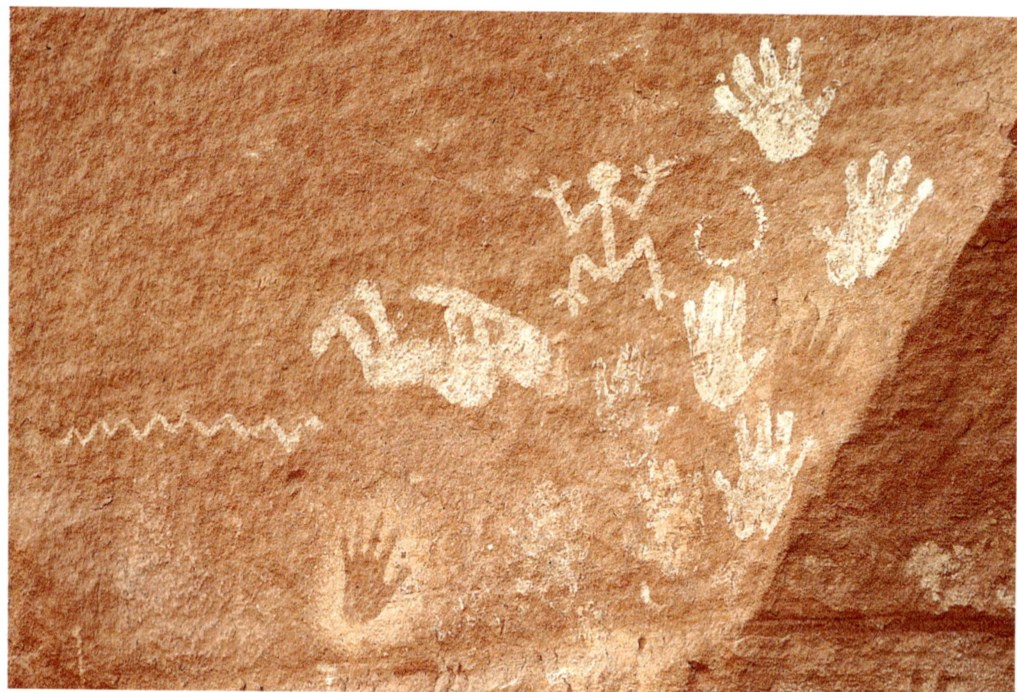

FIGURE 5.1. Ancestral Pueblo handprints stamped and stenciled in white near a reclining flute player, ca. AD 1100–1250, Canyon del Muerto, Arizona. Photograph by Polly Schaafsma.

these early polychromatic Basketmaker productions, Ancestral Pueblo people later (ca. AD 600–1300) painted smaller, monochromatic images. In general, rock paintings became simplified, suggesting that their ritual and social roles were reduced following Basketmaker times.

After around AD 1100 or 1150, Pueblo people created stenciled handprints by spattering paint around the hand pressed to the rock, while positive handprints, though less frequent, continued being made by stamping a paint-laden hand against the rock face (Figure 5.1). One asks whether these contrasting modes of leaving a handprint in a rockshelter were motivated by different purposes and therefore conveyed different meanings. A stamped print would seem to have the mark of individual identity, perhaps left as a petition to resident spirits. Spattered hand stencils—largely Pueblo III in origin—may have contained a more metaphorical significance.

As for the previously mentioned prevalence of red and white pigments for the small-scale renderings in many Pueblo rock paintings prior to the fourteenth century, there are exceptions. In some cases, nearby abundant clay sources may have resulted in more diversified use of color, especially when it came to earthy pigments, and an increase in the size of Ancestral Pueblo elements (Schaafsma 1966:Figures 11–14). Grant (1978:193) observes that in Canyon de Chelly, paintings made between AD 1100 and 1300 tend to be buff or white in hue and casually applied. Elements include stick-figure anthropomorphs, bighorn sheep, geometric designs, spirals, and snakes. Elsewhere in northern Arizona, it appears that easy access to more colorful clays resulted in elements rendered in pastel shades of cream, pink, and even lavender, in addition to white and buff.

Simultaneously, large elements in white that characterize many Pueblo sites on the Colorado Plateau merit further consideration. A line of white stepped elements high on the wall in Fluteplayer Cave in Tsegi Canyon strongly suggests white clouds. Below, superimposed across Basketmaker figures, is a five-foot long

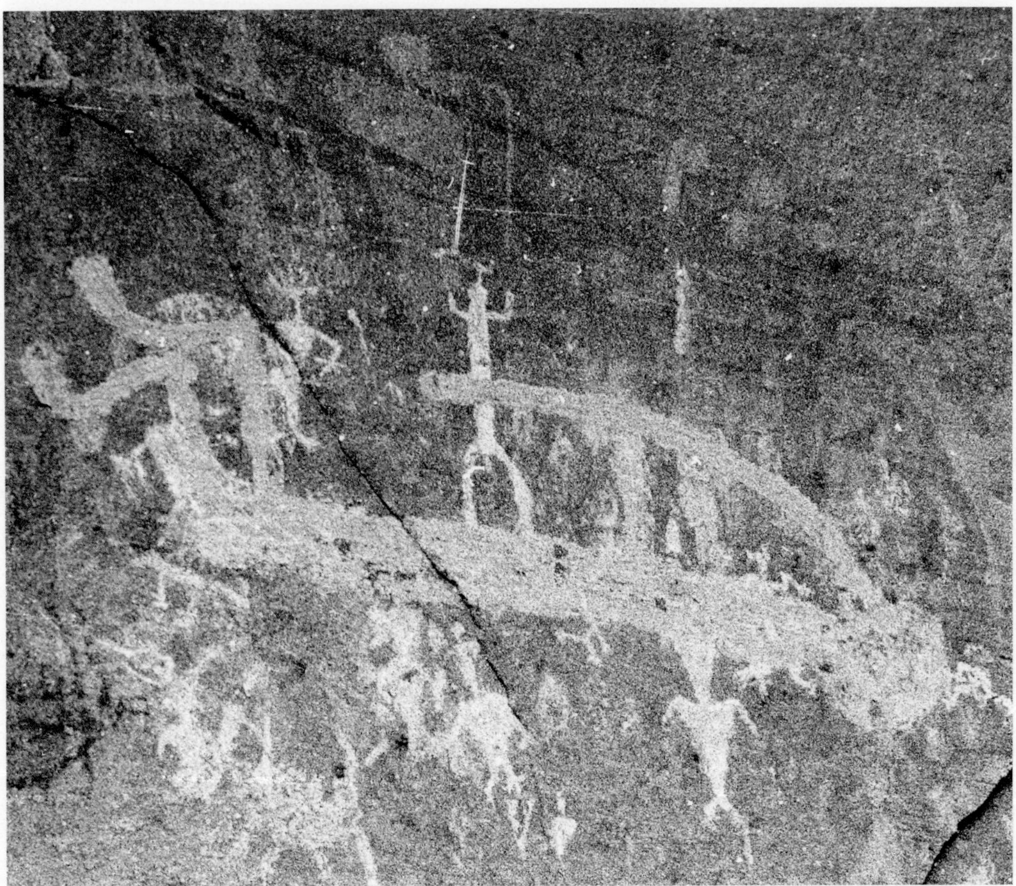

FIGURE 5.2. Reclining flute player nearly two meters in length, smeared in white clay over earlier paintings. Note the faint Basketmaker anthropomorphs (*upper left and center*). Tsegi Canyon, Arizona. Photograph by Polly Schaafsma.

reclining flute player in white clay, smeared on with the fingers (Figure 5.2). Elsewhere, a giant lizard, also in white and similarly applied, measures ten feet in length (Schaafsma 1966:Figures 11–13). Also scattered over earlier paintings are a white stick figure, long snakes, a centipede, and splotches of white paint. Formless blobs of white paint thrown at the cliff, obliterating earlier work, were noted in Canyon de Chelly (Grant 1978:193, Figure 4.44).

What is indicated by the often lavish use of whitish clays for seemingly casually produced rock paintings in the Four Corners region? Among contemporary Zunis, white paint has no ceremonies connected with its manufacture: "everyone has white paint" (Bunzel 1932b:859). Was white clay simply handy, able to be smeared on by hand with little advance preparation? Are these figures the products of children's play and nothing more? Or, alternatively, do these paintings represent painted gestures that were intended as petitions for rain? Are these figures smeared across the rocks with wet white clay the result of a synthetic process in which color, substance, and ritual act functioned as a synchronic whole to attract rain clouds, all contributing to the efficacy of the resulting image? If so, the meaning and significance of these figures is not diminished by their casual appearances and should not be evaluated according to Western standards of graphic skill, time investment, and attention to detail. As rain requests, their symbolic value lies in their white likeness to clouds, the wetness of the clay, and its possible sources in arroyos, seeps, and springs.

There is ethnographic support for this suggestion. In the 1880s and 1890s, Stephen (1936:701) described a man using muddy washes or white clay as body paint or for designs on kiva walls at Hopi:

> [He] dips his hands in the clay, and rubbing the clay in his hand with his saliva, passes round the kiva, rubbing with the palm of his right hand a white streak on the breast, back, each shoulder, mid-thigh, and each cheek of every person in the kiva.... It is a prayer to Cloud that he may see we desire the white clouds to hasten with rains. It is white on our bodies that Cloud may see.

Likewise, designs mud-washed on the beams of Hopi kivas were made to attract rain: "They want the rain to come and make the sand in the valley as is this sandy wash that they are now using" (Stephen 1936:198). The mud designs consisted of lightning clouds and handprints. This time-honored mimetic practice pervades Pueblo ritual (Bunzel 1932a:489–92; Young 1988:160) and may similarly explain the ancient large-scale, clay-painted figures in sandstone shelters.

The carefully painted white frets and textile designs from Canyon de Chelly form a distinct contrast to the large-scale, casual figures just discussed (Grant 1978:4.50a, c, and g and 4.52). The choice of white in Canyon de Chelly, with its allusion to cotton textiles, finds ethnographic parallels in the symbolic and ritual use of cotton in contemporary Pueblo rain rituals. Similar elaborate paintings in white with apparent reference to clouds and textiles appear on kiva walls contemporary with the rock paintings (Chapter 4). In an earlier paper, I discussed the representations of cotton textiles or their patterns in rock art on the Colorado Plateau after circa AD 1100 as symbolic appeals to the white clouds for rain, although most of these motifs occur as petroglyphs without color other than a simple light-dark contrast between the pecked figure and the darker patina on the rock surface (Schaafsma 2013). Along similar lines, Hays-Gilpin and VanPool (2009) address the cloud-like symbolic implications of black and white textile patterns on Tusayan white wares dating between the twelfth and thirteenth centuries, contemporaneous with the rock art under discussion.

Large white paintings of shields and shield bearers form a category of their own. Prominently displayed at defensively situated cliff dwellings in northern Arizona and southern Utah, these figures are carefully executed and measure up to a meter in diameter (Figure 5.3; see Plate 19). The occasional and parsimonious additions of other hues are incidental to their visual impact. I have proposed elsewhere that these paintings were related to the social stresses that eventually led to migrations out of the region around AD 1280 and that these designs had the magical protective roles ascribed to ethnographic shields (Schaafsma 2000:11–27). The white paint would have enhanced their visibility, and due to their perceived power, they would have functioned as both a warning and threat to marauders.

In summary, the use of color in Ancestral Pueblo rock paintings between AD 1000 and 1300 was relatively limited, and the mere availability of iron oxides and light-hued clays would have made them handy choices for paint without necessarily having any further implications. On the other hand, the choice of white clays may have been regarded as favored by rain-bringing spirits, with white being especially attractive to clouds. In contrast, the white paint used for shield paintings located high on walls above cliff dwellings appears to have been valued for its visibility.

### Pueblo IV (ca. AD 1325–1600)

The Pueblo IV era saw the florescence of Pueblo painting (Brody 1991:81–113). Following the migrations out of the Four Corners region, this was also a period of major changes in settlement patterns and pottery types (Cordell and McBrinn 2012). Rock art and mural iconography signal

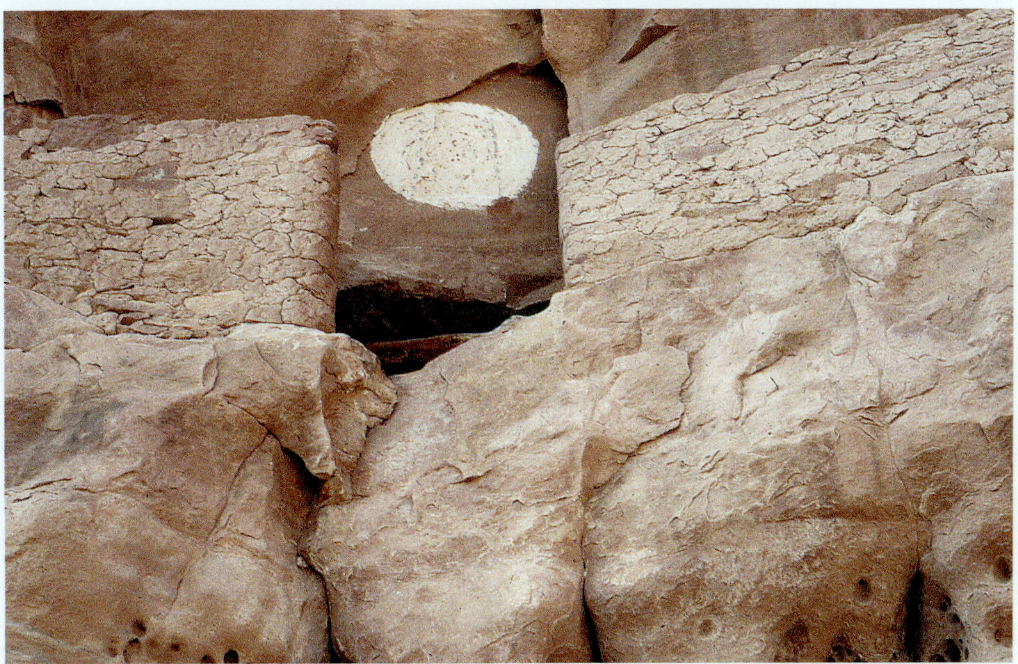

FIGURE 5.3. White shield about a meter in diameter painted above the entrance to the upper ledge of Jail House Ruin, ca. AD 1200–1280, Grand Gulch, Utah. The handprint below and right of the shield may be the mark of a war deity. Photograph by Polly Schaafsma.

major changes as well, in Pueblo religion and its graphic presentation. Rock art and kiva murals portraying new subjects reached a zenith of complexity and production, assuming a much more vigorous role in the visual communication of cosmological precepts (see Chapter 4). Shields and warriors, anthropomorphic and animal deities, katsina faces, ceremonial participants and rituals in progress, and other religious symbolism dominated the graphic arts. The variety of colors employed in Pueblo rock paintings increased significantly in tandem with new stylistic modes and content, facilitating the delineation of details pertinent to Pueblo cosmology. Among other uses, green, turquoise, and a variety of red, orange, yellow, and white pigments were selected to indicate facial markings and headgear composed of many types of feathers. Contrasting hues employed to delineate significant features of ceremonial importance were applied with small brushes of yucca and possibly other fibrous plants.

## Color Choices in Pueblo IV Rock Paintings

A search for meaning in color challenges the archaeologist. While reference to ethnographic information is often useful, adherence to symbolic color codes was hardly strict in Pueblo IV rock art. As in prior centuries, color choices for rock paintings during Pueblo IV were partly determined by the availability of pigments—thus the continuing common use of red and yellow ochres and white paint easily obtainable from mineral sources. Panels of rock paintings, however, display a more varied use of color than in the immediately preceding centuries. Color variability was so important that Miller and others (2012:48) propose that proximity to pigments may have been a determining factor in choosing shelters in which to paint. This proposal raises an issue discussed by Young (1988:173–178) about which is prior or prime: the power of the place where rock art was created or the power of the images? Miller and others (2012) cite as an example the richly painted overhang in Abo Pass in the Tompiro region, where naturally occurring green clays containing iron hydrate minerals are readily obtainable in the sediments in the immediate vicinity. Obviously, more evidence is needed to support this idea. In general, however, the greatest color diversity among Pueblo rock paintings of the Pueblo IV period occurs in the landscape of the southern Pueblo Piro and Tompiro region, where a diverse array of sediments provides access to colorful pigments.

Pueblo IV color selections were also increasingly governed by their aesthetic and symbolic values, or for clarity of communication. Painters often chose colors for their representational values, guaranteeing that the viewer understood exactly what was portrayed. Tiny yucca whips in the hands of star katsinas, for example, might go unnoticed but for the bright green paint used for this small detail, the whip being a significant aspect of a punitive katsina's identity and function (Schaafsma 2000:Figure 3.17b). Similarly, mountain lions are usually painted in yellow, and rare depictions of sunflowers are represented as small petaled bursts of yellow attached to green stalks. Likewise, the widely represented black-tipped white tail feathers of the young golden eagle are realistic and unmistakable.

There was much more at stake, however, than mere representation when it came to color choices because color itself harbors symbolic potential. The repeated use of a color for a particular image is likely to be symbolic, for example, if it contradicts the natural appearance of the subject, even if the significance of the color's symbolic usage is not understood. The seemingly enigmatic spotted felines painted in dull blue in the kiva murals at Pottery Mound and Awat'ovi are a case in point (but see Chapter 4). In many instances, however, symbolic color acquires its meanings in association with natural analogs, although this, too, involves complicating factors when additional meanings are added (see Chapter 1).

There may be more than one symbolic color choice for the same subject, or a color may be multivocal, standing for several things at once. Context provides clues when trying to determine the meanings of a color choice in any particular situation. A yellow sunflower might be used to denote flowers in general and beyond that to allude to sacred pollen, summer, sun, the growing season, and, more broadly, fertility (Hays-Gilpin et al. 2010:123). While yellow may reference fertility in some cases, in rock paintings it was used more commonly and consistently in depictions of mountain lions, which have symbolic connotations of their own. Although yellow is a natural color choice for this tawny creature, none of these mountain lions are portrayed as ordinary animals; rather, they are subject to ritualistic elaboration. As a patron of hunting and warfare, this feline is affiliated with the sun, who also figures prominently in warfare cosmology, and their symbolic connection is reinforced by their shared color (Schaafsma 2000:139). Further, when depicted in rock paintings and murals, the mountain lion's supernatural status is made apparent by added details in contrasting hues. These include red caps, attached red feathers, and in one case a necklace, ankle bands, and a "rainbow" in the upper body rendered in red, white, and green stripes (Figure 5.4; see Plate 20). Claws—the mountain lion's particular powerful attribute in its role of a hunt or war patron—are given special emphasis. Red tongues and outlines in contrasting black or white are further embellishments. Parsons (1939:287) specifically notes that at Zuni red feathers fastened to the animals of the six directions empower them to ask for rain, find wives, and to act as guards. May we surmise also that the little Piro mountain lion with red cap and feathers and rainbow-like stripes visually embodies symbolism of the war-fertility complex of Pueblo cosmology (Schaafsma 2000:154–157)? Are his white claws simply for emphasis in this painting, or do these white claws, with which he poetically obtains scalps, allude to the white clouds that the scalps—initiated as rain fetishes—will attract into the pueblo of the victor? Or both?

Although the mountain lion is associated with the yellow sun, the sun itself has a complex symbolic color repertoire of its own, including

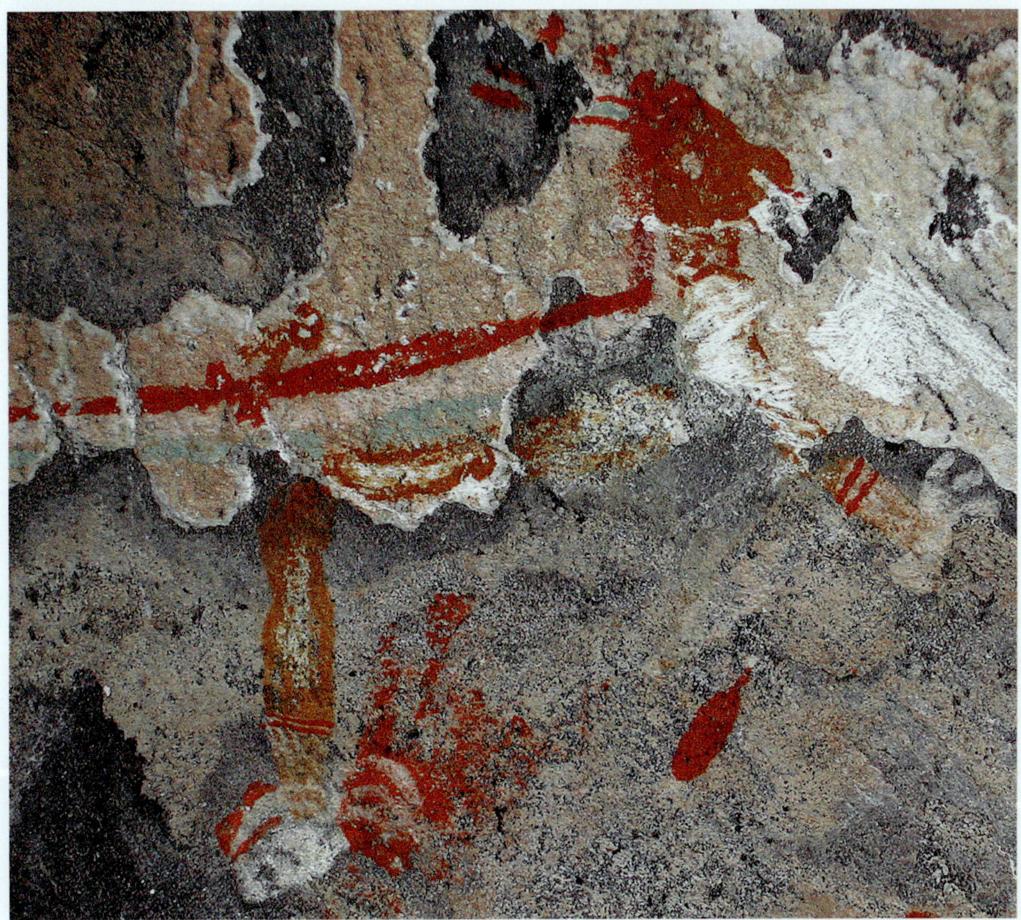

FIGURE 5.4. In orange, red, green, and white, this small mountain lion near Socorro, New Mexico, is outfitted with ceremonial attire, ca. AD 1325–1400. The white scratches are recent defacement. Photograph by Polly Schaafsma.

red, yellow, and white, as well as turquoise, all of which are apparent in rock art representations. Father of the War Twins, who have multiple powers, the sun is associated with rain, fertility, and the growth of maize as well as warfare. The use of turquoise for the sun contradicts its natural appearance, although according to Parsons (1939:102), the association of turquoise with the sun, who is regarded as male, is fitting since blue is regarded as a masculine color. The turquoise-sun relationship, symbolically contrived, is also prevalent in Mesoamerica (Izeki 2016; Townsend 1979:39, Figure 16). This shared color association is seemingly part of a pattern of broader relationships with Mesoamerica that are apparent in Pueblo cosmology after circa AD 1300 (Mathiowetz et al. 2015; Schaafsma 1999, 2000). As an aside, Florence Hawley Ellis was told by Santo Domingo Corn council members that San Marcos Pueblo (ca. AD 1325–1680), which is situated close to the Cerrillos Hills, was established and maintained by the Sun and Corn clans "primarily because of its proximity to turquoise and lead deposits in the Cerrillos Hills. The Sun Clan specialized in the production of turquoise and turquoise jewelry" (in Flint 2017:78). The Corn Clan, on the other hand, oversaw the lead obtained for pottery decoration. Following the Pueblo Revolt in 1680, these clans moved to Kewa (Santo Domingo)

Pueblo (Ellis 1977:3–4; Flint 2017:77–78). Today this is the basis for Kewa's claim to being traditional guardians of these mines.

Rock paintings contain images of turquoise suns and sun shields, as well as a turquoise-colored sun-shield bearer. The sun is also represented in white and yellow. Sun disks commonly have red or red and yellow borders, representing radiance, and eagle and macaw feathers may be attached to the rims, both of which have solar implications. A large sun-shield bearer in the Galisteo Basin is painted mostly in white, and a large yellow sunflower with red details is centered on the shield. Although a serrated border, a common feature of sun shields indicting rays, is clearly present, the original color of this detail has been lost, suggesting that it was not red or yellow. Was it turquoise?

Ethnographic references link the sun with all of these colors. Turquoise was considered an appropriate gift to the War Gods at Zuni, sons of the Sun. According to the Zuni,

> the sun itself is conceived as a shield of burning crystal, which the Sun Father, who is anthropomorphic, carries as he makes his daily journey from east to west. Prayers are addressed to the invisible and esoteric bearer…of the shield, who…is seated on a colossal turquois, wearing beautiful buckskin clothing. [Stevenson 1904:24, note b]

In addition, the sun is said to hide behind a mask: the mask is decorated with eagle and parrot plumes and "the hair around the head and face is red like fire and when it moves and shakes the people cannot look closely at the mask.… The heavy line encircling the mask is yellow and indicates rain" (Stevenson 1894b:35). Stevenson (1894b:29–30) also reports that the Zia perceived the sun as having been made of white shell, turquoise, red stone, and abalone shell. When the sun rose and he was far off his face was blue, but as he came nearer his face grew brighter. His face was also conceived of as a shield.

These ethnographic descriptions fit extremely well with the Pueblo IV rock art imagery. In contemporary replications of the sun's face, or shield, red horsehair may surround the disk, beyond which a serrated border is formed by pale corn husks, presumably indicating yellow rays (Fewkes 1897:Plate 104). I suggest that the serrated edges of the monochromatic petroglyphs of sun shields *imply* a radiant yellow border.

Ethnographically, high value was (is) ascribed to rare pigments such as blue-green or turquoise, especially when mixed with piñon gum (see Chapter 1). At Zuni, this paint was used exclusively for katsina faces, making them sacred or "valuable" (Bunzel 1932b:852–861). Today, the faces of katsinas are often painted with, or include, a turquoise shade of blue, seemingly in reference to water, although other colors are used as well (see Wright 1973).

For ancient rock art, turquoise color and bright green pigments (probably malachite, although direct confirmation is rare) were possibly acquired through trade, and used parsimoniously for selected subjects, due to the limited quantities available. Unfortunately, due to its composition, turquoise-colored paint flakes away easily and in many instances where it was used, today only remnants of paint remain. Bright turquoise and green pigments were used sparingly in rock paintings near Socorro to highlight details of katsinas and other beings and in these contexts may allude to water (Figure 5.5; see Plate 21). Turquoise-colored paint was also used for katsina faces and for pendent jewelry. In one notable example, a katsina face, possibly that of Somaikoli,[3] is painted on a plastered section of a rockshelter (Figure 5.6; see Plate 23). Fragments of brilliant turquoise-colored paint still in place indicate that it was used for details such as the narrow ears, as well as spaces between the horizontal red striping across the face.

Color symbolism for rain and moisture in Pueblo IV rock paintings includes white, black, turquoise, and possibly yellow, all of which have additional have symbolic connections to other cosmological entities, some of which have been discussed here. Thus the significance of these colors when they appear in late Ancestral Pueblo rock art may be ambiguous or multivalent, and their symbolic meanings ascertained on the basis of context. In particular, two tiny

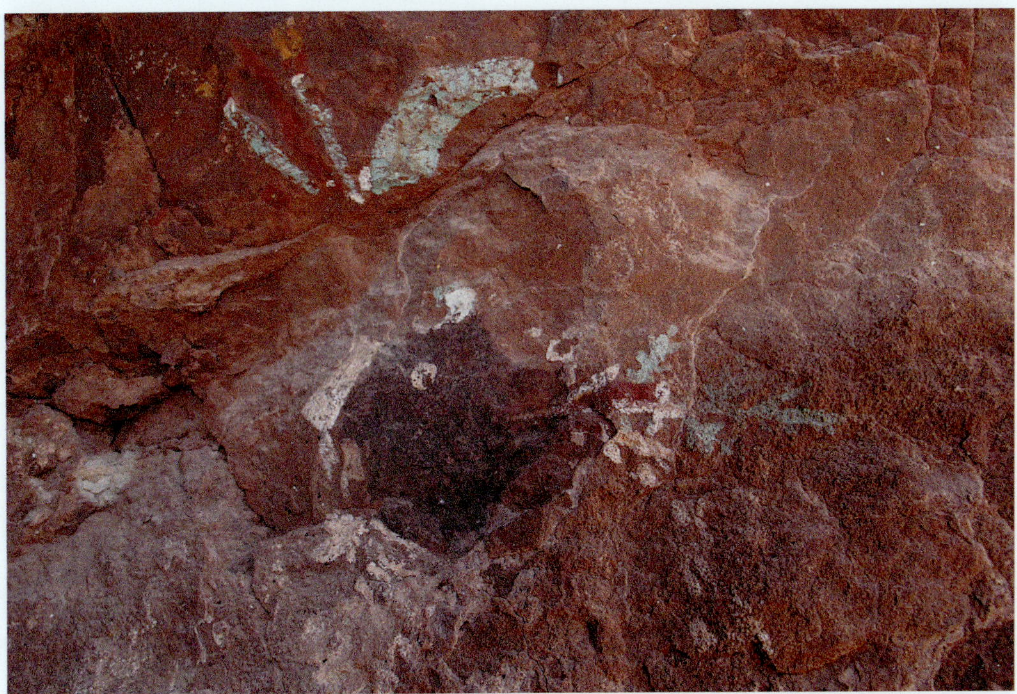

FIGURE 5.5. The black head of a horned serpent embellished with a green horn, feathers, and a plant, Abo, New Mexico, ca. AD 1350–1680. Photograph courtesy of John Pitts.

Tompiro turquoise katsina faces painted within a small rock depression may refer to water, the depression symbolically synthesizing concepts of the underworld, a water container, and the terrestrial sources of rain (Schaafsma 2009). These faces also have black beards. Depicted here and on other Tompiro katsinas, black beards may also symbolize rain, as they do among contemporary katsinas. At the same site, a jar-shaped katsina face with implications of a water container is painted in bright yellow; in this instance, yellow appears to have rain and fertility connotations (Bunzel 1932b:1024; Parsons 1939:275, 395).

As body paint and in kiva murals and rock paintings, the achromatic values of white and black may be both representational and symbolic in connection with rain-related symbolism. White and black are used in representations of clouds in kiva murals at Pottery Mound at and Kuaua (see Chapter 4), and I propose that the extensive use of black for images such as stepped cumulous clouds conveyed the same symbolic message in rock paintings. One impressive example is a large black cloud articulating with black and white water streaks beneath the lip of a rockshelter in the Casas Grandes hinterlands (Schaafsma 2015). Paintings spattered in black in Surratt Cave, near Gran Quivira, New Mexico, and white hand stencils, also spattered, from nearby Feather Cave may also allude to rainmaking ritual practices that took place deep within dark caves, the perceived residences of rain spirits and thus the place of origin of rain itself (Ellis and Hammack 1968; Greer and Greer 2002, 2015:26–30; Schaafsma 1999: 179–182, 2009). Surratt Cave is a dark-zone cave comprised of a vertical series of narrow passages and rooms formed by a collapsed limestone sink, with black paintings and charcoal drawings in various locations of clouds, snakes or lightning, katsina faces, hand stencils, and what appear to be tadpoles (Greer and Greer 2002, 2015:26–30). While some cloud designs are painted directly, a large number of marks and figures were produced by spattering or blowing

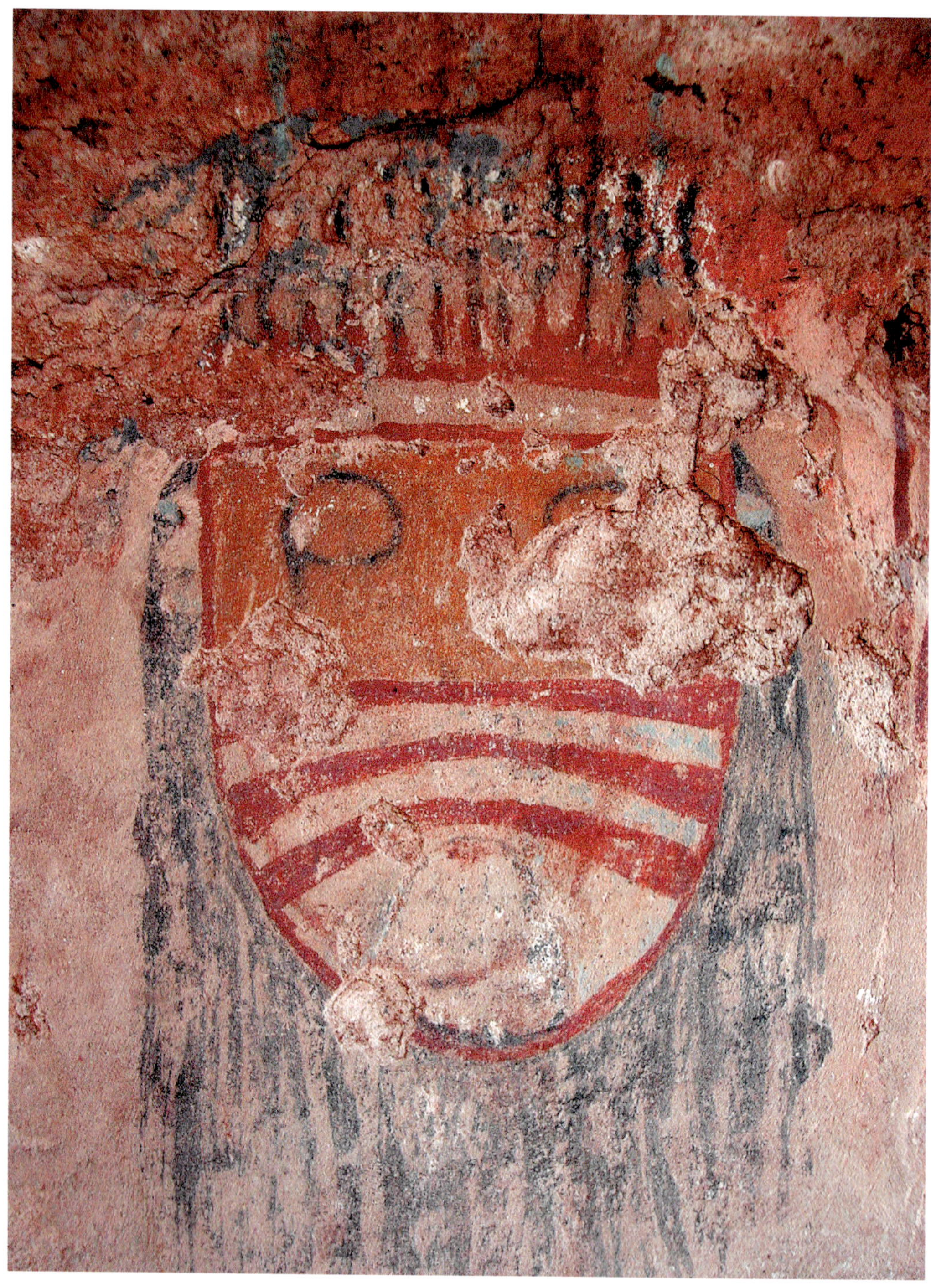

FIGURE 5.6. A nearly life-size katsina face painted on plaster in a rockshelter near Socorro, New Mexico. Traces of turquoise-colored paint remain on the ears and face, ca. AD 1325–1600. Photograph by Polly Schaafsma.

liquid paint, all reminiscent of rain itself and alluding to moisture and requests for rain. Spattered figures include the large black stepped cloud at the bottom of the cavity (Schaafsma 1999:Figure 12.17), stenciled hands, a large serpent, lightning, and various irregular shapes, and blown dot patterns, in addition to the various smears all of which are consistent with rainmaking symbolism. At the bottom of the cave complex, in a crack too narrow to access, perishable objects that probably served as offerings are visible (see also Caperton 1981). The large spattered cloud sits above this opening (Greer and Greer 2015:Figure 14). The finger-smeared applications of thick black paint or more rarely dark orange are reminiscent of the smeared images in white clay on the Colorado Plateau. In sum, evidence suggests that smearing and spattering are ritual acts related to rain-bringing that compound the meaning and power of the resulting images.

Near the outside entrance to the underground complex of Surratt Cave, pecked eyelike circles on either side of a vertical crack animate a large rock face, perhaps symbolizing a rain deity, a Southwestern version of the Mesoamerican Tlaloc (Greer and Greer 2002:38). This deity is pictured in a great many sites in southern New Mexico, and images often are integrated with the shape of the rock (Schaafsma 2015). Although the resemblance at Surratt Cave is not particularly close, this proposal is quite in line with the nature of the caves and their affinity to the underworld, from which clouds and rain are said to originate according to Mesoamerican and Pueblo cosmology (Schaafsma and Taube 2006).

As for paint spattering, the Hopi draw an analogy between rain drops and particles of corn meal that rain provides. Today and in the recent past, spattered paint is said to symbolize moisture and fertility, or, more specifically, rain drops and cornmeal (Hays-Gilpin et al. 2010:123; Sekaquaptewa and Washburn 2010:139). According to Sekaquaptewa and Washburn (2010:150, Figure 7.4), a hand with black cloud and lightning designs painted against a spattered background in a Sikyatki bowl signifies work to some contemporary Hopi consultants while the spatters allude to rain and the resulting cornmeal (see also Brody 1990:Plate 14 for a similar Sikyatki painting with clearer example of spatter work and an entirely different explanation). Hand stencils in rock art occur in contexts that are extremely different from those painted inside bowls that are receptacles for meal and water, so it may be unwise to project the same interpretation onto both.

The use of white paint to attract white clouds was discussed previously in conjunction with earlier sites on the Colorado Plateau, and today Pueblo ritual participants may be symbolically painted with blackish and white pigments to represent rain clouds (Stephen 1936:853). As such they function as "presumably chromatic rain prayer[s]" (Parsons 1939:397). In contemporary ceremony and ritual the frequent use of cotton in ritual paraphernalia and dance apparel is used to attract white cumulous rain clouds. Pictured as white highlights on ritual figures in Pueblo IV rock paintings, these white details presumably signify the same thing.

In general, Pueblo IV rock paintings do not make extensive use of white paint, although an exception resides in a Galisteo Basin shrine beneath an overhang, where white paint and content combine to focus on rainmaking. Several large white paint splotches against the rock possibly have symbolic connotations similar to those postulated for splashed paint in Pueblo III rock art described for Canyon de Chelly (see Grant 1978:193–94). The shelter also includes a panel of ceremonialists seemingly enacting a rain ceremony (Schaafsma 1990). One figure holds a small round object—probably a gourd—and a crook. Today, ceremonial gourds filled with spring water are used in pouring rites to mimic falling water or rain (Schaafsma and Taube 2006:25). Among their many ritual functions, crooks are used to "'pull down the rain' or to 'catch water from the sky'" (Parsons 1925:102; also see Schaafsma 1990:247). This scene is superimposed by at least two horned serpents painted largely in white, although the

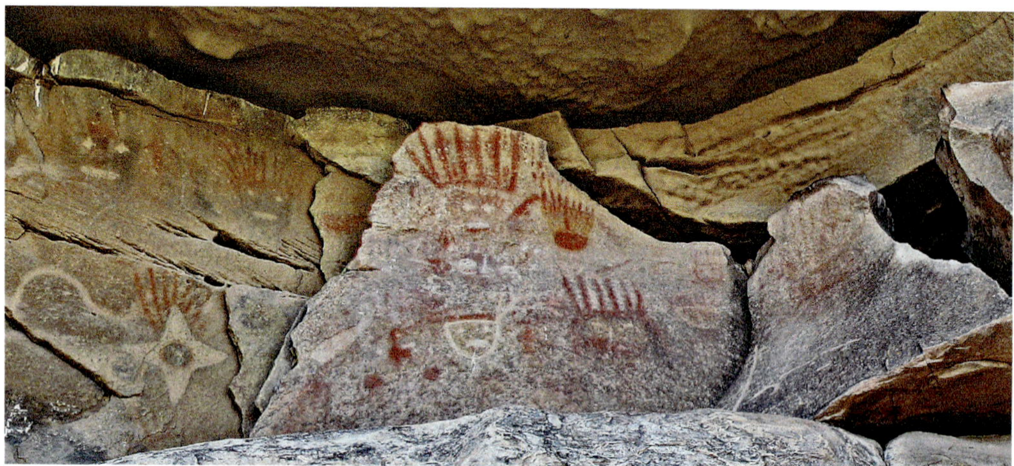

FIGURE 5.7. Paintings in red, black, and white display war themes above San Cristóbal Pueblo in the Galisteo Basin, New Mexico, ca. AD 1350–1680. Photograph by Curtis Schaafsma.

larger serpent's body is painted dark gray in the midsection. This painting is paralleled by a Hopi account involving cumulus cloud katsinas, water-filled gourds, the water serpent, and blackish and bluish gray clays, the latter reportedly from the bottom of springs where these serpent beings are often said to reside (Schaafsma and Taube 2006:273; Wright 1973:246–247).

At Abo Painted Rocks, a Tompiro site, two feathered serpents are painted bluish gray, bordered with white, and white feathers are attached to the edge of the body. Green dragonflies beside one of them further associate the serpent with water. Another serpent in the vicinity has a black head and a bright green horn, with a green plant-like object sprouting from the mouth (Figure 5.5). According to Parsons (1939:299), the northern Tewa offered black dirt to this deity after a rain.

As a powerful deity, the roles of the horned serpent vary, but his many representations in blue-gray pigment appear to reference sacred clays, sanctifying his image. Other clays, pinkish in hue and used as body paint for contemporary Zuni Mudhead personages, also carry profound symbolic meaning. Derived from sacred sources in ponds and springs described in Zuni historical traditions, this body paint ties the Zuni to their origins within their cultural landscape (Bunzel 1932:860–861a). The identity of the rare Mudhead painted in similar tones in Rio Grande rock paintings is unmistakable (Schaafsma 1990), although in this case the source of the paint is unknown.

Finally, black and red paints and their use in the iconography of war must be considered, as they comprise one of the most consistent symbolic uses of color in Pueblo IV rock paintings. A star with four red or white tapering points and a black face is identified as Morningstar and is associated with scalps that function as rain fetishes (Schaafsma 2000:144–150). In turn, this star shares a large packet of metaphorical connections with Venus as a fearsome Mesoamerican planet that shoots out lethal darts and plays a significant role in the war-fertility complex (Carlson 2005; Mathiowetz et al. 2015; Schaafsma 2000:146–157; Schaafsma 2014).

In Pueblo IV rock paintings, black-faced warriors and stars with red feathers, mouths, or outlines are typical images. In Tompiro rock art, star katsinas wearing dark red kilts have black faces and bodies, although their lower arms and legs are painted white. Likewise, the black faces with red feathered headgear painted under rock overhangs above San Cristóbal Pueblo are identifiable as warriors; significantly, a feathered star is displayed prominently among them (Figure 5.7; see Plate 22; and Parsons 1939:337, 530, note, 537).

In rock art, entire stars may be painted in red, and there are examples of Morningstar *petroglyphs* that were stained or painted red, the hue persisting today even on exposed cliff faces (Schaafsma 2000:146, Figures 3.26b and c and 4.32); the added paint likely contributed to the power of the image. Some black-faced Morningstar icons are depicted with feathered headdresses, usually of the tail feathers of the golden eagle, although the red feathers of others represent those from the red-tailed hawk. Appropriately, both birds are fierce predators and war patrons.

From Taos to Hopi, red has a prominent symbolic role in ethnographic contexts pertaining to warfare (Parsons 1939:275, 291, 337). At Cochiti Lange (1990:280) describes red as broadly signifying hail, epidemics, war, and starvation, all of which spell disaster. In the 1960s a Taos elder, observing a rare display of red northern lights, told me that they were a war omen. Stevenson (1894:122) reports that a Zia warrior returning with a scalp paints his face and lower legs red, "and the remainder" black. Sparkling black pigment is then spread over the face. From Hopi Titiev (1944:157) describes red and black used in concert for painting warrior marks (Elder War Twin's footprints) on cheeks—red first, with specular iron applied on top. A similar combination of superimposed red and black paint on a warrior's headdress is described from Pottery Mound (Chapter 4). At Laguna hunters paint their faces with the colors of the War Brothers in bands of black, red, black, red (Parsons 1939:395). Elsewhere, red and black pigments were offered to the sun (Isleta) and at War God shrines (Zuni; Parsons 1939:298–99, 337). At Taos scalps are rubbed with red pigment, and red pigment is offered to both stars and scalps (Parsons 1939:299). Red is symbolic of blood and—importantly within this cosmological complex in which a dynamic reciprocity is essential between humankind and the supernatural world—references are made to blood as fertilizing the earth (Parsons 1939:275, 397; Tedlock 1972:110–111; Young 1988:134). Red therefore has an important role in the war-fertility complex.

## Discussion and Conclusion

Cosmology is an organizing force that socially integrates and unites, and rock art imagery is one vehicle for promoting these functions. Via the use of color, rock paintings have a greater potential for communicating symbolic and cosmological information than do monochromatic petroglyphs. Different methods of applying paint, such as spattering and smearing, also contribute additional meaning to a representation. Beginning in the fourteenth century, when subjects and figurative styles underwent radical modifications, the increase in color use, and the details it enabled, made the new images more attractive, compelling, and above all, more informative than previous monochrome or bichrome productions. Imagery itself took on a more prominent role in Pueblo religion. A diversified palette was useful in actively promoting the shift in belief systems, and when color synthesizes meaning and symbol, the amount of information conveyed is increased.

As discussed at the beginning of this chapter, paint imbues objects with power. Paint alone may contribute to the sanctity of rock paintings, increasing their potency, thus making them more sacrosanct than petroglyphs. Bunzel (1932b:868) writes that "next to the mask, the face and body paint is the most sacred part of the dancer's regalia," adding that "this paint is very valuable and after the mask is painted with this, it is valuable [i.e., sacred]. Now it is finished; it is a person" (Bunzel 1932b:852). Parsons (1939: 397) notes that the application of paint makes katsina dolls sacrosanct, while a story from Zuni describes the careful painting of a dragonfly effigy—presumably an essential step to give it life (Cushing 1920:82–85). It is possible, even likely, that these values hold for painted rock art, especially if the paint used for them was carefully selected from sacred sources related to the times of origin or subject to ritual preparation (Young 1988:191–192). In addition, although rock paintings and petroglyphs share iconography that includes multitudinous katsina faces, deities, and ceremonial participants, the overall content of painted sites is more constrained, in that the miscellaneous elements of undetermined or ambiguous identity characteristic of so many petroglyph sites are absent or few in number. These factors, along with their restricted kiva-like settings under overhangs, suggest that these rock paintings were produced under ritual guidance (Munson 2011).

Further, many rock painting sites show evidence of numerous painting episodes, an accumulation of images that would have increased the ritual significance of the sites as paintings were added over time. Accumulation, a value itself and metaphor for power, involves repetition, superpositioning, and the juxtaposition of images as well as paint, all of which function to increase the power of what is portrayed as well as the place where it occurs (e.g., Young 1988:178–190). It could be argued that a similar principle applies to kivas with murals in which paintings were made on sequential layers of plaster.

In summary, Pueblo ritual and ceremony employ a variety of mimetic techniques performed or rendered in order to communicate with, not to mention *compel*, the spirit realm to comply with requests for rain and other blessings. Examples include dance movements, gestures, sound, regalia, and paraphernalia that mimic and echo the item of concern or whatever is desired. Since color also has mimetic qualities, the symbolic and natural use of color fits nicely into this Puebloan paradigmatic scheme and contributes to the power of the icon portrayed. Viewed thusly, within prescribed contexts reviewed in this chapter, color, beyond its symbolic connotations, has power in and of itself.

In addition to their social and religious impact on ritual participants and other Pueblo visitors to a site, colorful rock paintings must have played a major role in communicating with the ambient spirits in the land itself. In regard to katsinas, Bunzel (1932b:862) quotes a Zuni individual as saying:

> Sometimes the painting on the mask means something; sometimes not.... [T]hey paint something on the mask to please the earth and something to please the sky.... The red paint on the body is for the red-breasted birds and the yellow paint is for the yellow-breasted birds, and for the flowers and butterflies and all the beautiful things in the world. The white paint is for the sun.

Is it not also likely that the colorful imagery in its landscape settings was—and continues to be—pleasing to the earth or the sky and to the resident spirits in those places?

## Notes

1. I use the term "rock painting" as opposed to the common term "pictograph" when referring to all images painted on stone. Pictograph is derived from Latin "pingere," to paint, and while the word is commonly used to refer to pictorial images painted on stone, historically the term has been extended to petroglyphs, as well as to figures on birch bark, hides, and other media (Mallery 1893). In addition to being ambiguous, the term "pictograph" also carries connotations of "picture-writing" and all the evolutionary implications latent in that phrase. In my opinion, the term "pictograph" is a poor fit when it comes to rock art. "Rock painting," on the other hand, refers exactly to what is being discussed without cultural baggage and ambiguity.
2. In some instances, selected petroglyphs were also painted, although due to their exposed locations, remaining traces of paint on petroglyphs are scarce.
3. Similar katsina faces in the vicinity were identified as Somaikoli by Hopi artist Michael Kabotie (personal communication ca. 2001).

# 6

# The Sacred Colors and Materials of Ancestral Pueblo Jewelry

Jill E. Neitzel and David E. Witt

The inextricable combination of color and raw material was the most fundamental characteristic of Ancestral Pueblo jewelry. Hue and substance were intrinsic to each other; together, they made ornaments visually conspicuous, sacred objects. In addition to their striking appearance, white shell, blue-green turquoise, and black and red stone were imbued with diverse religious meanings that were more than just symbolic. At the most profound level, adornments with these colors and materials were spiritually alive.

This chapter considers the conjunction of jewelry colors, raw materials, and symbolism with animism, the understanding that supernatural spirits are present throughout the world (Harvey 2005; Tylor 1871). We analyze these topics from the perspective of artifact life history (Fogelin 2007; VanPool and Newsome 2012; VanPool and VanPool 2012; Walker 1999), and in our interpretations draw on ethnographic data from descendant groups, a strategy justified by the conservatism and continuity of religious traditions.

Our underlying premise is that the symbolism and embodied spirits of different color and raw material combinations strengthened and expanded during each successive stage in an ornament's life cycle. We also show that the extent of this amplification varied depending on a group's degree of social differentiation and ceremonial elaboration. Our discussion begins with raw materials, continues with craft production and then bodily adornment, and ends with ritual deposition. The involvement of unmodified substances, production debris, and incomplete ornaments in ritual deposition highlights the paramount importance of color and raw material.

## Raw Materials

Both literally and spiritually, the life cycle of Ancestral Pueblo jewelry began with raw materials whose most distinctive characteristic was their color (Figure 6.1; see Plate 24). But this correspondence was more nuanced than, for example, the general description of shell as white or turquoise as blue-green would suggest. Particular materials could vary considerably in their hues, and for some, their inclusions, textures, and sheen as well. Furthermore, different materials could be associated with the same color—shell, stone, and bone with white, jet, argillite, and shale with black, and argillite, shale, and shell with red-orange. Given that each of these colors and raw materials was imbued with a myriad of supernatural meanings, an ornament was a sacred object before it was even completed.

### *White Shell*

Marine species from the Gulf of California and the Pacific Coast were the raw material for Ancestral Pueblo shell ornaments (Brand 1938; Jernigan 1978:162–164; Mathien 1997; Smith 2002; Tower 1945). Most frequently used were the small gastropods *Olivella* and *Conus*. Other species included the large univalve *Haliotis*, the

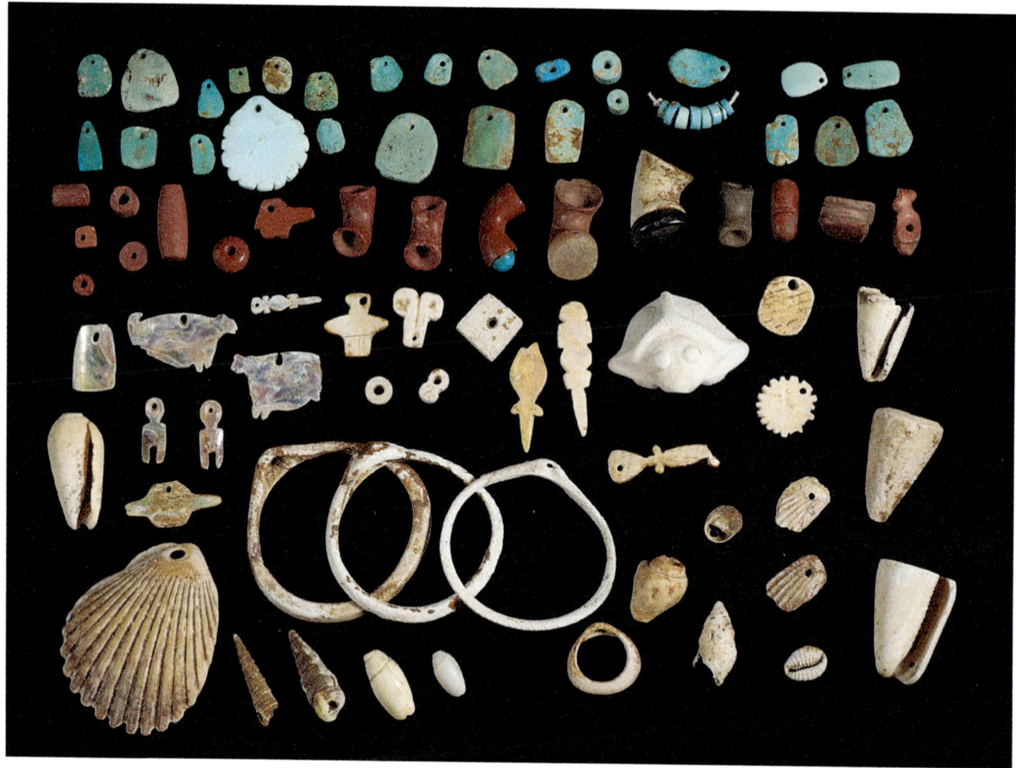

FIGURE 6.1. Colors and raw materials of diverse Ancestral Pueblo ornaments. *Top two rows*: turquoise. *Third row*: red stone with one piece of white stone and two turquoise and jet inlays. *Lower rows*: shell. Pueblo III period, Wupatki and Elden Pueblos, north central Arizona. Photo by Ryan Belnap and Daniel Boone. Courtesy of Northern Arizona University.

moderately sized bivalves *Glycymeris*, *Laevicardium*, and *Spondylus*, and the small gastropods *Turritella*, *Nassarius*, and *Columbella*.

These shells were distinguished not just by their shapes and sizes but also by the colors, sheen, and textures of their exterior and interior surfaces. The colors for finished ornaments were generally shades of white that for some species were tinted pink, beige, orange, or gray or were mottled with a darker hue (Figure 6.2, see Plate 25). For example, *Olivella* alternates brown or beige and white, and *Conus* is white with brown spots. Whatever its color, a shell's interior surface is smoother and shinier than its exterior, as best exemplified by *Haliotis*'s silvery sheen.

Historic period Pueblo people attributed an array of religious meanings to white, shell's most broadly defined color category (see Chapter 1). This symbolism included sacred directions, one of the katsinas' mountain homes, and white clouds, seeds, birds, butterflies, flowers, and trees. In addition, the gleam of a shell's interior surface may have signified the moon, the sun, deities, otherworldly origins, and great cosmic power (Miller and Hamell 1986; Teague and Washburn 2013).

Shells themselves were symbols of "birth, creation, and earliest time," and due to mollusks' high fertility rates, they also connoted rejuvenation (Claassen 2008:232). Their marine origins linked them to the primordial, underworld sea whose resident deities created the human world (James 1974). Because shells were among the deities' most precious possessions, their real world counterparts were sacred reminders of this supernatural realm.

Shells were also animate objects. In historic period Pueblo religion, all of Mother Earth's

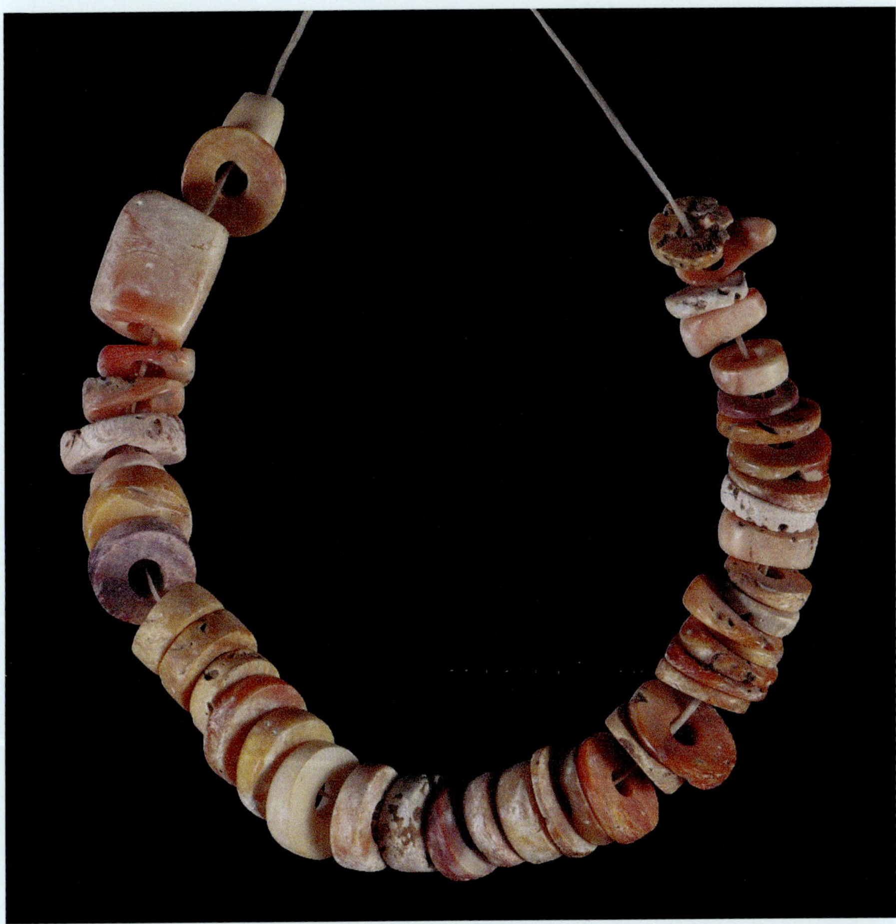

FIGURE 6.2. Shell bead necklace crafted from *Spondylus* species and one *Olivella* shell. Note variation in hues, mottling, sheen, and shapes. Pueblo III period, Wupatki, north central Arizona. Wupatki National Monument, National Park Service. Catalog number WUPA 440. Photo by Ryan Belnap and Daniel Boone. Courtesy of Northern Arizona University.

products share her cosmic spirit, which gives them nonhuman personhood (Brody and Swentzell 1996; Bunzel 1932a; Silko 1996). For shell, these Raw Beings could be associated with the physical object, with the living mollusk that it once protected, or both. As exemplified by conch shells, the kind of animating spirit also depended on the shell's biography and context (Mills and Ferguson 2008; also see Cohan 2010).

Most Ancestral Pueblo shell jewelry was imported from the Hohokam of south-central Arizona and later the Casas Grandeans of northwest Chihuahua (Bradley 1993; McGuire and Howard 1987; Mitchell and Foster 2000; Whalen 2013). But unworked shell and evidence of ornament production have been found at Ancestral Pueblo sites post-AD 900, most notably in Chaco Canyon (Mathien 1997; Windes 1993). Given the importance of the sea in Hopi cosmology, some of this raw shell may have been procured during ritual pilgrimages to coastal areas (Claassen 2008:232; Ferguson et al. 2009; Helms 1979; Titiev 1937). Travel over such long distances—from Chaco Canyon it is roughly 1,000 km to the Gulf of California and 1,300 km to the Pacific Coast—would have heightened the destination's cosmological significance and in turn added to the collected shells' sacredness.

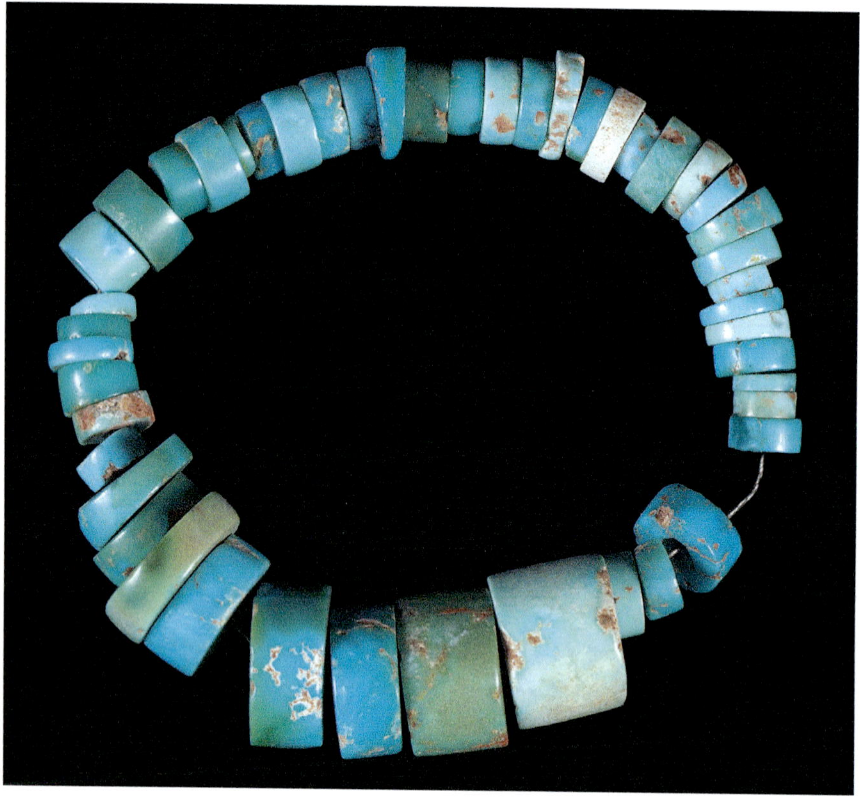

FIGURE 6.3. Turquoise disk bead bracelet. Note variation in the hues, inclusions, sheen, and shapes. Pueblo III period, Wupatki, north central Arizona. Wupatki National Monument, National Park Service. Photo by Ryan Belnap and Daniel Boone. Courtesy of Northern Arizona University.

### *Blue-Green Turquoise*

The colors of raw turquoise encompass shades of blue, blue-green, and green, variation that is the result of the mineral's chemical composition (Figure 6.3, see Plate 26). More copper makes it bluer; more iron makes it greener (Austin 1995). Some turquoise also has distinctive veiny inclusions, known as its matrix, whose color reflects the host rock's composition. Iron pyrite produces black matrix; rhyolite, yellow matrix; and iron oxides, such as hematite, brown matrix.

The religious meanings that historic period Pueblo people attributed to various shades of blue, blue-green, and green included sacred directions, another of the katsinas' mountain homes, the sky, clouds, and various flowers, seeds, trees, butterflies, birds, and other animals (see Chapter 1). Variable reports for the symbolism of blue, blue-green, and green suggest that even subtle color differences could be significant (Mattson 2016:131).

As a material, turquoise had its own sacred associations. It represented water, the sky, creation, and bountiful harvests. In addition to shell, turquoise was a precious possession of the underworld deities in the Hopi creation story (James 1974; McBrinn and Altshuler 2015). As one of Mother Earth's geological creations, turquoise was also animated by Raw Beings, who for the Zuni included the spirit of the blue mountain lion (Cushing 1883; also see Bower 1999; Clark 2015; Hallowell 1960).

Turquoise's underground source may have imbued the mineral with other supernatural connotations. For the Hopi, a kiva's sipapu and the sipapuni in the Grand Canyon are entrances to the underworld (James 1974). If a mine was another such entrance, then excavating pits,

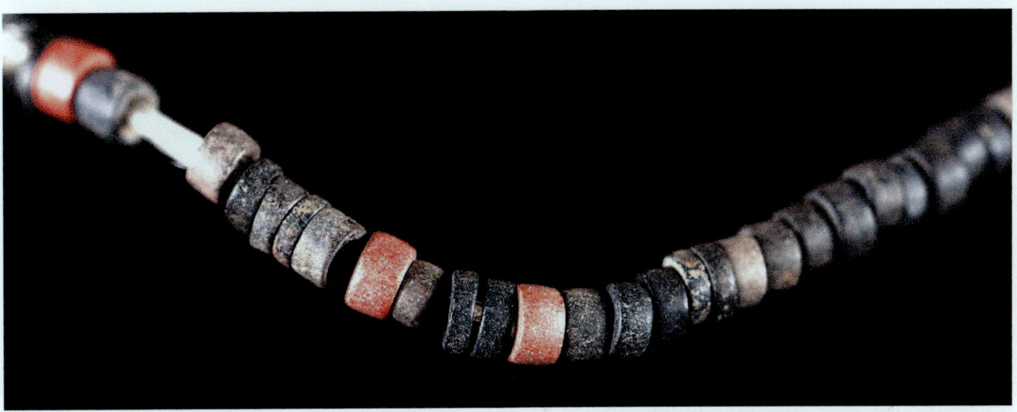

FIGURE 6.4. Black, gray, and red stone disk bead strand. Pueblo III period, northeast Arizona. Tsegi Canyon, Navajo National Monument, National Park Service. Catalog number NAVA-15451, photo by Ryan Belnap and Daniel Boone. Courtesy of Northern Arizona University.

shafts, and tunnels may have been a ritual activity whose religious significance increased at greater depths (Jernigan 1978:214; Northrop 1975:47–48, 435; Snow 1973:37–38). Thus, similar to clay, turquoise procurement may have required both sacred knowledge and rituals that added to the material's symbolism (Silko 1996; Trimble 2004; VanPool and Newsome 2012).

Ritual journeys to turquoise mines may have further increased these spiritual meanings. Such pilgrimages seem most likely for the Chacoans, who were the Southwest's major producers, consumers, and traders of turquoise ornaments and whose raw material sources included the Cerrillos Hills, located roughly 200 km to the east of Chaco Canyon, and other deposits in New Mexico, California, Nevada, and Colorado (Hull et al. 2014; Hull et al. 2008). Chaco pottery has been recorded near the Cerrillos mines, and unidentified Ancestral Pueblo artifacts have been recovered near the Halloran Spring mine in California's Mojave Desert (Rogers 1929; Warren and Mathien 1985; Wiseman and Darling 1986).

### *Black and Red Stone*

The Ancestral Puebloans' black ornaments were made of jet, argillite, and shale, whose hues encompassed shades of gray (Figure 6.4, see Plate 27). During the historic period, the color black's directional symbolism was with the nadir, and the color also represented storm clouds. Ancestral Puebloans also used red argillite for ornaments, whose hues ranged from deep red to orange-red to orange (Figure 6.4, See Plate 27). Similar to other colors, red symbolized sacred directions, and both black and red had their own associated clouds, seeds, birds, butterflies, flowers, and animals (see Chapter 1). Their materials were animated by Raw Beings, which for the Zuni were, respectively, the spirits of the black mountain lion and the red coyote (Cushing 1883; also see Bower 1999; Hallowell 1960).

In comparison to shell and turquoise, black and red stone were easier for most Ancestral Puebloans to obtain from nearby exposed strata and pit mines. Nevertheless, their sources and means of extraction may have added to the materials' supernatural connotations. The most notable deposits of jet were in Chaco Canyon and other locations in the surrounding San Juan Basin (Mathien 1997). Black argillite and shale may have been locally available to many communities. Red argillite occurred at a variety of locations in the San Juan Basin, the Rio Puerco of the East, and Sinagua area of north central Arizona (Colton 1941; Jernigan 1978; McGregor 1941; Stubbs and Stalling 1953).

## Production

After the raw material was procured, the next stage in an ornament's life history was its transformation into a finished piece of jewelry. When artisans created a basic form, such as a bead, pendant, or mosaic piece, they activated and

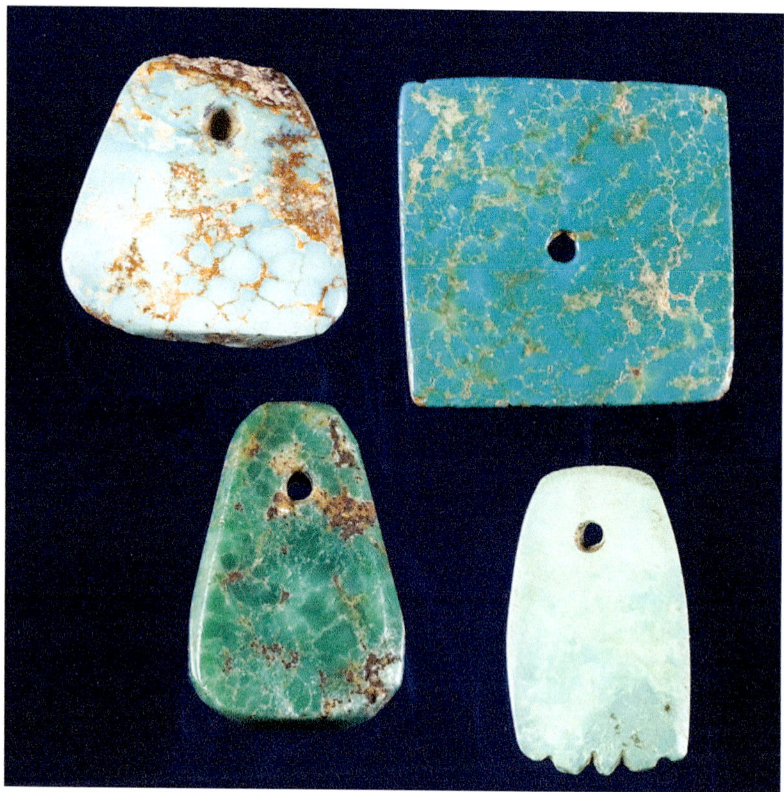

FIGURE 6.5. Turquoise pendants. Note variation in hues, inclusions, sheen, and forms. Pueblo III period, Flagstaff area sites, National Park Service. Photo by Ryan Belnap and Daniel Boone, courtesy of Northern Arizona University.

amplified the diverse symbolism that already imbued the color and material. They also displaced the original substance's Raw Beings with a new kind of spirit, that of Made Beings, whose impacts on the human world were much greater due to the ubiquity of adornments in everyday life (VanPool and Newsome 2012:247; VanPool and VanPool 2012:96). Subsequent embellishments to basic forms further strengthened and expanded this sacred content.

### *Creation*

When a basic form was crafted, the amount of material preparation and the complexity of the production tasks determined how much the preexisting color and material symbolism was bolstered and what new meanings were added. Simply perforating a whole shell for stringing required minimal effort, and any new religious connotations may have been limited to the ornament's distinctive shape, such as a gastropod's spiral (see Claassen 2008:235). But when the desired form was not visually obvious in the raw material, a series of tasks had to be completed with spiritual content being added during each. For example, to transform mined turquoise into a bead or pendant, an artisan first had to remove the material's host rock, which revealed its blue-green color and activated its myriad of symbolic meanings (Figures 6.3, 6.5, see Plates 26 and 28). Subsequent steps involved chipping, whittling, grinding, smoothing, polishing, and drilling to create the desired shape and sheen, each with its own supernatural significance. The crafting of large numbers of beads for a religious offering may have been a ritual activity that further heightened the ornaments' symbolism (Mills 2008).

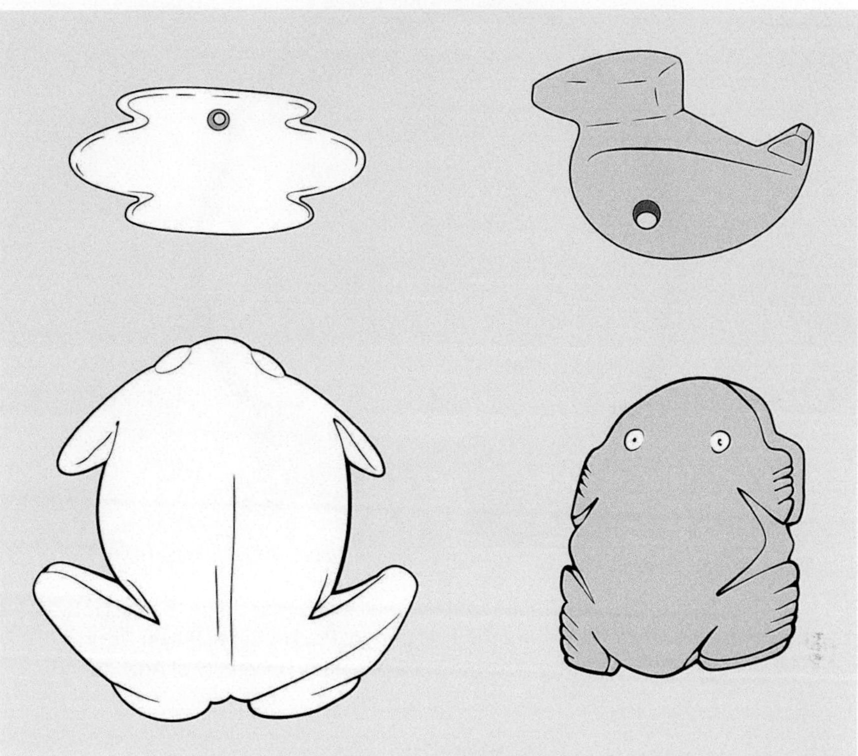

FIGURE 6.6. Bird and frog effigy pendants made of white shell (*left*) and blue-green turquoise (*right*). *Top row*: Pueblo II period Pueblo Bonito, Chaco Canyon. *Bottom row left*: Pueblo II–III period Kayenta. *Bottom row right*: Pueblo III period Mesa Verde. Based on Jernigan 1978: Figures 80–81; redrawn by Robert Schultz.

That finished forms were imbued with sacred meanings is most obvious for beads and pendants shaped as frogs, tadpoles, and birds, animals that historic period cosmology consistently associated with water and fertility (Fewkes 1903; Parsons 1939; also see Afrandilian 2007). When crafted from shell or turquoise, these effigies amplified the already present water-related symbolism of both raw materials and the color blue-green (Figures 6.1, 6.6). The Made Beings animating these ornaments would have included those of the animals themselves.

Geometric forms may have also had supernatural connotations. On Hopi katsina faces, dots represent stars, moisture, snow, flowers, corn kernels, and fertility (Colton 1959; Crown 1994; Fewkes 1903; Secakuku 1995). Disk beads may have carried some of these same meanings, with the extremely small size of some having added significance (Figure 6.1; and see Curcija 2018; Haury 1931). Pendants shaped as circles and serrated circles may have represented the sun and flowers, respectively (Figure 6.1, and see Crown 1994:Figure 9.1). These symbolic possibilities raise the question of whether other forms, such as bilobed beads and oval, square, and rectangular pendants, were also spiritually meaningful (Figures 6.1, 6.5; see Plates 24 and 28).

### *Embellishment*

Ancestral Pueblo artisans generally embellished individual forms by combining them with others, usually in strands and less frequently on mosaic pendants. This was the first life cycle stage in which the histories of basic forms diverged. While the vast majority were combined with other pieces, loose beads and tesserae could be used as ritual offerings, or a single

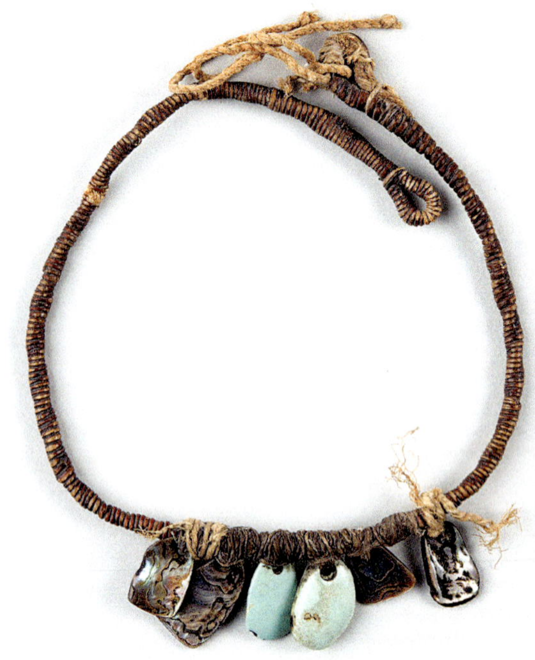

FIGURE 6.7. Cord necklace with *Haliotis* shell and turquoise pendants. Note *Haliotis* shells' sheen. Basketmaker III period, Pocket Cave, Prayer Rock district, northeast Arizona. Arizona State Museum, University of Arizona.

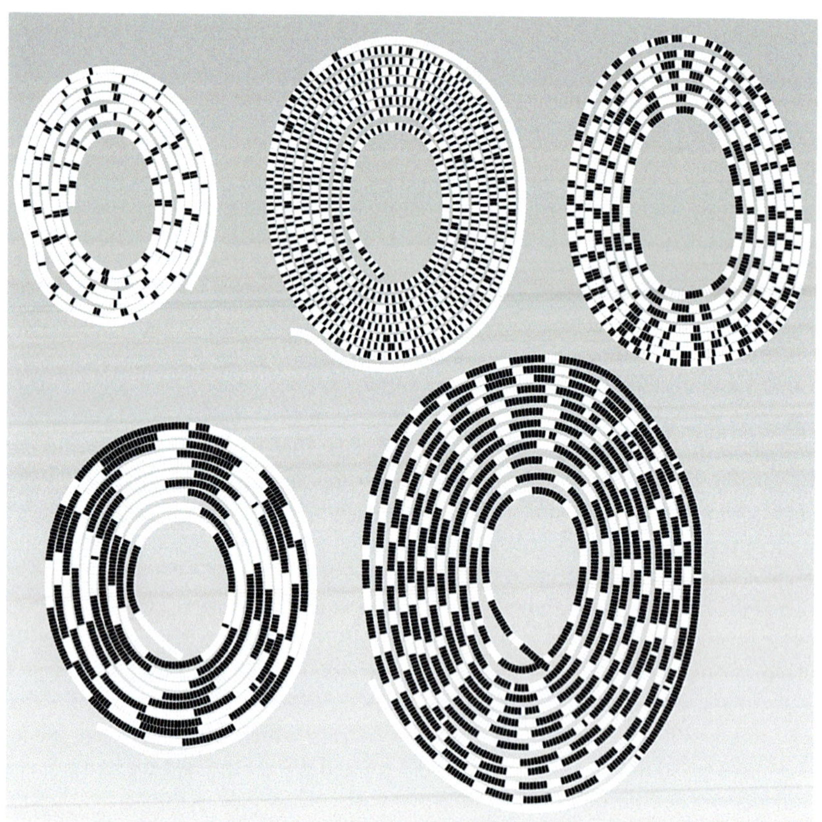

FIGURE 6.8. Schematic drawings of white shell and black stone disk bead strands. Note that the strands' ends consist of varying numbers of white *Olivella* shell beads, whose distinctive shapes are not depicted here. Pueblo II period Chetro Ketl, Chaco Canyon. Based on Hewett 1936:90–92; drawn by Robert Schultz.

bead or pendant could be strung on its own for a necklace.

The simplest embellishment was to string a few beads of the same color, material, and form (Figure 6.3; see Plate 26). This could be extended in several ways. One was to increase the numbers of beads, as illustrated most dramatically by Aztec Ruins' 17-m strand of 31,000 extremely small black-slate disk beads (Morris 1919a:99). Another was to alternate forms of the same material in a repeated pattern, such as a turquoise bracelet with groups of small turquoise beads separated by a larger disk (Jernigan 1978:Figure 85; Judd 1954:Plate 22). For shell strands, these configurations often involved different species, which could vary in their hue and sheen, such as a necklace with groups of *Olivella* beads separated by a shiny *Haliotis* tab pendant (Jernigan 1978:Plate 12).

Incorporating different colored materials provided more opportunities for embellishment. The simplest juxtaposition alternated two colors and materials of the same form, as seen in Prayer Rock Cave's cord necklace with *Haliotis* and turquoise pendants (Figure 6.7; see Plate 29). A more dramatic example is Chetro Ketl's two to five meter long strands of white shell and black stone disk beads, which illustrate the variety of patterns that could be achieved with just two colors and materials (Figure 6.8). Two different components could be combined into more complicated patterns, such as a necklace with groups of turquoise disk beads separated by *Haliotis* tab pendants (Jernigan 1978:Figure 86). A more complex arrangement from Wupatki incorporates two colors and materials: white shell and blue-green turquoise, a variety of bead types, and a large *Conus* pendant (Figure 6.9; see Plate 30).

A bead strand's sacred content was strengthened not just by incorporating greater numbers and more colors, raw materials, and forms but also by the symbolism associated with different bead and pendant shapes and with the patterned arrangement of these shapes and their colors and raw materials (Mills 2008:89). Recurring color combinations, such as white shell and black stone or white shell and blue-green turquoise, may have signified the dualism of Ancestral Pueblo religion (Teague and Washburn 2013).

A different type of embellishment involved inlaying small, thin, geometrically shaped pieces onto a backing to create a mosaic, usually a plaque pendant (Jernigan 1978:Figures 90–91). When only one material was used for the tesserae, it was blue-green turquoise that completely covered a wood or stone base. Bicolor mosaics pendants generally consisted of a fully exposed jet base inlaid with a few pieces of turquoise. In contrast, bicolor mosaics on the tops of wood combs were mostly turquoise inlay with a few pieces of jet.

More intricate mosaics incorporated a third color and material (see Jernigan 1978:Figures 90–91). Blue-green turquoise and black stone could be inlaid on a partially exposed shell base, which comprised the third color (Figure 6.10; see Plate 31). Or the three colors and materials could be the tesserae themselves, such as blue-green turquoise and black and red stone completely covering a shell base at Aztec Ruin (Figure 6.11; see Plate 32), or blue-green turquoise, white shell, and black stone completely covering a dark chert base at Poncho House Ruin (Guernsey 1931:Plate 1). Only rarely was a fourth material added, such as galena at Aztec Ruin (Figure 6.11; see Plate 32). In addition to their multiple colors and materials, these mosaics were distinguished by their shell and chert bases, overall shapes, tesserae shapes, and depicted designs.

Similar to bead strands, a mosaic's sacred symbolism became more powerful when greater numbers of tesserae and multiple colors and raw materials were used and was amplified further by the supernatural meanings associated with its overall shape, design, and color patterns. For example, circles may have represented the sun; serrated circles, flowers; and zigzag lines, lightning (Crown 1994:133). The most frequent bicolor combination was blue-green turquoise with black stone, which, similar to bead strands, may have signified religious dualism (Teague and Washburn 2013).

In addition to their sacred symbolism, bead strands and mosaics were animated by Made

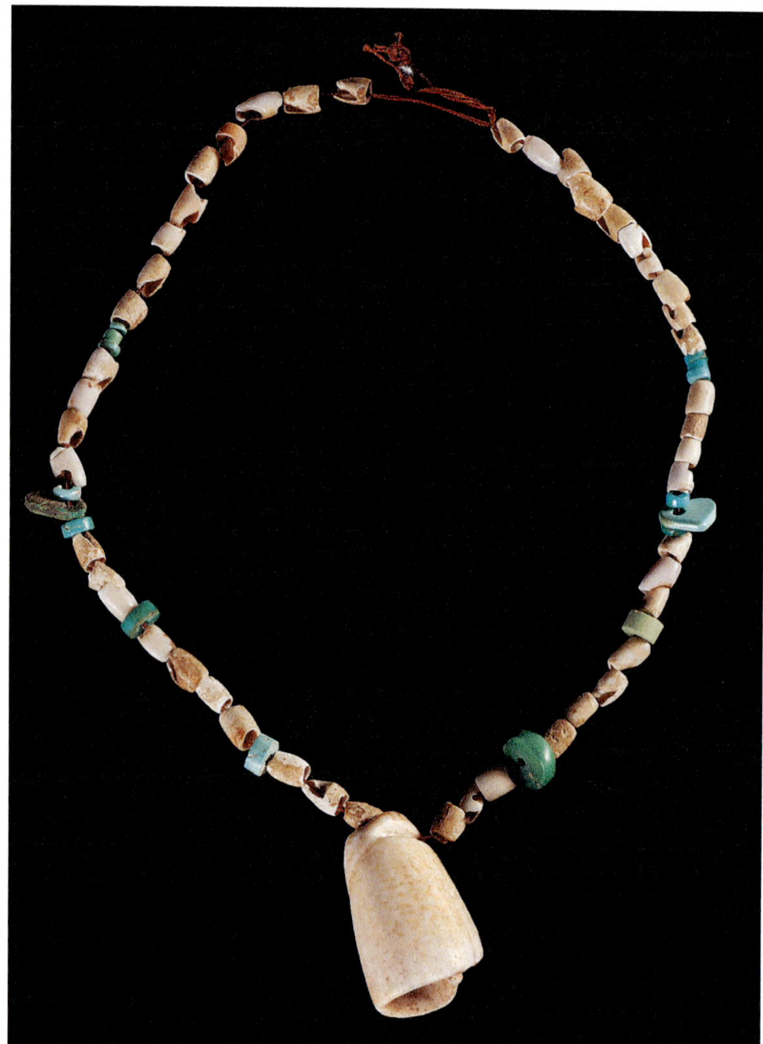

FIGURE 6.9. Necklace with *Olivella* shell and turquoise beads and *Conus* shell pendant. Note variation in *Olivella* beads' colors and sizes and turquoise beads' colors and forms. Pueblo III period, Wupatki. Wupatki National Monument, National Park Service. Catalog number WUPA 25468. Photo by Ryan Belnap and Daniel Boone. Courtesy of Northern Arizona University.

Beings. Before they were combined, each of the component pieces had its own embodied spirit, which could vary depending on the material and form. But juxtaposing greater numbers and different kinds of beads and pendants or tesserae did not simply aggregate their associated Made Beings. Instead, a new, more powerful Being could be created. Studies of katsina imagery suggest that different kinds of bead strands and mosaics may have embodied their own unique Made Beings whose power varied depending on how and by whom the jewelry was used and on the spirits' relative positions in their own nonhuman social system (Ladd 1994).

### Body Adornment

After their crafting was complete, ornaments were ready to be used, typically as bodily adornments for living people. When this function involved high-status persons or occurred during

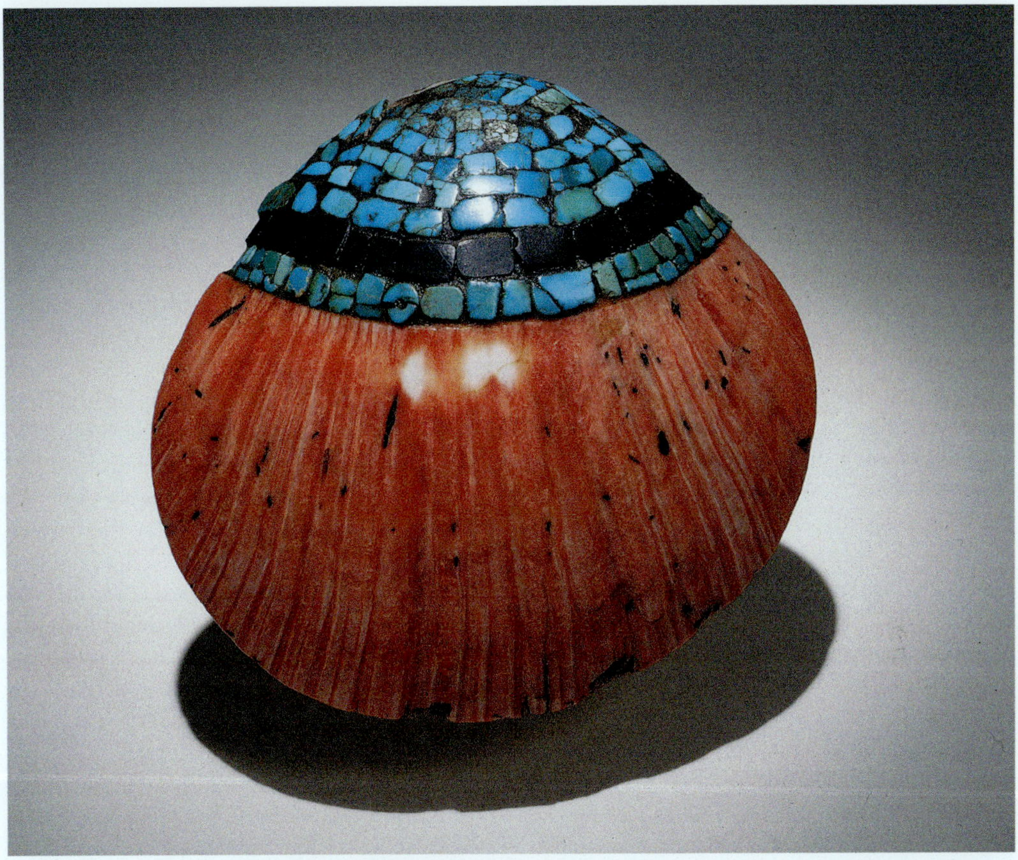

FIGURE 6.10. *Spondylus* shell brooch inlaid with turquoise and jet. Note the shell base's orange color. Pueblo II period, Pueblo Bonito, Chaco Canyon. National Museum of the American Indian, Smithsonian Institution, catalog number 7/1615. Photo by National Museum of the American Indian Photo Services.

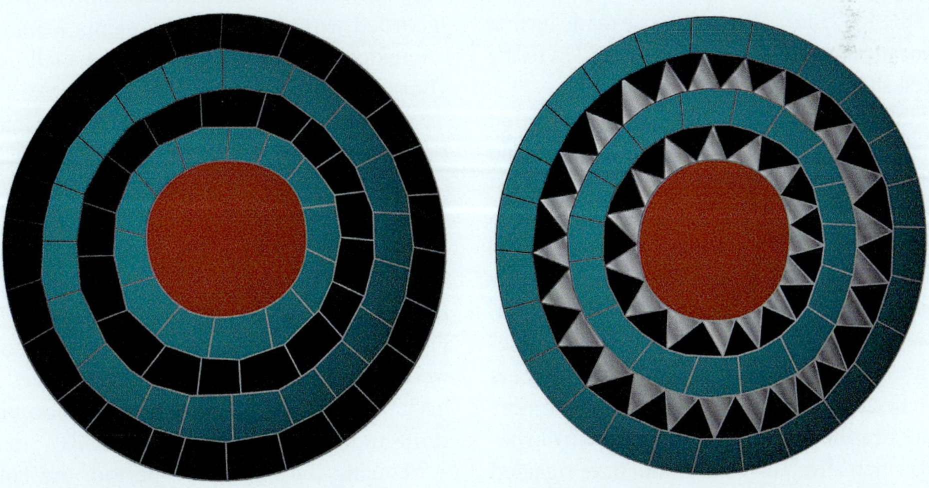

FIGURE 6.11. Brooches inlaid with blue-green turquoise, black and red stone, and silvery galena on shell base. Pueblo III period, Aztec Ruin. Based on Morris 1919a: Figure 73; redrawn and colorized by Robert Schultz.

religious ceremonies, the symbolic content of the jewelry's colors and raw materials increased in both power and scope. The particular contexts within which different kinds of bead strands and mosaics were worn also determined which of their possible Made Beings held sway.

### *High-Status Jewelry*

Ancestral Puebloans who were interred wearing jewelry evidence the synergy between colors, materials, and social status. Data recorded for these burials indicate that while adornments distinguished community members from one another during all periods, the degree of social differentiation varied tremendously (Barnes 2010:Appendix A). The symbolism and animating spirits associated with ornament colors and materials accrued to every adorned person, but new meanings were added for those with high status.

Prior to the Pueblo II period, mortuary adornments were usually few and simple, marking minimal to modest social differences. Basketmaker II period jewelry consisted of necklaces strung with 1–125 beads, mostly white shell followed by seeds, nuts, and black jet (Barnes 2010:271, 277, 288, 291, 293). White shell continued to predominate during the Basketmaker III and Pueblo I periods in necklaces with 1–1,500 beads, bracelets with 1–200 beads, or as a single *Glycymeris* bracelet (Barnes 2010:265, 271, 272, 273, 282, 289, 290). Also, turquoise made its first appearance, with roughly 10 beads added to the longest shell necklace (Barnes 2010:273).

The dramatic societal transformation that occurred in Chaco Canyon by the early Pueblo II period is epitomized by Pueblo Bonito's most richly adorned individual, Burial 14 (Akins 1986:117). This adult man was interred in Room 33, wearing a chest ornament, bracelets on both wrists, and anklets on both legs. All together, this jewelry included more than 6,000 blue-green turquoise beads and pendants, numbers that reflect a shift from modest social differences to elite stratification. By wearing so many ornaments when alive, this man would have signaled that he was much more powerful than both previous leaders and his contemporaries.

Furthermore, the prevalence of blue-green turquoise distinguished Burial 14 from his predecessors as a different kind of leader of a different kind of society. The sacred symbolism of blue-green turquoise and the different ornaments' Made Beings would have legitimized and enhanced Burial 14's ceremonial and sociopolitical roles. The same would have been true for Pueblo Bonito's second richest burial, Burial 14's crypt companion and probable relative, who was buried wearing ornaments entirely of blue-green turquoise (Akins 1986:117; Kennett et al. 2017; Plog and Heitman 2010). Thus, for the Pueblo II period Chacoans, blue-green turquoise acquired the new symbolism of representing elite status and the power of Chaco society as a whole. In comparison, the individual with the most adornments in the Pueblo II period from outside the limits of Chaco society wore a necklace of roughly 60 shell beads and a *Glycymeris* shell bracelet (Barnes 2010:265).

During the Pueblo III period, the major organizational changes that marked the decline of Chaco Canyon and the rise of Aztec Ruin were reflected in elite adornments. Large quantities of predominantly blue-green turquoise ornaments were no longer used to signify high status or Chaco society's power. Instead, the few individuals interred wearing jewelry at Aztec Ruin had much smaller quantities, and the primary material was once again white shell. The person recorded with the most ornaments wore only an anklet composed of 70 *Olivella* shell beads (Barnes 2010:266; Morris 1924:156–157).

The ornaments worn by the richest Sinagua burial were a mix of colors and materials (McGregor 1943). The so-called Magician from Ridge Ruin was adorned with turquoise bracelets and earrings (the latter inlaid with shell), knee bands composed of shell tinklers, and a red argillite nose plug inlaid with turquoise (see Figure 6.1 for example). In addition, his leggings were decorated with lines of shell tinklers and his cap was composed of roughly 4,000 black stone and several hundred shell beads.

During the Pueblo IV period, the colors and materials of mortuary adornments varied with geographic location. In the northern Rio

Grande Valley, Pecos Pueblo's worn jewelry was almost entirely white shell (Barnes 2010:280–281). In contrast, blue-green turquoise was worn most frequently in the southern San Juan Basin at the Ancestral Zuni site of Hawikku (Barnes 2010:273–274). At both pueblos, the numbers of ornaments suggest at most modest status differences—the maximum at Pecos was 200 and, at Hawikku, approximately 50 (Barnes 2010:273–274, 280–281). The prevalence of turquoise at Hawikku may be the historical legacy of Chaco Canyon's influence (Damp 2013). But while the sacred meanings and animating spirits associated with blue-green turquoise endured, the emphatic power symbolism that the color and material acquired during Chaco's heyday did not. In the absence of an elite-based hierarchy, these messages were no longer relevant.

### *Ceremonial Jewelry*

As depicted in Pueblo IV period kiva murals, jewelry was an integral part of Ancestral Pueblo ritual regalia (Dutton 1963; Hibben 1975). These ornaments were sacred objects whose supernatural content originated in their colors and raw materials and was amplified and clarified when worn during ceremonies.

Adornments in the Pottery Mound murals were mostly bead strands wrapped or hung around various parts of the body. Based on their colors, these necklaces, bracelets, and anklets were most frequently white shell, followed by black stone, and occasionally red or orange stone. Sometimes, white and black beads were combined, either alternating within individual strands or with multiple, homogeneous strands (Hibben 1975:Figures 74, 99). Although Pueblo IV period Ancestral Puebloans generally used blue-green turquoise more frequently for jewelry than red or orange stone, the color blue-green rarely appears in kiva murals, perhaps due to technical issues.

This absence raises the question of whether red or orange was a proxy for blue-green. A unique choker necklace with alternating orange and red beads clearly distinguishes the two colors (Hibben 1975:Figure 27). Support for the idea that one of them may have signified blue-green comes from depictions of white and red bird-shaped brooches. The contemporaneous Classic period Hohokam wore the same type of brooch crafted from white shell and blue-green turquoise (Hibben 1975:Figures 1, 35; Jernigan 1978:Plate 4). This concurrence suggests that mosaics and beads illustrated as either red or orange in kiva murals may have been made of blue-green turquoise (Hibben 1975:Cover, Figures 1, 8, 17, 18, 27, 35).

Wearing jewelry during a kiva ceremony amplified the sacred symbolism of its colors and raw materials in multiple ways. These ornaments were part of ritual regalia that included masks, headdresses, body paint, and garments, whose colors and designs were imbued with their own symbolic meanings (Kennard 2002; Roediger 1961; Wade and Evans 1973). The full regalia signaled specific ceremonial roles and prescribed sequences of prayers, songs, dances, processions, offerings, and feasts, each of which was loaded with supernatural significance (Dockstader 1954; Parsons 1939; Stephen 1936). These regalia and ritual activities compounded the jewelry's spiritual content and clarified which of its numerous symbolic meanings were paramount for the particular occasion.

The regalia and ritual activities also determined which of the jewelry's Made Beings predominated. Similar to historic period katsinas, a performer who wore a particular combination of adornments may have temporarily become the Being that animated them in this context and that spirit may have continued to be present in the assemblage after the event ended (Ladd 1994). Consequently, Ancestral Puebloans may have cared for ceremonial jewelry as their historic period descendants did for katsina friends (the term Hopis prefer to "mask") to ensure the Made Beings' physical and spiritual safety and to maintain positive interactions with these nonhuman persons.

### Deposition

Unless an ornament was accidentally lost, its life history ostensibly ended as a ritual offering deposited in a grave, religious structure, or some other sacred context. Ancestral Puebloans used jewelry for oblations due to its symbolism and animating spirits, both of which were amplified one last time by the liturgy of deposition. That finished ornaments were sometimes joined by broken and partially completed beads and pendants, production debris, and unmodified shell and turquoise highlights the fundamental importance of color and raw material and signifies the coexistence of Raw and Made Beings. After concealment, this spiritual power endured for those who knew about the offering's unseen presence, which extended an ornament's biography beyond its quotidian existence (Mills 2008:106–108).

### *Burial Offerings*

Mortuary offerings offer insights into the interaction between social differentiation and jewelry colors and raw materials that are consistent with those discussed previously for adornments worn by interred individuals. But one potentially significant contrast is that dressing the body before burial probably involved the person's own adornments, while offerings made during an interment ceremony or later may have belonged to others and reflected their social roles and agendas. Furthermore, the liturgies required to dress the body and to deposit offerings may have strengthened an ornament's supernatural significance and added new symbolism related to social position in different ways. The same may be true depending on whether an offering was deposited in an individual grave or a burial room at the time of interment or later.

Prior to the Pueblo II period, burial offerings usually consisted of a small number of beads, made of seeds early on and white shell later (Barnes 2010:280, 290). These deposits reflected minimal to modest status differences—the maximum number for seeds was 1,700 and for shell was 500—as well as religious beliefs associated with the ornaments' colors and raw materials. Support for religion's key role comes from the graves of infants and young children, whose offerings exceeded those of adults even though they hadn't lived long enough to distinguish themselves socially (Barnes 2010:272, 279).

The profusion of mortuary offerings that occurred among the Pueblo II period Chacoans is epitomized once again by Pueblo Bonito's Burial 14. More than 6,000 ornaments, of which more than 95% were blue-green turquoise, were added to his grave (Akins 1986:117). Deposited with the 12–14 related individuals interred in the room above his crypt were approximately 30,000 beads, pendants, and tesserae, which were more than 90% blue-green turquoise (Akins 1986:115). Through their quantities, color and raw material symbolism, and animating spirits, these offerings sanctified the unprecedented power of Burial 14 and his family. These messages were reinforced over a span of 300–400 years as additional bodies, more jewelry, and other sacred artifacts were added to the burial room (Akins 1986:115–116, 162; Kennett et al. 2017; Marden 2011:193–195; Plog and Heitman 2010:19622–19623).

At Pueblo III period Aztec Ruin, the quantities of jewelry deposited with some burials and in some burial rooms may have equaled those at Pueblo Bonito. But a change in how elites signified and sanctified their power can be seen in the mix of colors and raw materials. For example, the adult who wore the shell anklet was covered with beads and pendants made of shell, turquoise, jet, and bone (Barnes 2010:266–267; Morris 1924:155–156). Near him was a bird effigy jar containing 31,000 minute black disk beads (Morris 1924:154–156; also, Barnes 2010:268). Other offerings in this burial room included a cache of 8,500 pink stone beads and additional deposits that were roughly equal proportions of shell, turquoise, and stone (Barnes 2010:266–269; Morris 1924:99–100, 158).

Ornaments added to the Magician's burial at Ridge Ruin were also characterized by a mix of colors and materials (McGregor 1943). The view that these were sacred objects is reinforced by their association with a rich assemblage of ritual artifacts that may have represented the Magician's various ceremonial roles (O'Hara 2015). Furthermore, the inclusion of whole and fragmentary shell signifies the symbolic importance of colors and raw materials as well as the co-presence of Made and Raw Beings (Figure 2.4). The Magician's jewelry offerings are notable for their turquoise and shell mosaics, and several of his ceremonial sticks were also inlaid with turquoise and shell. This frequent use of turquoise, and especially an armband inlaid with more than 1,500 pieces of the blue-green material, may be evidence of Chaco's enduring legacy, as the armband resembles an inlaid basket interred with Pueblo Bonito's Burial 14.

Black stone dominated offerings in rich burials at other Pueblo III period sites. At a small site associated with a Chaco Great House in southwest Colorado, an adult female was interred with approximately 7,000 ornaments, which were two-thirds black stone and one-third turquoise (Barnes 2010:272). At the Kayenta site of RB568, an adult female was interred with a necklace of 50,400 beads and an adult male with an armband composed of 39,000 beads (Crotty 1983:32–23, 79, 83–85). More than 90% of both burials' ornament offerings were black stone, followed by red stone and turquoise (Crotty 1983:63).

As with worn jewelry, the colors and raw materials of Pueblo IV period offerings varied with geographic location. White shell again dominated in the northern Rio Grande Valley, comprising almost all deposits at the transitional Pueblo III–IV period site of Forked Lightning, and roughly two-thirds of those at Pecos Pueblo, where the rest were bone and turquoise (Barnes 2010:273, 280–282). Blue-green turquoise was again most frequent at the Ancestral Zuni site of Hawikku, but at roughly 40%, it was less dominant than shell in the northern Rio Grande Valley (Barnes 2010:273–277). Hawikku's secondary materials were shell and bone.

These Pueblo IV period oblations also indicate varying degrees of social differentiation. It was most pronounced at Forked Lightning where the maximum offering size was 5,000 white shell beads, and less so at Pecos Pueblo, where the maximum was roughly 300 beads that were mostly bone, followed by turquoise and shell (Barnes 2010:273, 280). In contrast, the largest offering at Hawikku consisted of just 39 turquoise and 5 shell beads (Barnes 2010:275). While this emphasis on turquoise may be further evidence of Chaco's enduring legacy, the offering's small size highlights the disappearance of powerful elites and the expanded meanings that had previously been associated with their jewelry.

### *Kiva Offerings*

Ancestral Puebloans deposited ornaments and related materials in religious structures because they were sacred objects. The fact that most great kiva and kiva offerings were composed primarily, if not entirely, of these items is compelling evidence of their spiritual value, which originated in the symbolism and animating spirits of their colors and raw materials. This supernatural content was amplified one last time by all aspects of the objects' placement—the ceremonial setting, the particulars of the occasion, and the liturgy of concealment.

In contrast with burials, great kiva and kiva oblations included partially crafted and broken ornaments, production debris, and unmodified materials much more often. While an offering of finished jewelry may have "dressed" the structure, which may itself have been a living presence (Mills 2008:91, 98), the related items could not be have been "worn." All forms may have been treated as equal because of their mutual involvement in the ritual production of ornaments (Mills 2008:98–99) as well as their shared color and raw material symbolism and animating spirits. These spirits would have included both Made and Raw Beings, which, depending on circumstances, could have coalesced into a singular, more powerful one.

Another contrast with burials is that great kiva and kiva deposits involved ceremonies related to the structures and their associated groups rather than to specific individuals. When placed below support beams, by benches, and on floors, offerings commemorated the rooms' initial construction, remodeling, and closure (Heitman 2015; Mattson 2016; Mills 2008). However, objects left in great kiva wall niches may have been periodically removed for ceremonies that ceased when the compartment was sealed.

Offerings in the earliest great kivas, which date to the Basketmaker III period in Chaco Canyon and the Pueblo I period outside the Canyon, contained just one to four items (Lightfoot et al. 1988; Mathien 2001:111; Roberts 1929; Windes 2015:111). Placed on or near benches, they included turquoise mosaic pieces, complete and fragmentary beads made of turquoise, shell, or bone, and unmodified turquoise. This diversity in colors, materials, and forms could represent different kinds of rituals, different groups, or (given the small numbers) simply what happened to be available at the time.

The ceremonial elaboration that was integral to Chaco society's unprecedented power during the Pueblo II period was manifested in the construction of increased numbers of great kivas and new, smaller kivas. Offerings placed in the two types of structures, as well as in different contexts within each, probably involved different kinds of ceremonies or different groups. Great kiva caches were generally larger, more diverse in their colors, materials, and forms, and placed in more varied contexts than in earlier great kivas and contemporaneous smaller kivas. In stark contrast with Pueblo Bonito's mortuary jewelry, both worn and added, blue-green turquoise did not predominate in either great kiva or kiva offerings. Instead, both finished ornaments and related items were variable mixes of white shell, blue-green turquoise, and black jet that were sometimes joined in great kivas by other kinds of ritual artifacts. This mixing indicates that the religious associations of great kivas and kivas differed, perhaps in complementary ways, from those of Chaco's elites and of the society as a whole.

Great kiva wall niches epitomize the diversity that could characterize offerings placed in the same type of context in the same type of structure. A compartment at Pueblo Bonito contained more than 250 ritual objects together with an assortment of 40 pendants, beads, bead blanks, mosaic pieces, worked fragments, and matrix, which were mostly blue-green turquoise, followed by white shell, bone, and slate (Judd 1954:323–324; Mills 2008:91–92, 94). In contrast, 10 wall niches at Chetro Ketl contained the previously mentioned long strands of black jet and white shell beads (the longest was more than 5 m, and the total bead count exceeded 17,000) along with a few shells and pieces of turquoise (Figure 6.8, and see Hewett 1936:87, 89–92; Mills 2008:88–90, 92). Further variation can be seen in other great kiva contexts at Chetro Ketl, whose offerings included leather bags filled with pulverized turquoise, jet and calcite beads with turquoise fragments, and bead strands and loose beads whose numbers and materials are unknown (Heitman 2015:227–228; Mills 2008:90–92).

The more limited and less diverse offerings placed in Chaco Canyon's small kivas included variable mixes of colors, materials, and forms along with an occasional non-jewelry item (Mattson 2016). For example, deposits at Pueblo Bonito contained different combinations of whole and fragmentary *Glycymeris* bracelets, turquoise, shell, and bone beads, broken pendants, probably made of shell and turquoise, worked turquoise and azurite, *Haliotis* shell, raw azurite, a hematite cylinder, and a duck bill (Judd 1954:322, Plate 89, 1964:184–186, 191–193; Mills 2008:95–96). At Pueblo del Arroyo, a kiva's pilasters contained approximately 450 whole and fragmentary beads and pendants made of turquoise and shell, turquoise mosaic pieces, and ornament production debris (Judd 1959: 60–62; Mills 2008:96–97).

During the Pueblo III period, the sizes and diversity of great kiva and kiva offerings declined at Chaco sites along the Middle San Juan River. At Aztec Ruin's great kiva, one deposit included shell beads, worked turquoise, and turquoise fragments, and another, a strand of *Olivella* shells, a turquoise pendant, and turquoise beads and mosaic pieces (Mathien 2001: 111–112; Mills 2008:92; Morris 1921:133). Salmon Ruin's offerings included numerous calcite beads and two pieces of turquoise in the great kiva and stone beads in the tower kiva (Reed 2006:153, 234).

With the dissolution of Chaco society and consequent closing of its great kivas, small kivas became the Ancestral Puebloans' primary religious structure during the Pueblo IV period. In the Rio Grande Valley, ritual offerings continued, but included ornaments and related items only rarely and in very small numbers. Nevertheless, they were sacred objects whose color and raw material symbolism and animating spirits were strengthened one last time by their ritual placement in a ceremonial room. A kiva at Tijeras Pueblo had two very small turquoise fragments and a mosaic inlaid with turquoise, shell, and hematite (Schuyler 2010). Offerings at the Leaf Water site in the Chama River Valley consisted of just two small pieces of raw turquoise (Luebben 1953). Post-occupational fill in Pottery Mound's kivas included small numbers of bone beads and other ornament-related items that may have commemorated the structures' closure (Schuyler 2016).

## Conclusion

The colors and raw materials of Ancestral Pueblo jewelry were inseparable—one simply did not exist without the other. As such, the sacred content of any ornament was multifaceted and powerful. The separate but overlapping sets of symbolic meanings associated with its color and material fused, and their religious significance was compounded by the material's animating spirits. While visibility and workability would have certainly been important practical considerations in selecting a particular color and raw material to make, for example, a bead or pendant, metaphysical qualities were probably just as compelling.

From initial procurement to final deposition, the activities, products, and contexts of each stage of an ornament's life history amplified the supernatural force of its colors and raw materials. The crafting process also transformed the materials' animating spirits from Raw to Made Beings. When a bead necklace or mosaic brooch was worn, its spiritual power was further strengthened by the presence of other adornments, the sounds the jewelry made when the person moved, the symbolism conveyed by the person's garments, the setting, and the occasion. When whole and broken ornaments, production debris, and raw materials were deposited as ritual offerings, their spiritual power was reinforced by the setting, the occasion, and all aspects of the liturgy—the sights, sounds, smells, participants, regalia, and choreography.

From the perspective of Ancestral Puebloans as a whole, the relative importance of different combinations of color and raw material was characterized by continuity, change, and variation. White shell was consistently most important through time. The peak for blue-green turquoise was among the Pueblo II period Chacoans, for whom it sanctified the unprecedented power of certain individuals, particular families, and the society as a whole. Chaco's legacy may be evident during the Pueblo III period in the Sinagua Magician's burial and during the Pueblo IV period at Hawikku. But elsewhere other colors and materials predominated or were combined.

Within these broad trends, a particular group's ornaments were almost always a variable mix of colors and raw materials. This co-occurrence was significant both in its presence and relative proportions. For example, when jewelry was worn, even a small number of secondary or tertiary colors and materials conveyed important information about different aspects of the person's societal roles, cultural identity, and probably much more. And the use of a rare color or material would have been especially eye-catching and effective in broadcasting these and other messages. The same was probably true for the diverse hues that characterized particular raw materials. As the illustrations in this chapter show, describing shell as white or turquoise as blue-green obscures considerable variation that would have been even more obvious to Ancestral Puebloans who encountered ornaments throughout their daily lives.

Future research on the conjunction of jewelry colors and raw materials will certainly be grounded in analyses of archaeological data, but religious interpretations will depend on ethnographic accounts of living descendants. Topics with great promise include variation in hues, sheen, and inclusions, recurrent combinations, correspondences with different forms, arrangements, and designs, and contextual patterns in burials, great kivas, and kivas. Conclusions about symbolic meanings and animating spirits will in turn contribute to more general questions about Ancestral Pueblo cosmology, rituals, and religion's role in leadership and sociopolitical relations. Patterns evident within and between contemporaneous sites and over time should illuminate broader cultural trends.

As with all studies of the ancient past, our understanding of jewelry's sacred content has limits. In the absence of written records, we will probably never be able to itemize with confidence any ornament's specific array of symbolic meanings. And while we can describe shell, turquoise, and black and red stone as being animated by spirits, comprehending what this means from an emic perspective is admittedly a challenge. Still, these constraints do not diminish the tremendous potential that jewelry colors and raw materials have for expanding our knowledge and appreciation of the Ancestral Pueblo world.

CONCLUSION

# The Chromatic Past

Marit K. Munson and Kelley Hays-Gilpin

Our survey of two millennia of color in the Pueblo Southwest demonstrates that Pueblo ancestors deployed colorful materials to enliven their personal adornments, household goods, buildings, and special places in the landscape. They lived in a colorful world, and their uses of color changed and varied across time, space, media, and contexts of use. In this chapter, we provide a chronological survey of the key aspects of color across the Ancestral Puebloan Southwest, highlighting the chromatic florescence of the 1300s. We then explore the enduring cultural contexts of colorful materials and imagery and the deliberate deployment of color as animate, transforming, and deeply meaningful in Ancestral Puebloan lives.

## Cross-Media Comparison and Temporal Patterns

Color choices varied widely across the Ancestral Pueblo world; rather than following a linear trajectory from simple to complex, the use of color ebbed and flowed, with different individuals and communities using color—and relating to colorful materials—in diverse ways. Basketmakers, for example, seem to have lived subtly colorful lives, drawing on a varied palette of locally available materials to enliven basketry, textiles, rock art and sometimes pottery. While bichrome combinations were typical of the Pueblo I–III periods, jewelry, mosaics, pigments, and elaborately painted paraphernalia found in Chaco Canyon and some Sinagua sites make it clear that early Pueblo people used polychrome combinations in elite contexts. Similarly, Ancestral Puebloans maintained an important distinction between black and white and polychrome even into the 1400s and beyond, displaying both black and white textiles and more colorfully painted cloths in the kiva murals of Pottery Mound (Hibben 1975:122–123, Figure 94). Clearly, Pueblo ancestors were always fully capable of coloring their world polychrome—but they made thoughtful choices about when and how to do so.

### *The Basketmaker Palette*

Research on Basketmaker period sites suggests that early farmers used colors derived from a diverse group of materials throughout their daily lives. Red and black were the most common colors across all media, probably because they were readily available. The array of colorful materials found in Basketmaker sites suggests that they did not necessarily favor any particular color or material over another.

Beads and other ornaments, for example, were made from materials such as white shell, black lignite, white limestone, red and green shale, green serpentine, red hematite, and white quartz and alabaster (Guernsey and Kidder 1921:47–48). Basketmaker rock paintings used a similarly broad palette, including red, green, yellow, white, and pink—more colors, in fact, than rock paintings from any other time until the Pueblo IV period. Despite the diverse range of available colors, painters did not use these hues to add detail or increase realism, as was typical in later Pueblo IV rock paintings. In fact, the most colorful rock paintings of this period are simple handprints.

Designs on textiles and basketry could be created by weaving, twining, or plaiting colored fiber into the structure of the object itself, or by painting directly on the finished item. In some cases, both techniques were used on the same piece (Guernsey and Kidder 1921:70). Baskets and textiles of the Basketmaker II period were generally decorated with simple black geometric patterns; by the Basketmaker III period, however, these objects displayed more color diversity. Most were decorated with black and red polychrome designs, both woven and painted, consisting of stripes or geometric patterns set against the yellowish background of natural fiber (Kent 1983:211; Morris and Burgh 1941). A few examples of painted textiles used up to four different colors, including yellow, dark blue, shiny black, and pink (Kent 1983:36–39, 211).

Twined Basketmaker III period sandals of the Four Corners area often display paired bands of bichrome geometric patterns, made with yucca fiber dyed red and yellow, paired with black or blue and white or tan. Teague and Washburn (2013:63–72) argue that these four-color, counterchange designs were connected with ritual activities relating to the movement of the sun and to the four directions as marked by the sunrises and sunsets of summer and winter solstices.

In contrast to textiles and rock painting, pottery dating to the Basketmaker II and III periods was generally plain brown or gray, sometimes with black paint and occasionally with red fugitive paint or slip late in the sequence (AD 600s–800s). It seems possible that the limited palette of early ceramics was determined in large part by the technical challenges of creating colors that would survive the firing process. However, other objects were also colored with red and black, such as dart shafts and hafted points from White Dog Cave (Guernsey and Kidder 1921:85–86). This suggests that the application of pigment or paint was a significant act that was meaningful in its own right, beyond mere decoration. Indeed, numerous Basketmaker period burials include small bags of pigments and paints as offerings or personal possessions of the dead, supporting the idea that the materials themselves were meaningful.

### *Pueblo I–III Palettes*

In contrast to earlier Basketmaker patterns, most media in the Pueblo I–III periods tended toward simple bichrome combinations. There was, however, some experimentation with ceramic color and significant use of polychromy in exceptional places such as Chaco Canyon and Sinagua sites.

Pueblo I–III wall paintings and rock paintings were made primarily with locally available clays and minerals in a range of reds, tans, browns, blacks, and whites. Such colorants would not have required a great deal of effort to obtain nor specialized knowledge to apply. Wall paintings, extremely rare during the Pueblo II period, were much more extensive in the subsequent Pueblo III period. This is particularly true in the Mesa Verde region, where the walls of kivas, rooms, and towers were painted with dado-triangle-dot designs or textile-type patterns.

Whether painting on rock faces or within rooms, most Pueblo II–III artists produced low-contrast designs and images with relatively subdued visual impact. A few more colorful paintings were created in locations where a wider range of colors was available. In some cases, color choices seem to reflect practical considerations relating to visibility, as in large-scale white shields painted at sites in defensive locations. In other contexts, white clays may have been chosen in order to reference clouds and cotton, which became increasingly significant in the Ancestral Pueblo world after AD 1100 (Teague 1998:24–26).

Red and white or various clay-based browns and tans were typical of most wall paintings, so perhaps it is not surprising that archaeologists have recorded few pigments and paints other than iron-based reds in Pueblo I–III sites. The application of a single color on a solid background seems to have been a deliberate choice on the part of painters, as they could easily have added detail using a contrasting color if they had wished to do so. This differs significantly from the Pueblo IV use of colors to highlight details or add to the realism of images.

Overall, the colors of ornaments seem to have been relatively limited at most Pueblo I–III sites, usually involving white, blue-green, black and red. Over time, white shell was the most common material, though at different times and places other colors and materials predominated and were mixed in varying proportions. As discussed below, the most dramatic was the prevalence of blue-green turquoise in Pueblo II period Chaco Canyon. During the Pueblo III period, black stone dominated two Kayenta and Mesa Verde sites, and a variety of colors and materials were combined in Aztec Ruin's burial rooms and Burial 16 at the Sinagua site of Ridge Ruin, also discussed later in this chapter.

Pottery traditions in the Pueblo I–III periods were dominated by fairly simple color combinations, albeit with higher contrast than most rock paintings and murals. By Pueblo I potters were adding white slips to ensure visibility of black-painted designs. Black-on-orange then black-on-red slipped pottery appeared in southeast Utah in the Pueblo I era, then spread more widely in the 900s and 1000s. Black-on-white and black-on-red pottery required specific materials and technical knowledge but was also relatively straightforward to produce. Once potters mastered the process, they produced bichrome vessels with relatively little variation or evident experimentation.

While the colors and materials used in Pueblo I–III media surely had important connotations and meanings for the individuals using them, most can be seen as a relatively expedient means of creating an image, decorating a pot, or evoking clouds and rain. However, the bichrome "rule" of the Pueblo I–III periods had two major exceptions: the extensive polychromy in elite contexts at Chaco and Sinagua sites, and potters' experimentation with new color combinations in the Western Pueblo area.

### Chaco Polychromy

In Chaco Canyon, that most exceptional of Southwestern places, the selective use of polychrome was an important element in elite contexts. Archaeologists working at Chaco encountered numerous ceremonial offerings, elite burials, and caches of religious paraphernalia, especially in Pueblo Bonito and other Great Houses (Duff et al. 2017:777; Heitman 2015:225–227). The bright and varied colors within these special contexts created a lasting impression on these researchers (e.g., Judd 1954:323), as they must have done for the canyon's original inhabitants a thousand years earlier.

Assembling precious materials and crafting them into powerful objects would have required a great deal of labor, time, and skill. Turquoise, the quintessential material of the Chacoan world, came from the Cerrillos Hills and other distant sources (Duff et al. 2017:778; Hull et al. 2014), then was cut, shaped, and polished at small sites and in Great Houses. Used alone or in combination with other meaningful materials, turquoise was transformed into items as diverse as bead necklaces, effigies of frogs, and mosaics on basketry, bone scrapers, and jewelry.

A variety of paints contributed to the rich symbolism of ritual paraphernalia at Chaco, such as the painted wooden birds and lightning lattice from Chetro Ketl (Vivian et al. 1978) and a painted stone mortar from Pueblo Bonito (Pepper 1920:264–267). Even the black-on-white cylinder jars recovered within the canyon may have been more colorful than they first appear, with hachure potentially standing in for blue-green (Plog 2003). Some of the jars were apparently reworked and renewed through the addition of new designs in black carbon paint and sometimes fugitive red paint as well (Crown and Wills 2003). Above all, assemblages associated with elite burials illustrate the use of extensive polychromy for ritual purposes, particularly in the complex burial deposits in the northern and western crypts at Pueblo Bonito (Plog and Heitman 2010), which contained large quantities of ritually and ceremonially significant objects.

How Chacoans thought of their colorful materials is difficult to know for certain. Was turquoise valued primarily as a tangible substance? Was azurite appreciated for its color, in an abstract sense? Were the feathers of a scarlet macaw meaningful because they evoked the birds' southern origins, combined with the symbolism of red and an unusually striking saturation and intensity of color? The prevalence of white kaolin and similar pigments, combined with the use of shell in creating ornaments, may suggest that white was valued, at least in part, as an abstract color.

At the same time, the pigments and paints used by the Chacoans do not seem to have been especially highly valued in their own right. Colorants were processed and prepared in expedient fashion, without the use of much specialized equipment (Judd 1954:285). And although raw pigments and paints were sometimes included in ritual deposits or burial assemblages (e.g., Judd 1954:323–324), colorants occur in small quantities that seem incidental when compared to the great quantities of turquoise, shell, and jet (Heitman 2015:225).

Chacoans may, however, have paid some attention to particular hues, as there is some evidence of varied preferences for different colors of turquoise. At Pueblo Alto, for example, most of the turquoise was toward the blue end of the spectrum (Mathien and Windes 1987a:423), while differences in the distribution of bluer versus greener turquoise within Pueblo Bonito may have reflected aspects of social identity, such as gender and group membership (Mattson 2016:130–131).

Regardless of hue, turquoise seems to have become an especially significant marker in the Chacoan world, not just of elite status of certain individuals, but, as Neitzel and Witt argue in Chapter 6, of "a different kind of society." The ideals and beliefs of that society, it seems, were built upon and expressed by an array of colorful materials, in the form of jewelry, mosaics, basketry, decorated tools, and painted wooden paraphernalia. Ceremonial or cosmologically significant deposits, such as caches or offerings in elite burials and in Great House architecture, included large quantities of raw turquoise, turquoise debris, and both finished and incomplete turquoise ornaments, as well as jet, black stone beads, and white shell, supplemented with macaw feathers and copper bells from the south. Color in the Chacoan world, it seems, centered on visually striking materials, often obtained from a great distance or from specific sources within the broader Chacoan landscape, used under the supervision of specialized religious leaders and elites.

### Sinagua Polychromy

A similar pattern appears to have extended beyond the Pueblo II period and into sites (contemporaneous with the Pueblo III period) in the Sinagua region, where colorful ornaments, pigments, and specialized ritual items were associated with religious leadership. This is most evident in Burial 16, the so-called Magician, at Ridge Ruin (McGregor 1943), although less elaborate burials from Nalakihu (King 1949:76, 107) and Lizard Man Village (Kamp and Whittaker 1990:114) also support the idea that certain Sinagua individuals held positions of religious or ceremonial leadership, facilitated in part through color (Kamp and Whittaker 1990:116).

Ridge Ruin's Burial 16 included more than 600 items, ranging from foodstuffs and tools to containers of pottery, basketry, and shell. Many of the items were elaborately decorated, including colorful stone and shell mosaics, a painted *Conus* shell ornament, a painted wooden cup, and a number of carved and painted staffs, rods, and arrows. The range of colors and variety of materials in the assemblage is stunning (Figure 2.4).

Many of the items from Burial 16 are similar to those from earlier contexts in the Chacoan world, including polychrome painted wooden plaques like those from Chetro Ketl, a mosaic-covered basketry armband that is similar to a basket from Pueblo Bonito, and painted, clay-coated baskets that appear to have antecedents at Chaco and Aztec Ruins (Neitzel 2017:Figure 3.8; Odegaard and Hays-Gilpin 2002). Turquoise, in the form of jewelry, mosaics, and effigies, was common in Burial 16, just as it was in the Chacoan world; two brightly colored parrots were placed in the same room as the burial. This evidence, combined with some aspects of the architecture of Ridge Ruin, suggests that polychromy in elite Sinagua contexts may be an important element within a broader Chacoan legacy.

In contrast, Sinagua pottery appears drab at first glance. Locally produced Sinagua vessels were plain brown or slipped red, often with deliberately polished and smudged interiors, perhaps a meaningful color treatment in its own right. Indeed, fire clouds and oxidized patches were frequent, and might have served as deliberate decorative elements, the way Hopi potters today value the "blush" or orange mottling produced by variations in firing atmosphere and temperature.

Sinagua pottery assemblages were in fact more colorful than suggested by simple brown or red ware alone. Some locally produced pottery bears white exterior designs, and some mimics the red-on-buff of Hohokam pottery from the south. At larger villages, like Ridge Ruin and Elden Pueblo, people imported large amounts of black-on-white, black-on-red, and orange polychrome pottery from their neighbors to the northeast. Clearly, some Sinagua communities were colorful places, incorporating aspects of Hohokam, Mogollon, and Colorado Plateau traditions into a unique post-Chaco world.

#### Ceramic Polychromy in the Pueblo III Period

Although most Pueblo III pottery was bichrome (especially black-on-white jars and black-on-red bowls), potters in the Kayenta, Hopi, Zuni, and White Mountain areas began experimenting with color around AD 1125 or 1150, creating increasing quantities of red- and orange-based polychrome. The advent of polychrome pottery required different materials and firing conditions than making black-on-white pottery (with rare exceptions, such as the iron-free clays from the Acoma area). Throughout the 1200s and into the 1300s, these colorful new traditions expanded in both range and variety, spreading throughout the Pueblo world.

At about the same time, the Pueblo world changed (Adams 1991; Adams and Duff 2004; Crown 1994). Drought, migration, aggregation into large, plaza-oriented pueblos, and the coming together of people from different cultural and linguistic backgrounds sparked innovation and change. Former cultural boundaries dissolved (Glowacki and Van Keuren 2011), and many aspects of the Pueblo world became far more colorful.

### *The Pueblo IV Period Palette*

The use of polychrome by ritual specialists in the Pueblo II–III periods foreshadowed the florescence of color in the Pueblo IV period, when media across the Ancestral Pueblo world were marked by "radical changes in artistic styles and aesthetic values" (Brody 1991:81). Archaeological evidence suggests that this florescence was complex and widespread, with close parallels in the symbolism, religions, and ritual practices of historic and contemporary Pueblo groups. Many aspects of color that are documented in the ethnographic literature seem to have fallen in place during the Pueblo IV period, perhaps as early as AD 1300, when Pueblo ancestors began to adopt new religious practices and transformed their world in ways both colorful and profound.

Notable ancestral and historic period correspondences include the mimetic symbolism of colors, such as the multicolored rainbows in Picuris' murals, black and white eagle feathers in murals at Kuaua, and red scarlet macaws in Pottery Mound's murals. In rockshelters near Abo Pueblo, paintings of star katsinas include blue-green yucca whips, while other rock paintings depict Morningstar and warriors with black faces and red four-pointed stars. Though petroglyphs are not normally thought of as colored, certain star depictions at San Cristóbal were stained with red pigment.

The contexts in which some colors were used in the Pueblo IV period suggest additional parallels to the historic Pueblos. Colors used in painted rockshelters, for kiva murals, or for the paraphernalia and activities of religious societies were probably restricted to knowledgeable individuals who had access to specific materials and to the specialized knowledge and expertise required to use them. In other cases, common people might use the same color (but perhaps not the same materials?) at feasts and other public events, wearing colorful textiles and jewelry, applying face or body paint, and displaying bright pottery and perhaps basketry as visible signs of their place of origin, status, or society membership (Mills 2007a).

The application of paint, and its accumulation over time, seems to have been quite meaningful in Pueblo IV contexts. In some rockshelters, for example, artists layered paint over and over again, until it became nearly impossible to distinguish individual images among the general wash of color. The process was akin to that of replastering kivas to refresh the walls and obscure existing murals, which suggests that the process of painting—and the presence of the paint itself—was more important than the creation of legible and durable images (Munson 2011). Some of the same rockshelters include both spattered and stamped handprints, recalling the rich symbolism of paint sprayed from the mouth, or the handprints and other designs smeared onto the beams of a kiva at Hopi in order to pull down the clouds and bring rain. Paint sprayed and splattered on iconographically rich Sikyatki polychromes and the droplets of water depicted in kiva murals at Kuaua evoke similar meanings, calling to mind the central Pueblo principle of like causing like.

Pueblo IV potters showed exquisite control over and understanding of their materials, manipulating clays, slips, paints, and firing conditions to produce a stunning array of colors and effects. This included, for the first time, yellow slips, which had long been technically possible but were never common before AD 1300. Potters also created glaze paints, produced from recipes incorporating compounds of lead, copper, and manganese. These melted into bright, glossy colors, including deep purples and greens that were not previously possible on fired vessels (Cordell and Habicht-Mauche 2012). Potters painted new icons on their vessels, even though the designs were sometimes obscured by the unpredictable drips, bubbles, and runs of the glazes. In fact, potters in the seventeenth-century Rio Grande Valley seem to have embraced a new looseness in their pottery painting, whether for pragmatic reasons, such as obscuring icons from the prying eyes of outsiders (Spielmann et al. 2006), or simply because they began to embrace a more process-oriented approach that deemphasized perfection in the painted line.

The diverse colors used in Pueblo IV murals served to define and highlight images, as well as to add symbolic meanings derived from various combinations of color and material. Like Pueblo IV potters and painters creating rock art, mural painters chose a wide range of techniques for applying paint, including brushes, dry-brushing, outlining, spattering, over-painting, smudging, scraping, and incising. As discussed in Chapter 4, Patricia Vivian's descriptions of painting techniques demonstrate that mural painters were fully engaged with the process, using a variety of tools and techniques to combine dry pigments and paints of different consistencies and opacities.

In contrast with the more straightforward painting style of Pueblo III, the act of creating Pueblo IV murals was an involved and time-consuming process, as if the movements of layering and outlining and scraping and spraying and incising created not only chromatic prayers but kinetic ones as well, embodied by the painters themselves. Even flat washes of color, without imagery, might have transformed ordinary rooms into sacred spaces, as in the fourteenth-century southern Sinagua cliff dwelling of Montezuma Castle, where interior walls of several rooms have specially prepared clay washes in red, yellow, and white (Guebard et al. 2018).

Even as polychromes flourished in the Pueblo IV period, Ancestral Pueblo people maintained a purposeful opposition between black and white pottery and textiles on one hand and black-on-red or polychrome counterparts on the other. A mural at Pottery Mound, for example, depicts polychrome blankets hanging from the wall, alternating with black and white dyed textiles (Hibben 1975:122–123, Figure 94). The polychrome textiles probably were painted (Webster 2007). Some have designs similar to banded black, red, and white decorations found on contemporaneous Rio Grande Glaze A pottery. Others resemble those seen on Sikyatki

Polychrome and Pottery Mound Polychrome, the latter being a kind of Glaze A with Sikyatki-style designs.

The same murals also show black and white textiles with grid-based, geometric designs such as the dot-in-square pattern or fields of white circles. These were probably produced with a tie-dye or resist dye technique, rather than with paints applied to their surfaces. Antecedents can be found in the sparse textile assemblages of Chaco, Aztec, Canyon de Chelly, and the Verde Valley site of Palatki (Webster et al. 2006), with more ancient tie-dyes found in Mexico.

Laurie Webster (2007) has suggested that the diverse inhabitants of Pottery Mound might have used textiles to recount histories of migration. Others suggest these textiles were associated with transmission of ritual sodalities by means of small-scale and short-term movements (Hays-Gilpin et al. 2018; Ware 2013). In both scenarios, people from the south were associated with tie-dye and weft-wrap openwork textile traditions, and those from the north were tied to long-standing traditions of polychrome painted textiles. It is tempting to see the black and white textiles as evocative of clouds and rain, while the polychromes might symbolize the vibrant Flower World (Hays-Gilpin et al. 2010; Hill and Hays-Gilpin 1999). It is also possible that the contrast reflected other distinctions, such as differences between elites and commoners, the presence of dual tribal sodalities (e.g., the Tewa Summer and Winter people), or a day- and night-based cycle of ritual responsibilities.

## Meanings and Persistence

Everyone wants to know, "what do colors mean?" But meaning is a challenging subject. We are reminded of that whenever we step inside the Museum of Northern Arizona's new collection center, which houses Native American artifacts and contemporary artwork. When local tribes were invited to consult about its design, they requested, among other features, a pattern in the floor to depict the colors of the four directions. The architect readily agreed, asking which colors and which directions. The Navajo consultants described one set of colors and directions; the Hopi consultants requested another. What to do? The architect designed a figure that places Hopi colors in four quarters of a circle, with the Navajo colors radiating outward.

The most interesting aspect of the Museum of Northern Arizona design collaboration was (and still is) listening to consultants explain the directional colors to visitors. The Hopi representatives start in the northwest with the color yellow, then move counterclockwise to blue in the southwest, red in the southeast, and white in the northeast. The Navajos start in the east with the color white, then move clockwise to turquoise blue in the south, yellow in the west, and black in the north. This clockwise pattern is shared by almost all Native North Americans in the northern part of the United States and throughout Canada, while the Hopi share the counterclockwise pattern with most other neighboring cultures in the Southwest, Southeast, and Latin America (DeBoer 2005). This, then, is what anthropologists can say about colors and directions: all Native Americans have traditions of directional symbolism, but they differ in emphasizing cardinal versus intercardinal directions, clockwise versus counterclockwise circuits, and the particular colors associated with each direction.

Is it any wonder, then, that archaeologists cannot reconstruct a consistent and persistent key to the meanings of particular colors in the ancient Pueblo world? After all, color symbolism is, by its nature, flexible and multifaceted, ideal for creating poetic nuances and subtle shadings of meaning.

As just one example, yellow has a great variety of connotations in Pueblo expression. Yellow is the quintessential flowery color, and yellow flowers may represent "all flowers, sacred pollen, and summer weather and the growing season" (Hays-Gilpin et al. 2010:123). In the Zuni language, these meanings are expressed through a verb form for yellow that refers to "any ripened or aged yellow object;" when used as a plural, however, "it is specialized to refer to pollen or corn meal" (Newman 1954:87–88). At the same time, yellow has a host of other potential meanings that could be evoked, especially in combination with other colors: the north, mountain lions (associated in turn with hunting and war), females or feminine gender, the moon, and the sun. The symbolic range of even a single color demonstrates that there is no uniform "code" of color meanings. And, ironically, it is that very range and complexity that assures us that color was (and still is) meaningful in a multitude of ways.

Cultural anthropology, particularly comparative ethnography, can suggest the kinds of factors that make colors meaningful. Natural resemblance is an obvious place to start, with white potentially referencing clouds, red blood, and green vegetation. Even when such mimetic symbolism is present, though, it is joined by a multitude of additional associations and meanings, derived from other factors.

The materiality of color is clearly an important factor in terms of meaning. Pigments and other colorful items may gain prestige from their association with distant places (Helms 1988), much as Europeans valued lapis lazuli that was imported from over the sea to be sold as ultramarine. In the Ancestral Pueblo Southwest, distance was surely a factor in the value placed upon colorful macaws and other parrots, shining copper bells with their clear musical sound, and glistening, iridescent shell from distant oceans. Even turquoise, though available within the Southwest, could only be obtained from mines in a few locations. Colors associated with cosmologically significant places gained even more layers of meaning, from red pigments from the Grand Canyon to black clay from the place of Emergence. Even the Flower World (a way of being more than an actual place) added meanings to polychrome or variegated color combinations.

The persistence of pigment sources as meaningful places through time, and the resilience and dynamism of the meanings of color may be attributed at least in part to the perception of paint and other colored materials as animate and animating substances, with agency in this world and in spiritual realms. Pueblo ethnographies demonstrate that some colorful materials are effective in communicating with nonhuman beings. White clay, for example, can attract clouds and rains when smeared or wiped onto walls, while yellow paint may represent pollen that similarly summons rain.

As animate materials, pigments and paints have the potential to effect change, provided they are handled with spiritually appropriate care and knowledge. Imagine the disastrous result should a ritual specialist bring down hail on the corn fields by using a winter black paint during the summer months, or the consequences if a kiva leader inadvertently chooses a green paint whose scent the katsinas find offensive. Although it is difficult to trace these kinds of choices back in time, the use of paints from specific sources across different contexts at Homol'ovi suggests that such factors may have been in play as early as the 1300s (Meyers 2007).

The ways in which colors were meaningful were not necessarily static. Put simply, the transformation of raw materials into finished artifacts by human labor and skill was, in Pueblo terms, the transformation of Raw Beings into Made Beings. Some materials transformed significantly in the heat of a fire, including yellow minerals used as red paint on pottery or certain cherts that were heat-treated before being knapped into tools. Heat-treating lithic materials for color change as well as flaking characteristics might date as early as Paleoindian times. Ancestral Puebloan interest in color as process was probably in place at least by the Pueblo II period, when potters in several regions first began to create red ware vessels that underwent a dramatic color transformation during firing. The complex, mottled colors of Ancestral Hopi polychromes and the shiny, sometimes brightly colored glaze paints of the Pueblo IV period Rio Grande and Zuni areas seem to indicate that potters paid a great deal of attention to the changes wrought by fire.

Turquoise itself would change color throughout its life history, in response to being worn, handled, or exposed to sunlight (Mattson 2016: 131). The meanings of turquoise, or any material, could also change and expand in combination with other materials, as when beads were strung together to create a necklace or when inlay was added to the handle of a bone tool. The layering of meanings happened in a literal sense in the replastered and repainted kiva murals of the Pueblo IV period, and probably in the reslipped and repainted cylinder jars in Chaco Canyon as well. Such transformations create complex life histories that strengthen, expand, and modify previous meanings. Even the techniques used in creating a design may add to meanings, as in the paints spattered or sprayed on rock paintings, in Pueblo IV kiva murals, and on Hopi yellow wares.

## Final Thoughts

The archaeological evidence discussed in this volume demonstrates that color uses and meanings varied across and within Ancestral Pueblo communities. Examining how colors became meaningful, in a general sense, and how these meanings changed over time are important directions for future research. The next and even more challenging step is to consider *why* the meanings of colors changed. At present, the list of possibilities includes migration and aggregation, negotiating new identities and rejecting old ones, losing access to sources of materials (or gaining access to new ones), expanding trade networks and emulating distant trade partners, developing new technologies, and adopting new religious concepts. We recognize that this list of possibilities is as broad as life itself, but that does not trouble us. Color is, after all, both material and sublime, the stuff of daily life and an effective actor in the holiest of places.

This understanding of color can seem quite foreign to many archaeologists, who tend to view color as a superficial trait—an idea constantly reinforced by the Munsell system, by frequent references to the work of Berlin and Kay, and by pottery typologies that classify ceramics by ware color. We argue, however, that archaeologists must be willing to move beyond recording basic color terms and Munsell codes to seek information relevant to how people acquired, processed, and used colors (and at times refrained from using them). For example, microscopic analyses may reveal evidence for pigment processing, while trace element analyses may distinguish similar hues derived from different sources. Experimental archaeology, replication studies, and ethnoarchaeological studies with artists who still practice or are reviving traditional technologies might offer insights beyond the usual "time and labor" studies.

Researchers should also consider the ways in which colors can change over time. While some colors encountered in the archaeological record are inherent and relatively permanent, such as the red of hematite or the black of jet, many others have the capacity to transform, ripen, or fade. This is particularly important for yellow pigments or paints, which can be heated to produce red. Finally, archaeologists should consider visual properties beyond color, including contrast, glossiness, sparkle, and iridescence, which may be important qualities in addition to—or even instead of—color (Guebard et al. 2018; Stone 2018; Wierzbicka 2008).

The Munsell chart has its place, as does the color name "red," but limiting ourselves to recording colors in this fashion means that we will inevitably fail to consider fully the sources, meanings, and powers of color. Imagine how much richer our view of the past can be when we make room to appreciate that color in the Pueblo world was—and is—as much about animacy, place, and process as about hue.

# References


Adams, E. Charles

1991 *The Origin and Development of the Pueblo Katsina Cult.* University of Arizona Press, Tucson.

1994 The Katsina Cult: A Western Pueblo Perspective. In *Kachinas in the Pueblo World*, edited by P. Schaafsma, pp. 35–46. University of New Mexico Press, Albuquerque.

Adams, E. Charles, and Andrew I. Duff (editors)

2004 *The Protohistoric Pueblo World, A.D. 1275–1600.* University of Arizona Press, Tucson.

Adams, Jenny L.

2002 *Ground Stone Analysis: A Technological Approach.* University of Utah Press, Salt Lake City.

Afrandilian, David

2007 Frogs, Snakes, and Agricultural Fertility: Interpreting Illinois Mississippian Representations. In *What Are the Animals To Us? Approaches from Science, Religion, Folklore, Literature, and Art*, edited by D. Afrandilian, pp. 53–88. University of Tennessee Press, Knoxville.

Akins, Nancy

1986 *A Biocultural Approach to Human Burials from Chaco Canyon, New Mexico.* Reports of the Chaco Center 9. National Park Service, Santa Fe.

Allison, James R.

2008 Exchanging Identities: Early Pueblo I Red Ware Exchange and Identity North of the San Juan River. In *The Social Construction of Communities in the Prehispanic Southwest*, edited by M. D. Varien and J. M. Potter, pp. 41–68. Altamira Press, Lanham, Maryland.

Amsden, Charles Avery

1934 *Navaho Weaving, Its Technic and History.* Southwest Museum, Santa Ana, California.

Anter, Karin Fridell

2008 Book Review: Colouring the Past—On Colour in Archaeological Research. *Color Research and Application* 33(4):327–334.

Austin, Gordon T.

1995 Turquoise. In *An Overview of Production of Specific U.S. Gemstones*, unpaginated. US Bureau of Mines Special Publication 14–95.

Baker, Pamela

2009 Painted Sites of the Ancestral Puebloans in Chaco Canyon National Historical Park, New Mexico. *American Indian Rock Art* 35:13–26.

Ball, Philip

2001 *Bright Earth: Art and the Invention of Color.* Farrar, Straus, and Giroux, New York.

Barber, E. J. W.

1999 Colour in Early Cloth and Clothing. *Cambridge Archaeological Journal* 9(1):117–120.

Barnes, Zonna

2010 Social Identity and Ornamentation in the Ancestral Puebloan Southwest: Basketmaker II to Pueblo IV. Master's thesis, Department of Anthropology, University of Colorado, Boulder.

Baty, Patrick

2017 *The Anatomy of Color: The Story of Heritage Paints and Pigments.* Thames and Hudson, London.

Beals, Ralph L., George W. Brainerd, and Watson Smith

1945 *Archaeological Studies in Northeast Arizona: A Report on the Archaeological Work of the Rainbow Bridge-Monument Valley Expedition.* University of California Publications in American Archaeology and Ethnology 44(1), Berkeley.

Bellorado, Benjamin

2017 The Context, Dating, and Role of Mural Paintings in Gallina Society. *Kiva* 83(4): 494–514.

Benedict, Ruth
1931 *Tales of the Cochiti Indians.* Bureau of American Ethnology Bulletin 98. Smithsonian Institution, Washington, DC.

Berlin, Brent, and Paul Kay
1969 *Basic Color Terms: Their Universality and Evolution.* University of California Press, Berkeley.

Blaszczyk, Regina Lee
2012 *The Color Revolution.* MIT Press, Cambridge.

Blinman, Eric
1989 Potluck in the Protokiva: Ceramics and Ceremonialism in Pueblo I Villages. In *The Architecture of Social Integration in Prehistoric Pueblos,* edited by W. D. Lipe and M. Hegmon, pp. 113–124. Occasional Paper. Vol. 1. Crow Canyon Archaeological Center, Cortez, Colorado.

Blinman, Eric, Kari L. Schleher, Tom Dickerson, Cynthia L. Herhan, and Ibrahim Gundiler
2012 Making a Glaze: Multiple Approaches to Understanding Rio Grande Glaze Paint Technology. In *Potters and Communities of Practice: Glaze Paint and Polychrome Pottery in the American Southwest, A.D. 1250–1700,* edited by L. S. Cordell and J. A. Habicht-Mauche, pp. 107–116. Anthropological Papers of the University of Arizona. Vol. 75. University of Arizona Press, Tucson.

Bliss, Wesley L.
1935 Kuaua Mural Notes. Document on file at Museum of Indian Arts and Culture/ Laboratory of Anthropology, Santa Fe.
1948 Preservation of the Kuaua Mural Paintings. *American Antiquity* 13(3):218–223.

Bower, Bruce
1999 When Stones Come Alive. *Science News* 155(23):360–362.

Bradley, Richard
1998 *The Significance of Monuments.* Routledge, London.
2000 *An Archaeology of Natural Places.* Routledge, New York.

Bradley, Ronna J.
1993 Marine Shell Exchange in Northwest Mexico and the Southwest. In *The American Southwest and Mesoamerica: Systems of Prehistoric Exchange,* edited by J. E. Ericson and T. G. Baugh, pp. 121–158. Plenum Press, New York.

Brand, Donald D.
1938 Aboriginal Trade Routes for Sea Shells in the Southwest. *Yearbook of the Association of Pacific Geographers* 4(1):3–10.

Brand, Donald D., Florence M. Hawley, and Frank C. Hibben
1937 *Tseh So, A Small House Ruin: Chaco Canyon, New Mexico.* University of New Mexico Bulletin. University of New Mexico, Albuquerque.

Braun, David
1983 Pots as Tools. In *Archaeological Hammers and Theories,* edited by J. A. Moore and A. S. Keene, pp. 103–137. Academic Press, New York.

Brew, John O.
1946 *Archaeology of Alkali Ridge, Southeastern Utah.* Papers of the Peabody Museum of American Archaeology and Ethnology 21. Peabody Museum of Archaeology and Ethnology, Cambridge, Massachusetts.

Bricker, Victoria R.
1999 Color and Texture in the Maya Language of Yucatan. *Anthropological Linguistics* 41(3): 283–307.

Brody, J. J.
1990 *Beauty from the Earth.* University Museum of Archaeology and Anthropology, University of Pennsylvania, Philadelphia.
1991 *Anasazi and Pueblo Painting.* University of New Mexico Press, Albuquerque.
2007 Kuaua Kiva Mural Project, 1/1/07–5/30/07: Final Report. In *Museum of Indian Arts and Culture/ Laboratory of Anthropology,* Santa Fe.

Brody, J. J., and Rina Swentzell
1996 *To Touch the Past: The Painted Pottery of the Mimbres People.* Hudson Hills Press, New York.

Brusatin, Manlio
1991 *A History of Colors.* Shambhala, Boston.

Bunzel, Ruth
1932a Introduction to Zuni Ceremonialism. In *Forty-Seventh Annual Report of the Bureau of American Ethnology, 1929–1930,* pp. 467–544. Government Printing Office, Washington, DC.
1932b Zuni Katcinas: An Analytical Study. In *Forty-Seventh Annual Report of the Bureau of American Ethnology, 1929–1930,* pp. 837–1086. Government Printing Office, Washington, DC.

Burger, Richard L.
1988 Unity and Heterogeneity within the Chavin Horizon. In *Peruvian Prehistory*, edited by R. W. Keatinge, pp. 99–144. Cambridge University Press, Cambridge.

Caperton, Thomas J.
1981 An Archaeological Reconnaissance. In *Contributions to Gran Quivira Archaeology, Gran Quivira National Monument, New Mexico*, edited by A. C. Hayes, pp. 4–11. Publications in Archaeology. Vol. 17. National Park Service, Washington, DC.

Carlson, John B.
2005 Transformations of the Mesoamerican Venus Turtle Carapace War Shield: A Study in Ethnoastronomy. In *Songs from the Sky*, edited by V. D. Chamberlain, J. B. Clarson, and M. J. Young, pp. 99–122. Center for Archaeoastronomy, College Park, Maryland.

Casson, Ronald W.
1992 On Brightness and Color Categories: Additional Data. *Current Anthropology* 33(4):395–397.
1994 Russet, Rose, and Raspberry: The Development of English Secondary Color Terms. *Journal of Linguistic Anthropology* 4(1):5–22.
1997 Color Shift: Evolution of English Color Terms From Brightness to Hue. In *Color Categories in Thought and Language*, edited by C. L. Hardin and L. Maffi, pp. 224–239. Cambridge University Press, Cambridge.

Cattanach, George S., Jr.
1980 *Long House: Mesa Verde National Park.* Publications in Archeology 7H, Wetherill Mesa Studies. National Park Service, Washington, DC.

Caywood, Louis R.
1936 Fitzmaurice Ruin. In *Two Pueblo Ruins in West Central Arizona*, edited by E. H. Spicer, pp. 87–115. University of Arizona Press, Tucson.

Chaco Research Archive
2018 Artifact Database. *The Chaco Research Archive.* www.chacoarchive.org. Accessed November 2, 2018.

Chapman, John
2002 Colourful Prehistories: The Problem with the Berlin and Kay Colour Paradigm. In *Colouring the Past: The Significance of Colour in Archaeological Research*, edited by A. Jones and G. MacGregor, pp. 45–72. Berg, Oxford.

Charley, Karen, and Lea S. McChesney
2007 Form and Meaning in Indigenous Aesthetics: A Hopi Pottery Perspective. *American Indian Art* 32(4):84–93.

Christensen, Don D., Jerry Dickey, and Steven M. Freers
2013 *Rock Art of the Grand Canyon Region.* Sunbelt Publications, San Diego.

Christie, Robert M.
2015 *Colour Chemistry.* Royal Society of Chemistry, Cambridge.

Claassen, Cheryl P.
2008 Shell Symbolism in Pre-Columbian North America. In *Early Human Impact on Megamolluscs*, edited by A. Antczak and R. Cipriani, pp. 231–236. Vol. S1865. British Archaeological Reports, Oxford.

Clark, J. Dylan
2015 Life Stone and Death Stone: Animate Power and Representations in Natural Material of the Mogollon Culture Region. In *Collected Papers from the 18th Biennial Mogollon Archaeology Conference, October 2014*, edited by L. C. Ludeman, pp. 175–180. Friends of Archaeology, Las Cruces.

Clarke, Mark
2001 *The Art of All Colours: Mediaeval Recipe Books for Painters and Illuminators.* Archetype Publications, London.

Cohan, John A.
2010 *The Primitive Mind and Modern Man.* Bentham Books, Sharjah.

Cole, Sally J.
2006 Imagery and Tradition: Murals of the Mesa Verde Region. In *The Mesa Verde World: Explorations in Ancestral Pueblo Archaeology*, edited by D. G. Noble, pp. 92–99. School for Advanced Research Press, Santa Fe.
2009 *Legacy on Stone.* Revised ed. Johnson Books, Boulder.

Colton, Harold S.
1941 Prehistoric Trade in the Southwest. *Scientific Monthly* 52(4):308–319.
1953 *Potsherds: An Introduction to the Study of Prehistoric Southwestern Ceramics and Their Use in Historic Reconstruction.* Northern Arizona Society of Science and Art, Flagstaff.
1959 *Hopi Kachina Dolls with a Key to Their Identification.* University of New Mexico Press, Albuquerque.

Colton, Harold S., and Lyndon L. Hargrave
1937 *Handbook of Northern Arizona Pottery Wares.* Museum of Northern Arizona Bulletin 11. Northern Arizona Society of Science and Art, Flagstaff.
Colton, Mary-Russell F.
1965 *Hopi Dyes.* Museum of Northern Arizona Press, Flagstaff.
Conklin, Harold C.
1955 Hanunóo Color Categories. *Southwestern Journal of Anthropology* 11:339–344.
1964 Hanunóo Colour Categories. In *Language in Culture and Society*, edited by D. H. Hymes, pp. 189–192. Harper and Row, New York.
Cordell, Linda S., and Judith A. Habicht-Mauche (editors)
2012 *Potters and Communities of Practice: Glaze Paint and Polychrome Pottery in the American Southwest, A.D. 1250–1700.* Vol. 75. University of Arizona Press, Tucson.
Cordell, Linda S., and Maxine E. McBrinn
2012 *Archaeology of the Southwest.* 3rd ed. Left Coast Press, Walnut Creek, California.
Crotty, Helen K.
1983 *Honoring the Dead: Anasazi Ceramics from the Rainbow Bridge- Monument Valley Expedition.* UCLA Museum of Cultural History Monograph Series 22. University of California, Los Angeles.
1995 Anasazi Mural Art of the Pueblo IV Period, A.D. 1300–1600: Influences, Selective Adaptation, and Cultural Diversity in the Prehistoric Southwest. Ph.D. dissertation, University of California, Los Angeles.
1999 Kiva Murals and Iconography at Picuris Pueblo. In *Picuris Pueblo through Time: Eight Centuries of Change at a Northern Rio Grande Pueblo*, edited by M. A. Adler and H. W. Dick, pp. 149–187. William P. Clements Center for Southwest Studies, Southern Methodist University, Dallas, Texas.
2007 Western Pueblo Influences and Integration in the Pottery Mound Painted Kivas. In *New Perspectives on Pottery Mound Pueblo*, edited by P. Schaafsma, pp. 85–107. University of New Mexico Press, Albuquerque.
Crown, Patricia L.
1994 *Ceramics and Ideology: Salado Polychrome Pottery.* University of New Mexico Press, Albuquerque.
Crown, Patricia L., and W.H. Wills
2003 Modifying Pottery and Kivas at Chaco: Pentimento, Restoration or Renewal? *American Antiquity* 68(2):511–532.
Crow-wing
1925 *A Pueblo Indian Journal, 1920–1921.* George Banta Publishing, Menasha, Wisconsin.
Curcija, Zachary S.
2018 Reevaluating the Prehistoric Disc Bead Industry. *Kiva* 84(1):27–45.
Cushing, Frank Hamilton
1883 Zuni Fetiches. In *Second Annual Report of the Bureau of American Ethnology, 1880–81*, pp. 9–45. Smithsonian Institution, Washington, DC.
1886 A Study of Pueblo Pottery as Illustrative of Zuni Culture Growth. In *Fourth Annual Report of the Bureau of American Ethnology*, pp. 467–522. Smithsonian Institution, Washington, DC.
1920 *Zuñi Breadstuff.* Indian Notes and Monographs 8. Museum of the American Indian, Heye Foundation, New York.
Damp, Nicholas E.
2013 Zuni Chacoan Communities: The Archaeology of Village of the Great Kivas and the Chaco Era in the Zuni Region. Master's thesis, Department of Anthropology, University of Colorado, Boulder.
Davidoff, Jules
1997 The Neuropsychology of Color. In *Color Categories in Thought and Language*, edited by C. L. Hardin and L. Maffi, pp. 118–134. Cambridge University Press, Cambridge.
DeBoer, Warren R.
2005 Colors for a North American Past. *World Archaeology* 37(1):66–91.
Dick, Herbert W., Daniel Wolfman, Curtis F. Schaafsma, and Michael Adler
1999 Prehistoric and Early Historic Architecture and Ceramics at Picuris. In *Picuris Pueblo through Time: Eight Centuries of Change at a Northern Rio Grande Pueblo*, edited by M. A. Adler and H. W. Dick, pp. 43–99. William P. Clements Center for Southwest Studies, Southern Methodist University, Dallas, Texas.
Dick, Herbert W., Daniel Wolfman, Curtis F. Schaafsma, and Marianne Wolfman
1965 Introduction to Picuris Archaeology. Manuscript on file at the Laboratory of Anthropology, Santa Fe.
Dockstader, Frederick J.
1954 *The Kachina and the White Man: Influences of White Culture on the Hopi Kachina*

*Religion*. Bulletin 35. Cranbrook Institute of Science, Bloomfield Hills, Michigan.

Doyel, David E.

2015 Specialized Hohokam Production and Exchange Prior to the Ballcourt and Market System. *Journal of Arizona Archaeology* 3(1–2):157–172.

Duff, Andrew I., Judith A. Habicht-Mauche, and M. Steven Shackley

2017 Minerals. In *The Oxford Handbook of Southwest Archaeology*, edited by B. J. Mills and S. M. Fowles, pp. 767–785. Oxford University Press, Oxford.

Dumarest, Noel

1919 *Notes on Cochiti, New Mexico*. Memoirs of the American Anthropological Association Vol. 6(3). American Anthropological Association, Lancaster, Pennsylvania.

Dutton, Bertha P.

1963 *Sun Father's Way*. University of New Mexico Press, Albuquerque.

Eckert, Suzanne L.

2006 Black-on-White to Glaze-on-Red: Migration, Ritual and Exchange in the Middle Rio Grande. In *The Social Life of Pots: Glaze Wares and Cultural Dynamics in the Southwest, AD 1250–1680*, edited by J. A. Habicht-Mauche, S. L. Eckert and D. L. Huntley, pp. 163–178. University of Arizona Press, Tucson.

Ellis, Florence Hawley

1936 *Field Manual of Prehistoric Southwestern Pottery Types*. University of New Mexico Press, Albuquerque.

1977 The Basis for Santo Domingo Pueblo's Claim to the Turquoise Mines Area. Plaintiffs Exhibit, Indian Claims Commission, Pueblo of Santo Domingo vs. United States. Dockett No. 355. In *Collection 2010.53*. Catalogue 2010.53. 277 vols. Maxwell Museum of Anthropology.

Ellis, Florence Hawley, and Laurens Hammack

1968 The Inner Sanctum of Feather Cave, a Mogollon Sun and Earth Shrine Linking Mexico and the Southwest. *American Antiquity* 33(1):25–43.

Feinman, Gary M., Steadman Upham, and Kent G. Lightfoot

1981 The Production Step Measure: An Ordinal Index of Labor Input in Ceramic Manufacture. *American Antiquity* 48(4):871–884.

Ferguson, T. J., G. Lennis Berlin, and Leigh Kuwanwisiwma

2009 Kukhepya: Searching for Hopi Trails. In *Landscapes of Movement: Trails, Paths, and Roads in Anthropological Perspective*, edited by J. E. Snead, C. L. Erickson, and J. A. Darling, pp. 20–41. University of Pennsylvania Museum of Archaeology and Ethnology, Philadelphia.

Fewkes, J. Walter

1897 Tusayan Katcinas. In *Fifteenth Annual Report of the Bureau of American Ethnology, 1893–94*, pp. 245–313. Smithsonian Institution, Washington, DC.

1898 Archeological Expedition to Arizona in 1895. In *Seventeenth Annual Report of the Bureau of American Ethnology, 1895–1896*, pp. 527–744. Smithsonian Institution, Washington, DC.

1903 Hopi Katcinas, Drawn by Native Artists. In *Twenty-first Annual Report of the Bureau of American Ethnology to the Secretary of the Smithsonian Institution, 1899–1900*, edited by J. W. Powell, pp. 3–126. Government Printing Office, Washington, DC.

1904 Two Summers' Work in Pueblo Ruins. In *Twenty-second Annual Report of the Bureau of American Ethnology, 1900–1901*, pp. 1–122. Smithsonian Institution, Washington, DC.

1909 *Antiquities of the Mesa Verde National Park: Spruce Tree House*. Bureau of American Ethnology Bulletin 41. Smithsonian Institution, Washington, DC.

1911 *Antiquities of the Mesa Verde National Park: Cliff Palace*. Bureau of American Ethnology Bulletin 51. Smithsonian Institution, Washington, DC.

1916 The Cliff-Ruins in Fewkes Cañon, Mesa Verde National Park, Colorado. In *Holmes Anniversary Volume*, pp. 96–117, Washington, DC.

Fiero, Kathleen

1999 *Balcony House: A History of a Cliff Dwelling, Mesa Verde National Park, Colorado*. Archeological Research Series No. 8. Mesa Verde Museum Association, Mesa Verde National Park.

Finlay, Robert

2007 Weaving the Rainbow: Visions of Color in World History. *Journal of World History* 18(4):383–431.

Finlay, Victoria

2003 *Color: A Natural History of the Palette*. Random House, New York.

Flint, Richard

2017 San Marcos Pueblo and the Galisteo Basin from First Contact to the Pueblo Revolt.

In *The Archaeology and History of Pueblo San Marcos: Change and Stability*, edited by A. Ramenofsky and K. L. Schleher, pp. 23–31. University of New Mexico Press, Albuquerque.

Fogelin, Lars
2007 The Archaeology of Ritual. *Annual Review of Anthropology* 36:55–71.

Ford, Richard I.
1980 The Color of Survival. *Discovery* 1:17–29.

Frankel, D.
1980 Munsell Colour Notation in Ceramic Description: An Experiment. *Australian Archaeology* 10:33–37.

Fraser, Pamela
2019 *How Color Works: Color Theory in the 21st Century.* Oxford University Press, New York.

Fratt, Lee
2001 Homol'ovi III Ground Stone. In *Homol'ovi III: A Pueblo Hamlet in the Middle Little Colorado River Valley*, edited by E. C. Adams, pp. 227–238. Arizona State Museum Archaeological Series. Vol. 193. Arizona State Museum, Tucson.

Gage, John
1993 *Colour and Culture: Practice and Meaning from Antiquity to Abstraction.* Thames and Hudson, London.
1999 *Colour and Meaning: Art, Science, and Symbolism.* Thames and Hudson, London.

Gage, John, Andrew Jones, Richard Bradley, Kate Spence, E. J. W. Barber, and Paul S. C. Taçon
1999 Viewpoint: What Meaning Had Colour in Early Societies? *Cambridge Archaeological Journal* 9(1):109–126.

Geib, Phil R.
2011 *Foragers and Farmers of the Northern Kayenta Region: Excavations along the Navajo Mountain Road.* University of Utah Press, Salt Lake City.

Gettens, Rutherford J., and Elisabeth West Fitzhugh
1966 Azurite and Blue Verditer. *Studies in Conservation* 11(2):54–61.
1974 Malachite and Green Verditer. *Studies in Conservation* 19(1):2–23.

Giardino, Marco, Richard Miller, Rachel Kuzio, and Dean Muirhead
1998 Analysis of Ceramic Color by Spectral Reflectance. *American Antiquity* 63(3): 477–483.

Gilpin, Dennis, and Kelley Hays-Gilpin
2012 Polychrome Pottery of the Hopi Mesas. In *Potters and Communities of Practice: Glaze Paint and Polychrome Pottery in the American Southwest, A.D. 1250–1700*, edited by L. S. Cordell and J. A. Habicht-Mauche, pp. 45–54. Anthropological Papers of the University of Arizona. Vol. 75. University of Arizona Press, Tucson.

Gladwin, Winifred, and Harold S. Gladwin
1930 *A Method for the Designation of Southwestern Pottery Types.* Medallion Papers 7. Gila Pueblo, Globe, Arizona.

Glowacki, Donna M., and Scott Van Keuren (editors)
2011 *Religious Transformation in the Late Pre-Hispanic Pueblo World.* University of Arizona Press, Tucson.

Goldfrank, Esther S.
1927 *The Social and Ceremonial Organization of Cochiti.* Memoirs of the American Anthropological Association. Vol. 33. American Anthropological Association, Lancaster, Pennsylvania.

Grant, Campbell
1978 *Canyon De Chelly: Its People and Its Rock Art.* University of Arizona Press, Tucson.

Greer, John, and Mavis Greer
2002 Dark Zone Pictographs at Surratt Cave, Central New Mexico. In *Forward Into the Past: Papers in Honor of Teddy Lou and Francis Stickney*, edited by R. N. Wiseman, T. C. O'Laughlin, and C. T. Snow, pp. 37–46. Vol. 28. Archaeological Society of New Mexico, Albuquerque.
2015 Rock Art and Ritual Cave Use in the Southwestern US and Northern Mexico. *American Indian Rock Art* 41:23–42.

Guebard, Matthew C., Angelyn Bass, and Douglas Porter
2018 Colored Washes and Cultural Meaning at the Montezuma Castle Cliff Dwelling and Casa Grande Great House. *Journal of Arizona Archaeology* 5(2):101–113.

Guernsey, Samuel J.
1931 *Explorations in Northeastern Arizona: Report on the Archaeological Fieldwork of 1920–1923.* Papers of the Peabody Museum of American Archaeology and Ethnology, Harvard University 12, No. 1. Peabody Museum, Cambridge, Massachusetts.

Guernsey, Samuel J., and A. V. Kidder
1921 *Basket-Maker Caves of Northeastern Arizona: Report on the Explorations, 1916–17.* Papers of the Peabody Museum of Ameri-

can Archaeology and Ethnology, Harvard University 8, No. 2. Peabody Museum, Cambridge, Massachusetts.

Habicht-Mauche, Judith A., Suzanne L. Eckert, and Deborah L. Huntley (editors)
2006 *The Social Life of Pots: Glaze Wares and Cultural Dynamics in the Southwest, AD 1250–1680*. University of Arizona Press, Tucson.

Hallowell, A. Irving
1960 Ojibwa Ontology, Behavior, and World View. In *Culture in History: Essays in Honor of Paul Radin*, edited by S. Diamond, pp. 20–52. Columbia University Press, New York.

Hardin, C. L., and Luisa Maffi (editors)
1997 *Color Categories in Thought and Language.* Cambridge University Press, Cambridge.

Harrington, John P.
1916 *The Ethnogeography of the Tewa Indians.* Twenty-Ninth Annual Report of the Bureau of American Ethnology 1907–1908. Smithsonian Institution, Washington, DC.

Harvey, Graham
2005 *Animism: Respecting the Living World.* Columbia University Press, New York.

Haury, Emil W.
1931 Minute Beads from Prehistoric Pueblos. *American Anthropologist* 33(1):80–87.

Haury, Emil W., and Lisa W. Huckell
1993 A Cotton Cache from the Pinaleño Mountains: Dating the Cache. *Kiva* 59(2):105–119.

Hawley, Florence M.
1929 Prehistoric Pottery Pigments in the Southwest. *American Anthropologist* 31(4): 731–754.

Hayes, Alden C., and James A. Lancaster
1975 *Badger House Community, Mesa Verde National Park, Colorado.* Publications in Archeology 7E, Wetherill Mesa Studies. National Park Service, Washington, DC.

Hayes, Alden C., Jon Nathan Young, and A. Helene Warren (editors)
1981 *Excavation of Mound 7: Gran Quivira National Monument, New Mexico* Vol. 16. National Park Service, Washington, DC.

Hays-Gilpin, Kelley
2008 Ceramic Decoration. In *Prehistory of the Northern Kayenta Anasazi Region: Archaeological Excavations along the Navajo Mountain Road*, edited by P. R. Geib. University of Utah Press, Salt Lake City.

2011 Pueblos. In *Oxford Handbook of the Archaeology of Ritual and Religion*, edited by T. Insoll, pp. 601–622. Oxford University Press, Oxford.

2014 Sikyatki Polychrome: Style, Iconography, Cross-Media Comparisons, and Organization of Production. *Kiva* 79(2):175–204.

Hays-Gilpin, Kelley, Dennis Gilpin, Suzanne L. Eckert, John A. Ware, David A. Phillips Jr., Hayward H. Franklin, and Jean H. Ballagh
2018 There and Back Again. In *Interaction and Connectivity in the Greater Southwest*, edited by K. G. Harry and B. Roth, pp. 54–83. University Press of Colorado, Boulder.

Hays-Gilpin, Kelley, and Steven A. LeBlanc
2007 Sikyatki Style in Regional Context. In *New Perspectives on Pottery Mound Pueblo*, edited by P. Schaafsma, pp. 109–136. University of New Mexico Press, Albuquerque.

Hays-Gilpin, Kelley, Elizabeth A. Newsome, and Emory Sekaquaptewa
2010 *Siitalpuva*, "Through the Land Brightened with Flowers": Ecology and Cosmology in Mural and Pottery Painting, Hopi and Beyond. In *Painting the Cosmos: Metaphor and Worldview in Images from the Southwest Pueblos and Mexico*, edited by K. Hays-Gilpin and P. Schaafsma, pp. 121–138. Museum of Northern Arizona Bulletin 67. Museum of Northern Arizona, Flagstaff.

Hays-Gilpin, Kelley, and Polly Schaafsma (editors)
2010 *Painting the Cosmos: Metaphor and Worldview in Images from the Southwest Pueblos and Mexico.* Museum of Northern Arizona, Flagstaff.

Hays-Gilpin, Kelley, and Emory Sekaquaptewa
2006 *Siitalpuva*: "Through the Land Brightened with Flowers." *Plateau* 3(1):13–25.

Hays-Gilpin, Kelley, Louise Senior, and Patrick Lyons
2001 Homol'ovi III Ceramics. In *Homol'ovi III: A Pueblo Hamlet in the Middle Little Colorado River Valley*, edited by E. C. Adams, pp. 137–226. Archaeological Series 193. Arizona State Museum, Tucson.

Hays-Gilpin, Kelley, and Eric van Hartesveldt
1998 *Prehistoric Ceramics of the Puerco Valley, Arizona.* Museum of Northern Arizona Ceramic Series 7. Museum of Northern Arizona, Flagstaff.

Hays-Gilpin, Kelley, and Christine S. VanPool
2009 Red Earth, White Clouds: The Metaphorical World of Kayenta Pottery. Paper

Presented at 74th Annual Meeting of the Society for American Archaeology. Atlanta.
Hays-Gilpin, Kelley, Lori D. Webster, and Polly Schaafsma
2004 The Iconography of Tie-Dye Textiles in the Ancient Americas. *Cosmos* 20:33–56.
Heitman, Carrie
2015 The House of Our Ancestors: New Research on the Prehistory of Chaco Canyon, New Mexico, A.D. 800–1200. In *Chaco Revisited: New Research on the Prehistory of Chaco Canyon, New Mexico*, edited by C. C. Heitman and S. Plog, pp. 215–248. University of Arizona Press, Tucson.
Helms, Mary W.
1979 *Ancient Panamanian Chiefdoms*. University of Texas Press, Austin.
1988 *Ulysses' Sail: An Ethnographic Odyssey of Power, Knowledge, and Geographic Distance*. Princeton University Press, Princeton, New Jersey.
Herhahn, Cynthia
2006 Inferring Social Interactions from Pottery Recipes: Rio Grande Glaze Paint Composition and Cultural Transmission. In *The Social Life of Pots: Glaze Wares and Cultural Dynamics in the Southwest, AD 1250–1680*, edited by J. A. Habicht-Mauche, S. L. Eckert and D. L. Huntley, pp. 179–196. University of Arizona Press, Tucson.
Hering, Ewald
1964 *Outlines of a Theory of the Light Sense*. Translated by L. M. Hurvich and D. Jameson. Harvard University Press, Cambridge.
Hewett, Edgar L.
1936 *The Chaco Canyon and Its Monuments*. University of New Mexico Press, Albuquerque.
Hibben, Frank C.
1975 *Kiva Art of the Anasazi at Pottery Mound*. KC Publications, Las Vegas.
Hickerson, Nancy P.
1975 Two Studies of Color: Implications for Cross-Cultural Comparability of Semantic Categories. In *Linguistics and Anthropology: In Honor of C. F. Voegelin*, edited by M. D. Kinkade, K. L. Hale, and O. Werner, pp. 317–330. Peter De Ridder Press, Lisse.
Hieb, Louis A.
1979 Hopi World View. In *Handbook of North American Indians, Volume 9: Southwest*, edited by A. Ortiz, pp. 577–580. Smithsonian Institution, Washington, DC.
Hill, Jane H., and Kelley Hays-Gilpin
1999 The Flower World in Material Culture: An Iconographic Complex in the Southwest and Mesoamerica. *Journal of Anthropological Research* 55(1):1–37.
Holmes, William Henry
1886 Origin and Development of Form and Ornament in Ceramic Art. In *Fourth Annual Report of the Bureau of American Ethnology*. Smithsonian Institution, Washington, DC.
Hough, Walter
1914 *Culture of the Ancient Pueblos of the Upper Gila*. United States National Bulletin 87. Smithsonian Institution, Washington, DC.
Houston, Stephen, Claudia Brittenham, Cassandra Mesick, Alexandre Tokovinine, and Christina Warinner
2009 *Veiled Brightness: A History of Ancient Maya Color*. University of Texas Press, Austin.
Howell, Todd L.
1994 Leadership at the Ancestral Zuni Village of Hawikku. Unpublished PhD dissertation, Dept. of Anthropology, Arizona State University, Tempe.
1995 Tracking Zuni Gender and Leadership Roles Across the Contact Period in the Zuni Region. *Journal of Anthropological Research* 51:125–147.
Hull, Sharon, Mostafa Fayek, Frances J. Mathien, and Heidi Roberts
2014 Turquoise Trade of the Ancestral Puebloan: Chaco and Beyond. *Journal of Archaeological Science* 45(1):187–195.
Hull, Sharon, Mostafa Fayek, Frances J. Mathien, Phillip Shelley, and Kathy R. Durand
2008 A New Approach to Determining the Geological Provenance of Turquoise Artifacts Using Hydrogen and Copper Stable Isotopes. *Journal of Archaeological Science* 35(5):1355–1369.
Huntley, Deborah L.
2008 *Ancestral Zuni Glaze-Decorated Pottery: Viewing Pueblo IV Regional Organization through Ceramic Production and Exchange*. Anthropological Papers of the University of Arizona 72. University of Arizona Press, Tucson.
Huntley, Deborah L., Thomas Fenn, Judith A. Habicht-Mauche, and Barbara J. Mills
2012 Embedded Networks? Pigments and Long-

Distance Procurement Strategies in the Late Prehispanic Southwest. In *Potters and Communities of Practice: Glaze Paint and Polychrome Pottery in the American Southwest, A.D. 1250–1700*, edited by L. S. Cordell and J. A. Habicht-Mauche, pp. 8–18. Anthropological Papers of the University of Arizona. Vol. 75. University of Arizona Press, Tucson.

Huntley, Deborah L., Katherine A. Spielmann, and Judith A. Habicht-Mauche
2007 Local Recipes or Distant Commodities? Lead Isotope and Chemical Compositional Analysis of Glaze Paints from the Salinas Pueblos, New Mexico. *Journal of Archaeological Science* 34(7):1135–1147.

Izeki, Mutsumi
2016 La Turquesa: Una Piedra Verde Cálida. *Arqueología Mexicana* 141:34–38.

Jackson, William Henry
1876 Ancient Ruins in Southwestern Colorado. In *Bulletin of the United States Geographical and Geological Survey of the Territories Embracing Colorado and Parts of Adjacent Territories for 1874, Hayden Survey*, pp. 367–381. Government Printing Office, Washington, DC.

James, Harry C.
1974 *Pages from Hopi History*. University of Arizona Press, Tucson.

Jameson, Kimberly
2005 Why GRUE? An Interpoint-Distance Model Analysis of Composite Color Categories. *Cross-Cultural Research* 39(2):159–204.

Jameson, Kimberly, and Roy G. D'Andrade
1997 It's Not Really Red, Green, Yellow, Blue: An Inquiry into Perceptual Color Space. In *Color Categories in Thought and Language*, edited by C. L. Hardin and L. Maffi, pp. 295–319. Cambridge University Press, Cambridge.

Jernigan, E. Wesley
1978 *Jewelry of the Prehistoric Southwest*. School of American Research Press, Santa Fe.

Jones, Andrew, and Richard Bradley
1999 The Significance of Colour in European Archaeology. *Cambridge Archaeological Journal* 9(1):112–114.

Jones, Andrew, and Gavin MacGregor
2002 Wonderful Things: Colour Studies in Archaeology from Munsell to Materiality. In *Colouring the Past: The Significance of Colour in Archaeological Research*, edited by A. Jones and G. MacGregor, pp. 1–21. Berg, Oxford.

Judd, Neil M.
1930 The Excavation and Repair of Betatakin. *Proceedings of the United States National Museum*, pp. 1–77. Vol. 77, Art. 5. Smithsonian Institution, Washington, DC.
1954 *The Material Culture of Pueblo Bonito*. Smithsonian Miscellaneous Collections 124. Smithsonian Institution, Washington, DC.
1959 *Pueblo del Arroyo, Chaco Canyon, New Mexico*. Smithsonian Miscellaneous Collections vol. 138(1). Smithsonian Institution, Washington, DC.
1964 *The Architecture of Pueblo Bonito*. Smithsonian Institution, Washington, DC.

Kamp, Kathryn A., and John C. Whittaker
1990 Lizard Man Village: A Small Site Perspective on Northern Sinagua Social Organization. *Kiva* 55(2):99–125.
1999 *Surviving Adversity: The Sinagua of Lizard Man Village*. University of Utah Press Anthropological Papers. University of Utah Press, Salt Lake City.

Kay, Paul
2005 Color Categories Are Not Arbitrary. *Cross-cultural Research* 39(1):39–55.

Kay, Paul, Brent Berlin, Luisa Maffi, and William Merrifield
1997 Color Naming Across Languages. In *Color Categories in Thought and Language*, edited by C. L. Hardin and L. Maffi, pp. 21–56. Cambridge University Press, Cambridge.

Kennard, Edward A.
2002 *Hopi Kachinas*. Kiva Publishing, Walnut, California.

Kennett, Douglas J., Stephen Plog, Richard J. George, Brendan J. Culleton, Adam S. Watson, Pontus Skoglund, Nadin Rohland, Swapan Mallick, Kristin Stewardson, Logan Kistler, Steven A. LeBlanc, Peter M. Whiteley, David Reich, and George H. Perry
2017 Archaeogenomic Evidence Reveals Prehistoric Matrilineal Dynasty. *Nature Communications* 8:Article 14115.

Kent, Kate Peck
1983 *Prehistoric Textiles of the Southwest*. University of New Mexico Press, Albuquerque.

Kidder, Alfred Vincent
1932 *The Artifacts of Pecos*. Yale University Press, New Haven.

King, Dale S.
1949 *Nalakihu: Excavations at a Pueblo III Site on Wupatki National Monument, Arizona.* Museum of Northern Arizona Bulletin No. 23. Museum of Northern Arizona, Flagstaff.

Kintigh, Keith W.
2007 Late Prehistoric and Protohistoric Settlement Systems in the Zuni Area. In *Zuni Origins: Toward a New Synthesis of Southwestern Archaeology*, edited by D. A. Gregory and D. R. Wilcox, pp. 361–376. University of Arizona Press, Tucson.

Kluckhohn, Clyde, and Paul Reiter
1939 *Preliminary Report on the 1937 Excavations, BC 50–51, Chaco Canyon, New Mexico.* University of New Mexico Bulletin, Anthropological Series 3, No. 2, Albuquerque.

Kuehni, Rolf G., and Andreas Schwarz
2008 *Color Ordered: A Survey of Color Systems From Antiquity to the Present.* Oxford University Press, Oxford.

Kühn, Hermann
1970 Verdigris and Copper Resinate. *Studies in Conservation* 15(1):12–36.

Ladd, Edmund J.
1994 The Zuni Ceremonial System: The Kiva. In *Kachinas in the Pueblo World*, edited by P. Schaafsma, pp. 17–21. University of New Mexico Press, Albuquerque.

Lange, Charles H.
1990 *Cochiti: A New Mexico Pueblo, Past and Present.* University of New Mexico Press, Albuquerque.

Lange, Charles H., and Carroll L. Riley (editors)
1966 *The Southwestern Journals of Adolph Bandelier, 1880–1882.* University of New Mexico Press, Albuquerque.

Laski, Vera
1958 *Seeking Life.* American Folklore Society, Philadelphia.

Lekson, Stephen H. (editor)
1983 *The Architecture and Dendrochronology of Chetro Ketl, Chaco Canyon, New Mexico.* National Park Service, US Department of the Interior, Albuquerque.

Lewis, Candace K.
2002 Knowledge is Power: Pigments, Painted Artifacts, and Chacoan Ritual Leaders. Master's thesis, Department of Anthropology, Northern Arizona University, Flagstaff.

Lightfoot, Ricky R., Alice M. Emerson, and Eric Blinman
1988 Excavation in Area 5, Grass Mesa Village (Site 5MT23). In *Dolores Archaeological Program: Anasazi Communities at Dolores: Grass Mesa Village*, edited by W. D. Lipe, J. N. Morris, and T. A. Kohler, pp. 561–766. US Department of the Interior, Bureau of Reclamation, Denver.

Lister, Robert H., and Florence C. Lister
1987 *Aztec Ruins on the Animas: Excavated, Preserved, and Interpreted.* University of New Mexico Press, Albuquerque.

Livingstone, Margaret
2008 *Vision and Art: The Biology of Seeing.* Abrams, New York.

Lockett, H. C., and Lyndon L. Hargrave
1953 *Woodchuck Cave: A Basketmaker II Site in Tsegi Canyon, Arizona.* Northern Arizona Society of Science and Art, Flagstaff.

Loendorf, Larry
2010 Pigments of the Imagination: Ancestral Pueblo Painted Walls in Canyon Del Muerto, Arizona. In *Painting the Cosmos: Metaphor and Worldview in Images from the Southwest Pueblos and Mexico*, edited by K. Hays-Gilpin and P. Schaafsma, pp. 41–60. Museum of Northern Arizona Bulletin 67. Museum of Northern Arizona, Flagstaff.

Logan, Erik N., and Lee Fratt
1993 Pigment Processing at Homol'ovi III: A Preliminary Study. *Kiva* 58(3):415–428.

Lomawywesa (Michael Kabotie) and Coochsiwukioma (Delbridge Honanie)
2010 Painting "Journey of the Human Spirit": A Contemporary Hopi Mural. In *Painting the Cosmos: Metaphor and Worldview in Images from the Southwest Pueblos and Mexico*, edited by K. Hays-Gilpin and P. Schaafsma, pp. 179–196. Museum of Northern Arizona Bulletin 67. Museum of Northern Arizona, Flagstaff.

Lowengard, Sarah
2001 Colour Quality and Production: Testing Colour in Eighteenth-Century France. *Journal of Design History* 14(2):91–103.
2007 *The Creation of Color in Eighteenth-Century Europe.* Columbia University Press, New York.

Lucy, John A.
1997a Linguistic Relativity. *Annual Review of Anthropology* 26:291–312.
1997b The Linguistics of "Color." In *Color Categories in Thought and Language*, edited by C. L. Hardin and L. Maffi, pp. 320–346. Cambridge University Press, Cambridge.

Luebben, Ralph A.
1953 Leaf Water Site. In *Salvage Archaeology in the Chama Valley, New Mexico*, edited by F. Wendorf and S. A. Stubbs, pp. 9–33. Monographs of the School of American Research Vol. 17. School for Advanced Research Press, Santa Fe.

McAnany, Patricia
1982 LA 17360. In *Prehistoric Adaptive Strategies in the Chaco Canyon Region, Northwestern New Mexico, Vol. 2: Site Reports*, edited by A. H. Simmons, pp. 604–606. Navajo Nation Papers in Anthropology 9. Navajo Nation Cultural Resource Management Program, Window Rock, Arizona.

McBrinn, Maxine E., and Ross E. Altshuler
2015 *Turquoise, Water, Sky: Meaning and Beauty in Southwest Native Arts.* Museum of New Mexico Press, Santa Fe.

McGregor, John C.
1941 *Winona and Ridge Ruin, Part I.* Museum of Northern Arizona Bulletin 18. Museum of Northern Arizona, Flagstaff.
1943 Burial of an Early American Magician. *Proceedings of the American Philosophical Society* 86(2):270–298.

McGuire, Randall H., and Ann V. Howard
1987 The Structure and Organization of Hohokam Shell Exchange. *Kiva* 52(5):113–146.

MacLaury, Robert E.
1992 From Brightness to Hue: An Explanatory Model of Color-Category Evolution. *Current Anthropology* 33(2):137–186.

Mallery, Garrick
1893 Picture-Writing of the American Indians. In *Tenth Annual Report of the Bureau of American Ethnology*, pp. 3–807. Smithsonian Institution, Washington, DC.

Marden, Kerriann
2011 Taphonomy, Paleopathology and Mortuary Variability in Chaco Canyon: Using Bioarchaeological and Forensic Methods to Understand Ancient Cultural Practices. Ph.D. dissertation, Department of Anthropology, Tulane University, New Orleans.

Mathien, Frances Joan
1997 Ornaments of the Chaco Anasazi. In *Ceramics, Lithics, and Ornaments of Chaco Canyon: Analyses of Artifacts from the Chaco Project, 1971–1978. Volume III, Lithics and Ornaments*, edited by F. J. Mathien, pp. 1119–1219. Publications in Archeology: Chaco Canyon Studies. Vol. 18G. National Park Service, Santa Fe.
2001 The Organization of Turquoise Production and Consumption by the Prehistoric Chacoans. *American Antiquity* 66(1): 103–118.

Mathien, Frances Joan, and Thomas C. Windes (editors)
1987a *Investigations at the Pueblo Alto Complex, Chaco Canyon, New Mexico, 1975–1979. Volume III, Part 1. Artifactual and Biological Analyses.* National Park Service, Santa Fe.
1987b *Investigations at the Pueblo Alto Complex, Chaco Canyon, New Mexico, 1975–1979. Volume III, Part 2. Artifactual and Biological Analyses.* National Park Service, Santa Fe.

Mathiowetz, Michael, Polly Schaafsma, Jeremy Coltman, and Karl Taube
2015 The Darts of Dawn: The Tlahuizcaltpantecuhtli Venus Complex in the Iconography of Mesoamerica and the American Southwest. *Journal of the Southwest* 57(1):1–102.

Mattson, Hannah
2016 Ornaments as Socially Valuable Objects: Jewelry and Identity in the Chaco and Post-Chaco Worlds. *Journal of Anthropological Archaeology* 42:122–139.

Mayer, Ralph
1981 *The Artist's Handbook of Materials and Techniques.* 5th ed. Viking, New York.

Mera, H. P.
1943 *An Outline of Ceramic Developments in Southern and Southeastern New Mexico.* Laboratory of Anthropology Technical Series, Bulletin 11. Museum of New Mexico, Santa Fe.

Meyers, Julia Isabell
2007 Prehistoric Wall Decoration in the American Southwest: A Behavioral Approach. PhD dissertation, Department of Anthropology, University of Arizona, Tucson.

Miller, Christopher L., and George R. Hamell
1986 A New Perspective on Indian-White Contact: Cultural Symbols and Colonial Trade. *Journal of American History* 73(2): 311–328.

Miller, Myles R., Lawrence Loendorf, and Leonard Kemp
2012 *Picture Cave and Other Rock Art Sites on Fort Bliss.* Geo-Marine, Inc. Cultural Resources Report No. 10–36.

Mills, Barbara J.
2007a Performing the Feast: Visual Display and Suprahousehold Commensalism in the Puebloan Southwest. *American Antiquity* 72(2):210–239.

2007b A Regional Perspective on Ceramics and Zuni Identity, AD 200–1630. In *Zuni Origins: Toward a New Synthesis of Southwestern Archaeology*, edited by D.A. Gregory and D.R. Wilcox, pp. 210–238. University of Arizona Press, Tucson.

2008 Remembering while Forgetting: Depositional Practices and Social Memory at Chaco. In *Memory Work: Archaeologies of Material Practices*, edited by B.J. Mills and W.H. Walker, pp. 81–108. School for Advanced Research Press, Santa Fe.

Mills, Barbara J., and T.J. Ferguson

2008 Animate Objects: Shell Trumpets and Ritual Networks in the Greater Southwest. *Journal of Archaeological Method and Theory* 15:338–361.

Mitchell, Douglas R., and Michael S. Foster

2000 Hohokam Shell Middens along the Sea of Cortez, Puerto Peñasco, Sonora, Mexico. *Journal of Field Archaeology* 27(1):27–41.

Montgomery, Ross Gordon, Watson Smith, and John Otis Brew

1949 *Franciscan Awatovi: The Excavation and Conjectural Reconstruction of a 17th-century Spanish Mission Establishment at a Hopi Indian Town in Northeastern Arizona.* Papers of the Peabody Museum of American Archaeology and Ethnology 36. Harvard University, Cambridge.

Morris, Earl H.

1919a *The Aztec Ruin.* Anthropological Papers of the American Museum of Natural History 26(1). American Museum of Natural History, New York.

1919b Preliminary Account of the Antiquities of the Region Between the Mancos and La Plata Rivers in Southwestern Colorado. In *Thirty-third Annual Report of the Bureau of American Ethnology, 1911–1912*, pp. 155–206. Smithsonian Institution, Washington, DC.

1921 *The House of the Great Kiva at the Aztec Ruin.* Anthropological Papers of the American Museum of Natural History 26(2). American Museum of Natural History, New York.

1924 *Burials in the Aztec Ruin.* Anthropological Papers of the American Museum of Natural History 26(3). American Museum of Natural History, New York.

Morris, Earl H., and Robert F. Burgh

1941 *Anasazi Basketry.* Carnegie Institution of Washington Publications 533. Carnegie Institution of Washington, Washington, DC.

Morris, Elizabeth A.

1980 *Basketmaker Caves in the Prayer Rock District, Northeastern Arizona.* Anthropological Papers of the University of Arizona 35. University of Arizona Press, Tucson.

Munsell, Albert

1907 *Atlas of the Color-Solid.* Wadsworth-Holland, Malden, Massachusetts.

1915 *Atlas of the Munsell Color System.* Wadsworth-Holland, Malden, Massachusetts.

Munson, Marit K.

2011 Iconography, Space, and Practice: Rio Grande Rock Art, AD 1150–1600. In *Religious Transformation in the Late Pre-Hispanic Pueblo World*, edited by D.M. Glowacki and S. Van Keuren, pp. 109–129. University of Arizona Press, Tucson.

Neitzel, Jill E.

2017 *Recognizing People in the Prehistoric Southwest.* University of Utah Press, Salt Lake City.

Nelson, Kit, and Judith A. Habicht-Mauche

2006 Lead, Paint, and Pots: Rio Grande Intercommunity Dynamics from a Glaze Ware Perspective. In *The Social Life of Pots: Glaze Wares and Cultural Dynamics in the Southwest, AD 1250–1680*, edited by J.A. Habicht-Mauche, S.L. Eckert, and D.L. Huntley, pp. 197–215. University of Arizona Press, Tucson.

Newhall, S.M., D. Nickerson, and D.B. Judd

1943 Final Report of the Optical Society of America Subcommittee on the Spacing of Munsell Colors. *Journal of the Optical Society of America* 33:385–418.

Newman, Stanley

1954 Semantic Problems in Grammatical Systems and Lexemes: A Search for Method. In *Language in Culture*, edited by H. Hoijer, pp. 82–91. University of Chicago Press, Chicago.

Newsome, Elizabeth A.

2010 Mural Arts from Pueblo II to Pueblo IV. In *Painting the Cosmos: Metaphor and Worldview in Images from the Southwest Pueblos and Mexico*, edited by K. Hays-Gilpin and P. Schaafsma, pp. 61–71. Museum of Northern Arizona Bulletin 67. Museum of Northern Arizona, Flagstaff.

Newsome, Elizabeth A., and Kelley Hays-Gilpin

2011 Spectatorship and Performance in Mural Painting, 1250–1500: Visuality and Social Integration. In *Religious Transformation in* the Late Pre-Hispanic Pueblo World, edited by D. M. Glowacki and S. Van Keuren, pp. 153–174. University of Arizona Press, Tucson.

Newton, Isaac

1704 *Opticks: Or, a Treatise of the Reflections, Refractions, Inflections, and Colours of Light.* William Innys, London.

Nickens, Paul R.

1981 *Pueblo III Communities in Transition: Environment and Adaptation in Johnson Canyon.* Memoirs of the Colorado Archaeological Society 2. Colorado Archaeological Society, Boulder.

Nordenskiöld, Gustaf

1893 *The Cliff-Dwellers of the Mesa Verde.* P. A. Norstedt and Soner, Stockholm, Sweden.

Northrop, S. A.

1975 *Turquoise and Spanish Mines in New Mexico.* University of New Mexico Press, Albuquerque.

Odegaard, Nancy, and Kelsey Hanson

2019 The Technology of Capturing Color: Complementary Analyses of Pigment Cakes and Chalks. Paper Presented at the 84th Annual Meeting of the Society for American Archaeology, Albuquerque.

Odegaard, Nancy, and Kelley Hays-Gilpin

2002 Technology of the Sacred: Painted Basketry in the Southwest. In *Traditions, Transitions, and Technologies: Themes in Southwestern Archaeology*, edited by S. H. Schlanger, pp. 307–331. University Press of Colorado, Boulder.

O'Hara, Michael

2015 Suyanisqatsi/Koyaanisqatsi: Creating Balance in a Land of Little Water and Burning Rock: Cooperation, Competition, and Climate in the Flagstaff Region of the U.S. Southwest, A.D. 1000–1300. PhD dissertation, Department of Anthropology, Arizona State University, Tempe.

Orna, Mary Virginia

2013 *The Chemical History of Color.* Springer, New York.

Ortiz, Alfonso

1969 *The Tewa World: Space, Time, Being, and Becoming in a Pueblo Society.* University of Chicago Press, Chicago.

Ortman, Scott G.

2000 Conceptual Metaphor in the Archaeological Record: Methods and an Example from the American Southwest. *American Antiquity* 65(4):613–645.

2006 Ancient Pottery of the Mesa Verde Country: How Ancestral Pueblo People Made It, Used It, and Thought About It. In *The Mesa Verde World: Explorations in Ancestral Pueblo Archaeology*, edited by D. G. Noble, pp. 100–109. School for Advanced Research Press, Santa Fe.

2008 Architectural Metaphor and Chacoan Influence in the Northern San Juan. In *Archaeology without Borders: Contact, Commerce, and Change in the US Southwest and Northwestern Mexico*, edited by L. D. Webster and M. E. McBrinn, pp. 227–256. University Press of Colorado, Boulder.

Parsons, Elsie Clews

1925 *The Pueblo of Jemez.* Papers of the Phillips Academy Southwestern Expedition 3. Yale University Press, New Haven, Connecticut.

1932 Isleta, New Mexico. In *Forty-Seventh Annual Report of the Bureau of American Ethnology, 1929–1930*, pp. 193–466. Government Printing Office, Washington, DC.

1933 *Hopi and Zuni Ceremonialism.* Memoirs of the American Anthropological Association Vol. 39. American Anthropological Association, Lancaster, Pennsylvania.

1939 *Pueblo Indian Religion* 1 and 2. University of Chicago Press, Chicago.

1964 [1917]a *Notes on Zuni, Part I.* Kraus Reprint, New York.

1964 [1917]b *Notes on Zuni, Part II.* Kraus Reprint, New York.

1964 [1933] *Hopi and Zuñi Ceremonialism.* Kraus Reprint, New York.

Pastoureau, Michel

2001 *Blue: The History of a Color.* Princeton University Press, Princeton, New Jersey.

2008 *Black: The History of a Color.* Princeton University Press, Princeton, New Jersey.

Peckham, Barbara A.

1981 Pueblo IV Murals at Mound 7. In *Contributions to Gran Quivira Archaeology, Gran Quivira National Monument, New Mexico*, edited by A. C. Hayes, pp. 15–38. Publications in Archaeology. Vol. 17. National Park Service, Washington, DC.

Pepper, George H.

1920 *Pueblo Bonito.* Anthropological Papers of the American Museum of Natural History 27. American Museum of Natural History, New York.

Phagan, Carl J.

1993 The Stone Artifacts from Arroyo Hondo Pueblo. In *Arroyo Hondo Archaeological*

*Series*, pp. 202–239. Vol. 8. School of American Research, Santa Fe.

Pippin, Lonnie C.
1987 *Prehistory and Paleoecology of Guadalupe Ruin, New Mexico*. University of Utah Anthropological Papers 112. University of Utah Press, Salt Lake City.

Plog, Stephen
1989 Ritual, Exchange, and the Development of Regional Systems. In *The Architecture of Social Integration in Prehistoric Pueblos*, edited by W. D. Lipe and M. Hegmon, pp. 143–154. Occasional Paper. Vol. 1. Crow Canyon Archaeological Center, Cortez, Colorado.
2003 Exploring the Ubiquitous through the Unusual: Color Symbolism in Pueblo Black-on-White Pottery. *American Antiquity* 68:665–695.

Plog, Stephen, and Carrie Heitman
2010 Hierarchy and Social Inequality in the American Southwest, A.D. 800–1200. *Proceedings of the National Academy of Sciences* 107(46):19619–19626.

Pond, Gordon
1966 A Painted Kiva near Winslow, Arizona. *American Antiquity* 31:555–558.

Prudden, T. Mitchell
1914 The Circular Kivas of Small Ruins in the San Juan Watershed. *American Anthropologist* 16(1):33–58.

Rapp, George (Rip)
2009 *Archaeomineralogy*. Springer, Berlin.

Reed, Paul F. (editor)
2006 *Thirty-Five Years of Archaeological Research at Salmon Ruins*. Center for Desert Archaeology, Tucson, Arizona.

Reyman, Jonathan E.
1971 Mexican Influence on Southwestern Ceremonialism. PhD dissertation, Department of Anthropology, Southern Illinois University, Carbondale.

Rice, Prudence
1987 *Pottery Analysis: A Sourcebook*. University of Chicago Press, Chicago.

Riley, Carroll L.
1963 Color-Direction Symbolism: An Example of Mexican-Southwestern Contacts. *America Indigena* 23(1):49–60.

Roberts, Frank H. H.
1929 *Shabik'eshchee village: A Late Basket Maker Site in the Chaco Canyon, New Mexico*. Bureau of American Ethnology Bulletin 92. Smithsonian Institution, Washington, DC.

Roediger, Virginia More
1961 *Ceremonial Costumes of the Pueblo Indians: Their Evolution, Fabrication, and Significance in the Prayer Drama*. University of California Press, Berkeley.

Rogers, Malcolm J.
1929 *Report on an Archaeological Reconnaissance in the Mohave Sink Region*. Archaeological Papers 1(1). San Diego Museum of Man, San Diego.

Rohn, Arthur
1971 *Mug House, Mesa Verde National Park, Colorado*. Archeological Research Series 7D, Wetherill Mesa Excavations. National Park Service, Washington, DC.

Russell, Will G., Sarah Klassen, and Katherine Salazar
2018 Lines of Communication: Mimbres Hachure and Concepts of Color. *American Antiquity* 83(1):109–127.

Saunders, Barbara
1992 *The Invention of Basic Colour Terms*. ISOR, Utrecht.
2000 Revisiting Basic Color Terms. *Journal of the Royal Anthropological Institute* 6(1): 81–99.

Scarre, Chris
2002 Epilogue: Colour and Materiality in Prehistoric Society. In *Colouring the Past: The Significance of Colour in Archaeological Research*, edited by A. Jones and G. MacGregor, pp. 227–242. Berg, Oxford.

Schaafsma, Curtis F.
2007 Compilation of Excavated and Previously Reported Ceramics from Pottery Mound: Appendix D. In *New Perspectives on Pottery Mound Pueblo*, edited by P. Schaafsma, pp. 277–294. University of New Mexico Press, Albuquerque.

Schaafsma, Polly
1965 Kiva Murals from Pueblo Del Encierro (LA 70). *El Palacio* 72(3):7–16.
1966 *A Survey of Tsegi Canyon Rock Art*. Navajo National Monument, National Park Service, Santa Fe.
1980 *Indian Rock Art of the Southwest*. University of New Mexico Press, Albuquerque.
1990 The Pine Tree Site: A Pueblo IV Shrine in the Galisteo Basin, New Mexico. In *Clues to the Past: Papers in Honor of William M.*

*Sundt*, edited by M. S. Duran and D. T. Kirkpatrick. Papers of the Archaeological Society of New Mexico. Vol. 16. Archeological Society of New Mexico, Albuquerque.

1999 Tlalocs, Kachinas, Sacred Bundles, and Related Symbolism in the Southwest and Mesoamerica. In *The Casas Grandes World*, edited by C. F. Schaafsma and C. L. Riley, pp. 164–192. University of Utah Press, Salt Lake City.

2000 *Warrior, Shield, and Star: Imagery and Ideology of Pueblo Warfare*. Western Edge Press, Santa Fe.

2002 Pottery Metaphors in Pueblo and Jornada Mogollon Rock Art. In *Rock Art and Cultural Processes*, edited by S. A. Turpin, pp. 51–66. Special Publication 3. Rock Art Foundation, San Antonio, Texas.

2007a The Kuaua Murals: A Re-evaluation. *The Getty Re-Evaluation Project*. Manuscript on file, Museum of Indian Arts and Culture/ Laboratory of Anthropology, Santa Fe.

2007b *New Perspectives on Pottery Mound Pueblo*. University of New Mexico Press, Albuquerque.

2009 The Cave in the Kiva: The Kiva Niche and Painted Walls in the Rio Grande Valley. *American Antiquity* 74(4):664–690.

2010 Landscape and Painted Walls: Images in Place. In *Painting the Cosmos: Metaphor and Worldview in Images from the Southwest Pueblos and Mexico*, edited by K. Hays-Gilpin and P. Schaafsma, pp. 19–40. Museum of Northern Arizona Bulletin 67. Museum of Northern Arizona, Flagstaff.

2013 Petitions for Rain: Textile and Pottery Designs in Rock Art. *International Newsletter on Rock Art* 66:17–27.

2014 The Morningstar/Maize/Rain Complex in the American Southwest. In *Astronomy and Ceremony in the Prehistoric Southwest: Revisited, Collaborations in Cultural Astronomy*, edited by G. E. Munson, T. W. Bostwick, and T. Hull, pp. 19–28. Maxwell Museum Anthropological Papers No. 9. University of New Mexico Press, Albuquerque.

2015 Tlaloc and a Mesoamerican Cosmology in the American Southwest. *Tlaloque: Boletin Del Seminario: El Emblema De Tlaloc en Mesoamerica* 5(17):6–50.

2018 Human Images and Blurring Boundaries: The Pueblo Body in Cosmological Context: Rock Art, Murals, and Ceremonial Figures. *Cambridge Archaeological Journal*. 28(3):411–431.

Schaafsma, Polly, and Curtis F. Schaafsma

1974 Evidence for the Origins of the Pueblo Katchina Cult as Suggested by Southwestern Rock Art. *American Antiquity* 39: 535–545.

Schaafsma, Polly, and Karl Taube

2006 Bringing the Rain: An Ideology of Rain Making in the Pueblo Southwest and Mesoamerica. In *A Pre-Columbian World*, edited by J. Quilter and M. Miller, pp. 231–286. Dumbarton Oaks, Washington, DC.

Schaafsma, Polly, and Regge N. Wiseman

1992 Serpents in the Prehistoric Pecos Valley of Southeastern New Mexico. In *Archaeology, Art, and Anthropology: Papers in Honor of J. J. Brody*, edited by M. S. Duran and D. T. Kirkpatrick, pp. 175–183. Papers of the Archaeological Society of New Mexico. Vol. 18. Archaeological Society of New Mexico, Albuquerque.

Schachner, Gregson

2006 The Decline of Zuni Glaze Ware Production in the Tumultuous Fifteenth Century. In *The Social Life of Pots: Glaze Wares and Cultural Dynamics in the Southwest, AD 1250–1680*, edited by J. A. Habicht-Mauche, S. L. Eckert, and D. L. Huntley, pp. 124–141. University of Arizona Press, Tucson.

Schuyler, Lucy C.

2010 *The Jewelry of Tijeras Pueblo*. Technical Series No. 15. Maxwell Museum of Anthropology, Albuquerque.

2016 *The Jewelry of Pottery Mound with a Comparison to Tijeras Pueblo*. Technical Series No. 26. Maxwell Museum of Anthropology, Albuquerque.

Secakuku, Alph H.

1995 *Hopi Kachina Tradition: Following the Sun and Moon*. Northland Publishing, Flagstaff, Arizona.

Sekaquaptewa, Emory, and Dorothy K. Washburn

2010 Living in Metaphor: Hopi Traditions in Song and Image. In *Painting the Cosmos: Metaphor and Worldview in Images from the Southwest Pueblos and Mexico*, edited by K. Hays-Gilpin and P. Schaafsma, pp. 139–177. Museum of Northern Arizona

Bulletin 67. Museum of Northern Arizona, Flagstaff.

Shafer, Harry J.

1985 A Mimbres Potter's Grave: An Example of Mimbres Craft-Specialization? *Bulletin of the Texas Archeological Society* 56:185–200.

Shepard, Anna O.

1929 A Preliminary Study of Zuni Words Referring to Pottery and Pottery Designs. *Anna O. Shepard Collection.* Drawer 4, Folder 42. University of Colorado Museum of Natural History, Boulder.

1956 *Ceramics for the Archaeologist.* Carnegie In stitution of Washington, Washington, DC.

Silko, Leslie Marmon

1996 *Yellow Woman and a Beauty of the Spirit.* Simon and Schuster, New York.

Silver, Constance S.

1982 The Mural Paintings from the Kiva at LA 17360: Report on the Initial Treatment and Their Preservation. In *Prehistoric Adaptive Strategies in the Chaco Canyon Region, Northwestern New Mexico, Vol. 2: Site Reports*, edited by A. H. Simmons, pp. 715–728. Navajo Nation Papers in Anthropology 9. Navajo Nation Cultural Resource Management Program, Window Rock, Arizona.

Sivik, Lars

1997 Color Systems for Cognitive Research. In *Color Categories in Thought and Language*, edited by C. L. Hardin and L. Maffi, pp. 163–193. Cambridge University Press, Cambridge.

Smith, Watson

1952 *Kiva Mural Decorations at Awatovi and Kawaika-a, with a Survey of Other Wall Paintings in the Pueblo Southwest.* Papers of the Peabody Museum of American Archaeology and Ethnology 37. Harvard University, Cambridge.

1971 *Painted Ceramics of the Western Mound at Awatovi.* Papers of the Peabody Museum of Archaeology and Ethnology, Harvard University 38. Peabody Museum, Cambridge, Massachusetts.

1972 *Prehistoric Kivas of Antelope Mesa, Northeastern Arizona.* Papers of the Peabody Museum of American Archaeology and Ethnology 39, No. 1. Harvard University, Cambridge.

Smith, Watson, Richard B. Woodbury, and Nathalie F. S. Woodbury

1966 *The Excavation of Hawikuh by Frederick Webb Hodge.* Contributions from the Museum of the American Indian, Heye Foundation Vol. 20. Museum of the American Indian, Heye Foundation, New York.

Smith, William Hoyt

2002 Trade in Molluskan Religiofauna Between the Southwestern United States and Southern California. PhD dissertation, Department of Anthropology, University of Oregon, Eugene.

Snow, David H.

1973 Prehistoric Southwestern Turquoise Industry. *El Palacio* 79(1):33–51.

Solometo, Julie

2010 The Context and Process of Pueblo Mural Painting in the Historic Era. *Kiva* 75(4): 83–116.

Spicer, Edward H.

1936 Kings Ruin. In *Two Pueblo Ruins in West Central Arizona*, edited by E. H. Spicer, pp. 5–85. University of Arizona Press, Tucson.

Spielmann, Katherine A.

1998 Ritual Influences on the Development of Rio Grande Glaze A Ceramics. In *Migration and Reorganization: The Pueblo IV Period in the American Southwest*, edited by K. A. Spielmann, pp. 253–261. Anthropological Research Papers. Vol. 51. Arizona State University.

Spielmann, Katherine A., Jeannette L. Mobley-Tanaka, and James M. Potter

2006 Style and Resistance in the Seventeenth Century Salinas Province. *American Antiquity* 71(4):621–647.

Stephen, Alexander M.

1898 Pigments in Ceremonials of the Hopi. *Archives of the International Folk-Lore Association* 1:260–265.

1936 *Hopi Journal of Alexander M. Stephen.* Columbia University Contributions to Anthropology 23. Columbia University, New York.

Stevenson, James

1883 Illustrated Catalogue of the Collections Obtained from the Indians of New Mexico and Arizona in 1879. In *Second Annual Report of the Bureau of American Ethnology, 1880–81*, pp. 311–422. Smithsonian Institution, Washington, DC.

Stevenson, Matilda Coxe

1894a A Chapter of Zuni Mythology. In *Memoirs of the International Congress of Anthropology*, pp. 312–319.

1894b The Sia. In *Eleventh Annual Report of the Bureau of American Ethnology, 1889–90*, pp. 3–157. Smithsonian Institution, Washington, DC.
1904 The Zuni Indians: Their Mythology, Esoteric Societies, and Ceremonies. In *Twenty-Third Annual Report of the Bureau of American Ethnology, 1901–1902*, pp. 1–634. Smithsonian Institution, Washington, DC.

Stone, Tammy
2018 Smudged Wares: The Importance of Color and Iridescence as a Long-Lived Decorative Attribute in the Mogollon Highlands. *Kiva* 84(1):1–26.

Stubbs, Stanley A., and William S. Stalling Jr.
1953 *The Excavation of Pindi Pueblo, New Mexico*. Monographs of the School of American Research and the Laboratory of Anthropology No. 18. School of American Research, Santa Fe.

Swannack, Jervis D., Jr.
1969 *Big Juniper House, Mesa Verde National Park, Colorado*. Archeological Research Series 7C. National Park Service, Washington, DC.

Swink, Clint
2004 *Messages from the High Desert: The Art, Archaeology and Renaissance of Mesa Verde Pottery*. Redtail Press, Bayfield, Colorado.

Tanner, Clara Lee
1976 *Prehistoric Southwestern Craft Arts*. University of Arizona Press, Tucson.

Taube, Karl
2010 Gateways to Another World: The Symbolism of Supernatural Passageways in the Art and Ritual of Mesoamerica and the American Southwest. In *Painting the Cosmos: Metaphor and Worldview in Images from the Southwest Pueblos and Mexico*, edited by K. Hays-Gilpin and P. Schaafsma, pp. 72–120. Museum of Northern Arizona Bulletin 67. Museum of Northern Arizona, Flagstaff.

Taussig, Michael
2009 *What Color Is the Sacred?* University of Chicago Press, Chicago.

Teague, Lynn S.
1998 *Textiles in Southwestern Prehistory*. University of New Mexico Press, Albuquerque.

Teague, Lynn S., and Dorothy K. Washburn
2013 *Sandals of the Basketmaker and Pueblo Peoples: Fabric Structure and Color Symmetry*. University of New Mexico Press, Albuquerque.

Tedlock, Dennis
1972 *Finding the Center*. Dial Press, New York.
1979 Zuni Religion and World View. In *Southwest*, edited by A. Ortiz, pp. 499–508. Handbook of North American Indians, Vol. 9, W. C. Sturtevant, general editor, Smithsonian Institution, Washington, DC.

Thompson, Evan
1995 *Colour Vision: A Study in Cognitive Science and the Philosophy of Perception*. Routledge, New York.

Tilley, Christopher
1996 *An Ethnography of the Neolithic: Early Prehistoric Societies in Southern Scandinavia*. Cambridge University Press, Cambridge.

Titiev, Mischa
1937 A Hopi Salt Expedition. *American Anthropologist* 39:244–258.
1944 *Old Oraibi: A Study of the Hopi Indians of Third Mesa*. Peabody Museum of American Archaeology and Ethnology, 22. Harvard University, Cambridge.

Tower, Donald B.
1945 The Use of Marine Mollusca and Their Value in Reconstructing Prehistoric Trade Routes in the American Southwest. *American Anthropologist* 49(3):466–467.

Townsend, Richard F. (editor)
1979 *State and Cosmos in the Art of Tenochtitlan*. Dumbarton Oaks, Washington, DC.

Trimble, Stephen
2004 *Talking with Clay: The Art of Pueblo Potters*. 4th ed. School for Advanced Research Press, Santa Fe.

Turner, Victor
1967 *The Forest of Symbols: Aspects of Ndembu Ritual*. Cornell University Press, Ithaca, New York.

Tyler, Hamilton A.
1979 *Pueblo Birds and Myth*. University of Oklahoma Press, Norman.

Tylor, Edward B.
1871 *Primitive Culture*. G. P. Putnam's Sons, New York.

Van Keuren, Scott
2006 Decorating Glaze-Painted Pottery in East-Central Arizona. In *The Social Life of Pots: Glaze Wares and Cultural Dynamics in the Southwest, AD 1250–1680*, edited by J. A. Habicht-Mauche, S. L. Eckert and D. L. Huntley, pp. 86–104. University of Arizona Press, Tucson.

VanPool, Christine S., and Elizabeth Newsome
2012 The Spirit in the Material: A Case Study of Animism in the American Southwest. *American Antiquity* 77(2):243–262.
VanPool, Christine S., and Todd L. VanPool
2012 Breath and Being: Contextualizing Object Persons at Paquime, Chihuahua, Mexico. In *Archaeology of Spiritualities*, edited by K. Rountree, C. Morris, and A. A. D. Peatfield, pp. 87–106. Springer, New York.
Vivian, Gordon, and Tom W. Mathews
1973 *Kin Kletso: A Pueblo III Community in Chaco Canyon, New Mexico.* Southwestern Monuments Association, Technical Series, Part 1, Globe, Arizona.
Vivian, Patricia
1961 Kachina: The Study of Pueblo Animism and Anthropomorphism within the Ceremonial Wall Paintings of Pottery Mound and the Jeddito. Master's thesis, University of Iowa, Iowa City.
1994 Anthropomorphic Figures in the Pottery Mound Murals. In *Kachinas in the Pueblo World*, edited by P. Schaafsma, pp. 81–91. University of New Mexico Press, Albuquerque.
2007 The Kiva Murals of Pottery Mound: A History of Discovery and Methods of Study, Kivas 1–10. In *New Perspectives on Pottery Mound Pueblo*, edited by P. Schaafsma, pp. 75–83. University of New Mexico Press, Albuquerque.
Vivian, R. Gwinn, Dulce N. Dodgen, and Gayle H. Hartman
1978 *Wooden Ritual Artifacts from Chaco Canyon, New Mexico: The Chetro Ketl Collection.* University of Arizona Press, Tucson.
Voth, H. R.
1903 *The Oraibi Summer Snake Ceremony.* Field Columbian Museum, Anthropological Series III, No. 4. Field Columbian Museum, Chicago.
Wade, Edwin L., and David Evans
1973 The Kachina Sash: A Native Model of the Hopi World. *Western Folklore* 32(1):1–18.
Wade, Edwin L., and Lea S. McChesney (editors)
1980 *America's Great Lost Expedition: The Thomas Keam Collection of Hopi Pottery from the Second Hemenway Expedition, 1890–1894.* Heard Museum, Phoenix, Arizona.
Walker, William H.
1999 Ritual, Life Histories, and the Afterlives of People and Things. *Journal of the Southwest* 41(3):381–405.
Ware, John A.
2013 *A Pueblo Social History: Kinship, Solidarity, and Community in the Northern Southwest.* School for Advanced Research Press, Santa Fe.
Warren, A. Helene, and Frances Joan Mathien
1985 Prehistoric and Historic Turquoise Mining in the Cerrillos District: Time and Place. In *Collected Papers in Honor of Albert H. Schroeder*, edited by C. H. Lange, pp. 93–127. Papers of the Archaeological Society of New Mexico. Vol. 10. Archaeological Society of New Mexico, Albuquerque.
Watchman, Alan
1997 Analysis of Kuaua Kiva Mural Pigments. Manuscript on file at the Laboratory of Anthropology, Santa Fe.
Webster, Laurie D.
2007 Ritual Costuming at Pottery Mound: The Pottery Mound Textiles in Regional Perspective. In *New Perspectives on Pottery Mound Pueblo*, edited by P. Schaafsma, pp. 167–206. University of New Mexico Press, Albuquerque.
Webster, Laurie D., Kelley Hays-Gilpin, and Polly Schaafsma
2006 A New Look at Tie-Dye and the Dot-in-a-Square Motif in the Prehispanic Southwest. *Kiva* 71(3):317–348.
Whalen, Michael E.
2013 Wealth, Status, Ritual, and Marine Shell at Casas Grandes, Chihuahua, Mexico. *American Antiquity* 28(4):624–639.
White, Leslie A.
1932 *The Pueblo of San Felipe, New Mexico.* Memoirs of the American Anthropological Association Vol. 38. American Anthropological Association, Lancaster, Pennsylvania.
1935 *The Pueblo of Santo Domingo, New Mexico.* Memoirs of the American Anthropological Association Vol. 43. American Anthropological Association, Lancaster, Pennsylvania.
1942 *The Pueblo of Santa Ana, New Mexico.* Memoirs of the American Anthropological Association Vol. 60. American Anthropological Association, Lancaster, Pennsylvania.

1943 Keresan Indian Color Terms. In *Papers of the Michigan Academy of Science, Arts, and Letters*, pp. 559–563. Vol. 28. Michigan Academy of Science, Arts, and Letters.

1945 Notes on the Ethnobotany of the Keres. In *Papers of the Michigan Academy of Science, Arts, and Letters*, pp. 557–568. Vol. 30. Michigan Academy of Science, Arts, and Letters.

1962 *The Pueblo of Sia New Mexico*. Bureau of American Ethnology Bulletin 184. Smithsonian Institution, Washington, DC.

Whittlesey, Stephanie M.

2014 Subjective Color in Mimbres Black-on-White Pottery. *Kiva* 80(1):45–70.

Wierzbicka, Anna

2005 There Are No "Color Universals" but There Are Universals of Visual Semantics. *Anthropological Linguistics* 47(2): 217–244.

2008 Why There Are No "Colour Universals" in Language and Thought. *Journal of the Royal Anthropological Institute* 14(2): 407–425.

Wilson, C. Dean, Lori S. Reed, and Kelley Hays-Gilpin

2000 Basketmaker Ceramic Technology: From Early Ceramic Horizon to the Development of Regional Traditions. In *Foundations of Anasazi Culture: The Basketmaker—Pueblo Transition*, edited by P. F. Reed, pp. 203–220. University of Utah Press, Salt Lake City.

Windes, Thomas C.

1987a *Investigations at the Pueblo Alto Complex, Chaco Canyon, New Mexico, 1975–1979. Volume II, Part 1. Architecture and Stratigraphy*. Publications in Archeology 18F, Chaco Canyon Studies. National Park Service, Santa Fe.

1987b *Investigations at the Pueblo Alto Complex, Chaco Canyon, New Mexico, 1975–1979. Volume II, Part 2. Architecture and Stratigraphy*. Publications in Archeology 18F, Chaco Canyon Studies. National Park Service, Santa Fe.

1993 *The Spadefoot Toad Site: Excavations at 29SJ629 in Marcia's Rincon and the Fajada Gap Pueblo II Community, Chaco Canyon, New Mexico*. Reports of the Chaco Center No. 12. National Park Service, Santa Fe.

2015 *Early Puebloan Occupations in the Chaco Region Volume 1: Excavations and Survey of Basketmaker III and Pueblo I Sites, Chaco Canyon New Mexico*. Reports of the Chaco Center No. 13. National Park Service, Santa Fe.

Wiseman, Regge N., and J. Andrew Darling

1986 The Bronze Trail Site Group: More Evidence for a Cerrillos-Chaco Turquoise Connection. In *By Hands Unknown: Papers in Honor of James G. Bain*, edited by A. Poore, pp. 115–143. Papers of the Archaeological Society of New Mexico. Vol. 12. Ancient City Press, Santa Fe.

Woodbury, Richard B.

1954 *Prehistoric Stone Implements of Northeastern Arizona*. Papers of the Peabody Museum of American Archaeology and Ethnology 34. Peabody Museum, Cambridge, Massachusetts.

Wright, Barton

1973 *Kachinas: A Hopi Artist's Documentary*. Northland Publishing, Flagstaff, Arizona.

Young, Jon Nathan

1981 Stone Artifacts of Mound 7. In *Excavation of Mound 7: Gran Quivira National Monument, New Mexico*, edited by A. C. Hayes, J. N. Young, and A. H. Warren, pp. 104–139. Publications in Archeology. Vol. 16. National Park Service, Washington, DC.

Young, M. Jane

1988 *Signs From the Ancestors: Zuni Cultural Symbolism and Perceptions of Rock Art*. University of New Mexico Press, Albuquerque.

# Index